To John

from your Dad

For my wife, Paula, whose motherly duties
caused her to miss much of the fun,
and to Christine, Michael and Sally-Anne.

The Grand Prix Carpetbaggers

The Autobiography of John Cooper
with John Bentley

Foreword by Ken Tyrrell

DOUBLEDAY & COMPANY, INC.
GARDEN CITY, NEW YORK
1977

ISBN: 0-385-03081-9
Library of Congress Catalog Card Number 76-2763
Copyright © 1977 by John Cooper and John Bentley
All Rights Reserved
Printed in the United States of America
First Edition

Library of Congress Cataloging in Publication Data

Cooper, John, 1923–
    The Grand Prix carpetbaggers.

    Includes index.
    1. Cooper, John, 1923–   2. Automobile racing drivers—Great Britain—
Biography.   3. Grand Prix racing.   I. Bentley, John, 1908–   joint
author.   II. Title.
GV1032.C68A35   796.7'2'0924 [B]

Grateful acknowledgment is made to *Autosport* for permission to reproduce
the chart of Cooper cars which appears in the Appendix.

Contents

Foreword

By Ken Tyrrell

Because a man like John Cooper is a legend in his own lifetime, it's hard to talk about him in the past tense. He still has that infectious enthusiasm for everything he does, and that makes him a larger-than-life character about whom you could tell stories all night. John really enjoyed motor racing and when he was having a good time, so was everyone else.

I suppose John Cooper taught me the rudiments of Grand Prix team management when I ran a team of Formula 2 Coopers using his Grand Prix drivers. Formula 2 races were often the supporting events to a *Grande Épreuve* and I was able to watch the energy and precision John injected into the pit work. He had the gift of making quick decisions and I took note of what he did during a race and of the sort of decisions he made. This was an education for me.

After John's near fatal accident in the twin-engined Mini, I was asked to go in and manage the Cooper Grand Prix team for a few races, but it was a team that didn't really need managing. It almost looked after itself, in large measure because of an excellent team of mechanics. In fact I learned as much about team managing from mechanics in those days as I have since done from anyone else.

John was in charge of the team that did to Grand Prix racing in 1959 and 1960 what Ferrari does today, but it was a different era then. It wasn't Big Business (although it probably seemed big enough at the time) and there seemed to be more fun and more characters like John.

One thing I recall with amusement. When Roy Salvadori and Jack Brabham were driving the works Coopers, everyone used to watch everyone else like a hawk. Each was convinced that he was being short-changed of his just due by everyone else, and after a race the drivers would go with John Cooper to the race office, where the start and prize money was usually paid by check. That was so that everyone would know how much the club was paying and not how much John *said* they were paying! Then the trio would take off for the bank with John to cash the check—Roy on one side and Jack on the other, acting as two "security guards." The fact was they were not worried about the money being nicked from John; they were concerned about him nicking the money from *them!* Still, it all happened in a spirit of good clean fun.

For some reason, mechanics never seem to get the mention (let alone the credit) they deserve for their fantastic and selfless work, without which no race car could even start a race—let alone finish it. Endless hours of back-breaking toil and sleepless nights one after another are too often taken for granted by many drivers and most of the public.

Mechanics, of course, come in all sizes, types and temperaments. "Noddy" Grohman, who was chief mechanic on the Cooper team in the Championship years was a fantastic individual, but strictly a loner. I remember that when Brabham crashed at Monaco and twisted the space frame of his car, there was barely a week to go before the Dutch Grand Prix at Zandvoort. So we hitched the car on a trailer behind our Formula Junior transporter and brought it back to England. Noddy started work on the car the moment it arrived, removed the engine, put the chassis on a jig and straightened it out. He kept working around the clock, non-stop, refusing assistance from *anyone.*

John, who felt guilty about the work load on Noddy, decided to help him out on what was probably the third night. Noddy's eyes were popping out of his head with fatigue and he was getting more and more bad-tempered. When John arrived that evening with his box of tools and started climbing into a pair of overalls, Noddy took one look and gathered up his tools. Since he usually worked with about six inches of tools piled high all around him and never packed them until ready to leave for a race, this was a bad sign. John couldn't believe what he saw as the car was still far from finished.

"What's the matter, Noddy?" he asked.

"If you're starting, I'm stopping," came the laconic answer.

So John went home and Noddy finished the car—and Jack won the Dutch Grand Prix with it the following Sunday.

I must say, though, that if John Cooper didn't spare himself, neither did he handle his drivers with kid gloves. I'll never forget the Formula 2 race at Reims before the Grand Prix, the year when a tremendous heat wave hit the area. The road surface was literally melting and drivers came in exhausted by the heat and bleeding from flying stones. They had a scant two hours to recover before the Grand Prix but could probably have used two days! Bruce McLaren and Masten Gregory were the works drivers that year and Bruce was laid out to recuperate in the shade. About four laps after the start of the Grand Prix, Masten came in slowly and coasted to a stop. When John asked him what he was stopping for, Masten replied haltingly, "Because I'm hot!"

His mechanic promptly dashed a bucket of water into the cockpit and John told Masten to get the hell back into the race. When the latter drove off, John turned to me indignantly and said, "It cost me £20,000 to build that car for him and he tells me he's hot after four laps . . . !" Words failed him.

There was one occasion at Reims when I didn't regard John as the life and soul of the party, though. He and I had driven over in a Mini van loaded with spare engines for our Formula 2 cars and it turned out that we had reservations at the same hotel. The only thing was that when we finally arrived, dead beat, at about midnight, there was only one room to spare. So, quick as a flash, John grabbed the key, said, "Good night," and locked the door behind him, leaving me with my mouth wide open! He didn't even offer me floor space. But that was another of the lightning Cooper decisions I learned about.

I could go on for pages about John's dedication to the Mini and how his unflagging enthusiasm and vision turned this little wonder car into a world best seller. And about the day we realized Jackie Stewart's tremendous potential during a tryout and grabbed him from Esso so that he was able to drive for me under the Shell banner. And much, much more. But all this has been pretty thoroughly gone over in this book, the title of which I must say I really like! For a long time, especially during the early 500 cc days, when famous drivers lined up to buy their Coopers for the next season, they didn't realize they would practically have to build their own car at the factory! It was that much of a shoestring operation! Yet it led straight to the World Championship and it taught other race car builders a great deal!

Anyway, I was delighted at the invitation to write this Foreword to John's book because it's a story that has long needed to be told, as opposed to the dreary catalogues of races which so often pass for autobiographies.

John Cooper was great for motor racing. He was a colorful character in a colorful era, and the stories he tells in this book have put an indelible stamp of humor and suspense on his own Grand Prix generation.

KEN TYRRELL
Ockham, Surrey
May 1976

1

One Engine Too Many

Racing drivers don't always have their most serious shunts on a track or road course. Unfortunately, I had mine while testing an experimental car, even though at the time (in 1962) I was already an established car builder whose products had twice won the World's Formula 1 Championship. I was, in fact, returning from the Fairoaks Flying Club, where, along with Jack Brabham, I had learned to fly and where we had both obtained our pilot's licenses. At the time, I happened to own a Piper Tri-Pacer, and about eight months earlier Maurice Smith, D.F.C., of *Autocar* magazine had come up with what they thought was a great suggestion. They would take pictures of racing drivers who were interested in flying and who would be willing to demonstrate their skill over Fairoaks in Kent. For my part, I had only just obtained my ticket and wasn't very experienced, but on the chosen day quite a collection of personalities connected with motor racing turned up. Colin Chapman was there with his Piper Commanche, and I think John Webb, the then owner of Brands Hatch racecourse was also there with his Piper, as was Ken Gregory—Stirling Moss's manager—in yet another Piper.

Also present was the editor of *Autocar,* and his staff was getting ready to take pictures of us flying around a couple of thousand feet up. Anyway, it turned out then when we arrived at Fairoaks on that particular Sunday afternoon it was a pretty windy day. There were some very heavy crosswinds—so bad in fact that my father, who was with me, strongly objected.

"Look," he said, "you're not going to fly in this sort of weather, surely? You'll kill yourself!"

"You're probably right," I agreed.

I sought out ex-Wing Commander Arthur, who had taught both Jack and me to fly, and told him, "Frankly, I'm not experienced enough to cope with the present flying conditions."

"In that case," he said, "I'll send someone up with you."

That seemed reasonable, more so as it turned out that my "co-pilot" had also been one of my flying instructors. His name was "Sport" Martin and he was a captain in Dan-Air, where I believe he still flies jumbo jets. Anyway, I took the plane off and followed the flight plan and the magazine got some good shots of us in midair. Colin Chapman had already had his picture taken, so he decided to come up with us as a rear-seat passenger, just for the fun of it. He was to wish that he had not done so!

When it came to our turn to land, as we lost height I handed over the aircraft to Martin, who, by then, had become used to flying four-engined aircraft. He therefore made a very fast approach—much too fast, I thought, for such a small plane—but it did cross my mind that he was probably intending to buzz the airfield, so I was quite unprepared for what happened next. No sooner had we touched down than the nosewheel folded up and the aircraft went tail over nose. Colin Chapman was knocked unconscious but I was unhurt and so was "Sport" Martin, although the plane lay upside down. Jack Brabham, who was passing overhead, saw what had happened and immediately landed and rushed over to see if he could help. Just as I was about to drag Chapman out of the plane, he woke up and his first words were, "Is everything switched off?"

This was typical of his efficient manner. Anyway, we got out of the aircraft and walked away from it, which was pretty good going, all things considered. The Piper was badly damaged, but I can honestly say that, because of the crosswind, although I was in the number one seat, it was not I who had been flying the aircraft or handled the controls.

The plane was duly righted and shipped off to Kenneth McAlpine's workshop for repairs, in Luton, Bedfordshire. McAlpine was a car manufacturer in his own right who had built the famous Connaught race car. He had also started his own aircraft business, which was where my Piper was being shipped off for repairs. Fortunately, it was an insurance job, but it seemed to take forever. After about eight months had elapsed while the damage was being fixed, I finally received a notice that the aircraft was ready for collection. So I went over to Luton, picked up my plane and flew it back to Fairoaks, which is where this story really begins.

At the time, I happened to be using a twin-engine Mini destined to cause me a lot of grief. I had driven this car from our Surbiton garage to Fairoaks, left it there while I got a lift up to Luton by plane, where I picked up my Tri-Pacer and flew it back to Fairoaks.

I had no sooner landed than someone told me there was an air display at Biggin Hill in Kent, that day, so a couple of the boys asked if they could cadge a lift and we went on by air to Biggin Hill to watch the aerobatics. When we got ready to fly back, "Sport" Martin, who was with me, remarked, "Have you inspected your plane, John? You're supposed to do that before takeoff, you know."

"But it's just been repaired," I said.

"Take a look anyway," he insisted. And sure enough the tail of the aircraft was all bent over. Someone obviously had run into it while it was parked but had not even taken the trouble to leave a note. So once again the plane was pushed into the local Piper agent's hangar, that happened to be at Biggin Hill, for still another repair session. I phoned Fairoaks Flying Club to see if they could send anyone to pick us up. They could and did. They sent a man with a private pilot's license (which he had only just obtained) to fetch us, and besides getting lost on the way home I must admit this chap frightened us to death! But somehow we made it back to Fairoaks in one piece and I got into my Mini for the delayed drive home.

Talk about jumping from the frying pan into the fire! That night I was having dinner with Roy Salvadori at his house in Esher, along with Bruce McLaren. My wife, Paula, was going to be there, together with the other wives and the whole thing had been planned in advance. But Fate decreed otherwise. On the way home from Fairoaks to Surbiton (where I planned to stop off and change for dinner), something let go in the Mini while I was on the Kingston Bypass. The car went end over end with almost no warning, and the next thing I knew was that I woke up in hospital without knowing where I was or how I had got there. My first re-action, in fact, was a vague belief that the jockey who had flown us back from Biggin Hill to Fairoaks had become involved in some terrible shunt.

One often wonders if when there is trouble ahead, things tend to build up to the final situation. First, there had been the incident of the bent tail on my damaged plane, which I had nearly flown back without knowing it. Suppose we had taken off—what would have happened? We might have run into serious trouble. Then that harrowing return flight to Fairoaks with our lives in the hands of some character who didn't seem to know much. Our landing a bit late and my hurrying off in the Mini to get home and change, although in the ordinary course of events I wasn't one to go very fast along the highways. My racing days were already a decade past.

Then, as I lay there in my hospital bed, things began to sort themselves out. I remembered driving along the Kingston Bypass and being pleasantly aware of the tremendous power of my little car, with two Mini-Cooper engines stuffed into one chassis! I recalled experiencing a sense of great pleasure at the terrific road-holding and neutral steering character of the car. I even got as far as a vague recollection that something had let go at the back, though in that split second I had no idea what it was. Later examination did establish the cause of the accident, which, I think, could fairly be called unusual.

This particular Mini actually had two front subframes, installed back to back so as to accommodate both engines—one up front and the other at the rear. The subframe fitted at the back had, of course, been modified to perform its particular job, although it was basically the same as its front counterpart. We had removed the rack and used the steering links as another suspension arm which pivoted on the subframe. Unfortunately, it was one of those steering links that let go. To get into slightly more detail, it was the ball joint on the end of the link which we had secured to the subframe instead of the rack itself. We had been testing this car some time previously in the snow, because these twin-engine Minis were very good under severe conditions. Following a demonstration to the Press boys, the car had been put aside so that we might install some better engines with a view to racing it. I think that what happened was pretty clear. One of the ball joints had somehow got snow in it, which produced enough rust to make the whole thing seize up and break off. As a result, a rear wheel suddenly made a sharp right turn—there no longer being anything to keep it going straight—and as I was motoring along at probably 100 mph, the result wasn't hard to imagine. A sudden veering to one side, followed by a number of somersaults!

I wasn't strapped in when all this happened. A lot of people later said that if I had been using my seat belt I probably would have killed myself, but I think the opposite would have been true and I might have escaped serious injury, particularly since the car didn't catch fire. What did the real damage was when I hit my head on the doorpost during one of the rolls.

The place where the accident occurred was a very fast stretch on the Kingston Bypass, and interestingly enough, after all these years, there is still a deep gash along the wall where the car finished up.

At this point it might be appropriate to talk about the origin of this interesting machine. In those days, Alec Issigonis (a brilliant automotive engineer with BMC—the British Motor Corporation—about whom I shall have a lot more to say later) was a great one for thinking up new ideas, and it was he who had discussed with me the notion of putting two engines in a Mini. The layout was so compact and took up so little room because of the transverse mounting of both units, that it seemed like a natural to try out. By then, Alec had spent a lot of time—both his own and that of BMC —developing a machine called "The Moke," which was intended primarily for the Army. It was in fact a Mini-Jeep, so built that the windshield would fold flat and the steering wheel could be collapsed, allowing these vehicles to be stacked into an aircraft or a ship like layers of biscuits, one on top of the other. The very small wheels and general compactness were of course a great asset.

The first twin-engine setup was in fact installed in a Moke, which was also Alec Issigonis' idea. The thinking behind all this was very good, intensely practical and typical of the man. Normally, the most expensive item on a four-wheel-drive vehicle is the transfer box, in addition to which—or perhaps because of which— handling problems always seem to arise. At least they did in those days. But the idea behind the twin-engine Mini was much simpler. Each power unit operated independently of the other, and fitting a second engine was cheaper and simpler than the complications and cost involved with the usual transfer gear. Admittedly, a small amount of load-carrying capacity had to be sacrificed, but with transverse engines it didn't amount to much. Against this, the actual performance was enormously improved.

There were other considerations, too. If the car was on a flat road you could use the front engine alone, or the rear. There was no need to use both. The inactive one simply stayed in neutral. What in fact this amounted to was that you always had a spare engine available for use on difficult terrain such as, for example, the desert. The same was true under conditions of snow and mud. With both engines going, you would then have the finest imaginable vehicle for these conditions. And the cost was less than using a transfer box for four-wheel drive with a conventional layout. I think, despite my accident, that the advantages easily overruled the drawbacks. Our military people on the other hand, disagreed. They decided they would sooner spend the money on a transfer box than on an extra engine. I think they made a big mistake, and most certainly my accident was in no way related to the basic principles upon which the twin-engine Mini was designed. Until the moment of that shunt, the little car had run beautifully and displayed great potential.

Unfortunately, Issigonis did not have any interest in marketing a twin-engine Mini for sale to the general public. His sole interest was beamed toward the use of this car for military purposes. I don't think he really saw any future in a passenger car so equipped, although for my part, as soon as I got involved with this setup I immediately started to build a regular bodied, twin-engine Mini for my own use—with the help of Issigonis, of course. My idea was to produce a thousand of these cars to get the design homologated by the FIA and win saloon (sedan) car races and rallyes. I am still convinced that with more development work—strengthening the gearbox among other things—this dual-engine Mini would have been a great success and a sure bet to win rallyes and closed circuit races as well. It would have been a natural, for example, at the Nürburgring.

We had started off with two 1000 cc engines, but the car in which I crashed had two 1300 cc power units, which was really going some! These were just stock 1300's, but our intention had been to put in two full-house racing power units! What this would have meant is not hard to imagine when you consider that our later, fuel-injected 1300 cc engines were producing 135 bhp apiece! We could also have used ZF self-locking differentials front and rear, instead of the normal production type. Given 270 bhp in a car weighing about 12 cwt (1,344 pounds), we would have obtained a power–weight ratio of under five pounds per bhp, which at any time and even in straight-out competition cars would mean terrific acceleration and performance.

As to the next two days after my crash, I really don't remember much and it seems to me that even a brief description of the rather unique little car that got me involved in the worst shunt I have ever experienced, would be more interesting than trying to recapture the hushed tones and antiseptic smells of a hospital, or the swish of carefully starched nurses' uniforms, the quick jab of pain-killing needles in my arms or the slithery cold of a thermometer in mouth, which already tasted more or less like the inside of a bus driver's glove!

I found out afterwards that a lady and her husband whose car I had just passed and who must have seen me go end over end were in fact the first on the scene. There was not much they could do besides reporting the accident to the police, but the lady was so shocked by what had happened that she suffered a "nervous breakdown" and tried to claim compensation from my insurance company! It was certainly a new twist and worth a try, but I don't think she collected anything, or some kind of strange precedent might have been set for awarding damages!

The police drove round to our home, where my wife was already changed and ready to go to the Salvadori dinner party. They told Paula that I was badly injured and she should accompany them to the Kingston Hospital. In fact, when the ambulance picked me up the attendants thought I had had it. My father also came to the hospital and in his own stolid way didn't—so he later said—give much for my chances of recovery. I was black and blue all over; my skull was fractured and I had injured my back rather badly. The skull fracture occurred when I hit my head on the door pillar as the car rolled. In fact, I was thrown clean out of the car during one of the loops and that's probably what saved my life. This accident was perhaps the exception that proves the rule, because after that I made sure I used a seat belt if I wanted to go quickly.

I was in hospital about three weeks, which, all things considered, was not really that long. But then I had to go through quite an extended convalescence at home and spent another two or three weeks at Littlehampton getting the sea air at the Beach Hotel. And that was how we came to settle in this part of the world. We just liked it so much we decided to move to the South Coast for good.

People have asked me whether I suffered from ill effects as the result of this crash. Well, at the time I had a heavy racing program on—it was the period when the International Formula was being changed—as well as many drivers and it's pretty hard to shut your mind off to a dozen different problems all requiring attention. So fretting around and feeling helpless didn't exactly speed up my recovery. For a long time after, I couldn't get a decent night's sleep, due—as the doctors explained it—to my injuries. I also suffered from bad headaches and still do so to this very day. But it's hard to say whether the end result would have been any different, even had I not had a care in the world at the time.

Probably, that shunt was the turning point of my career. One gets a warning to ease off and take things in a more leisurely fashion. Whereas before the accident I could work on cars and seemingly never get much sleep, from then on it was a different story. I had to regulate my life in a much more normal manner and go to bed at a reasonable hour.

At the time of the Mini accident, as I've mentioned, I had long since given up driving cars in competition. My active race driving had ended in 1952 and the Mini shunt took place a decade later. I had, of course, continued extensive testing at Silverstone and Goodwood, trying out suspension and handling improvements on every new car we produced at the Cooper works, but that was something else, even though our own Bruce McLaren did lose his life in a freak accident of that sort. However, although this is not a book about John Cooper, racing driver, I do recall with satisfaction that I had a fair spell at the wheel to look back on, especially with 500 cc cars. Going back a lot further, when I was only eight years old, my father, who was then running a garage at Surbiton, had built me a single-seater car with a Villiers lawn mower engine in it. I remember what a fine time I had driving that little machine around the garage and at various carnivals. I was the envy of the other boys at school because it was a lovely little motorcar.

Later on, when I was thirteen years old, my father built me another Special, which had a highly tuned Austin Seven engine to propel it along. He had actually modified this engine with the intention of using it for his home-built Flying Flea airplane, but later decided to substitute a Henderson motorcycle engine, which was lighter. In fact this very nice little car became known as our Number One Cooper Special.

When my father was mechanic to the famous Kaye Don, I remember he used to drive me to Brooklands track, which was very famous in those days, and while they were busy sorting out problems in practice, I would drive my little Cooper Special around the paddock and along the access roads, without a driving license, of course. I even drove around Brooklands at the age of eleven—unofficially, it need hardly be said!

Then in 1946 the first production race car built by my father made its appearance, and that was the start of the famous 500 era. I remember that the Bristol Aeroplane Club's Motor Section had written up a new Formula which would be cheap and simple to produce and therefore accessible to many would-be race drivers. Specifications called for a motorcycle engine and gearbox with chain drive in a very light, streamlined single-seater race car. At that point we decided to start building the 500 as a commercial proposition. And how we got around to that is a story worth the telling, even though you may very likely have heard it before.

It so happened that we had a crashed Fiat 500 in the garage with a virtually undamaged front end, and since Kaye Don was a friend of J. A. Prestwich, the owner and designer of JAP engines, which were very hard to get after the War, that made things a lot easier for us. We therefore looked for and found another Fiat 500 front end, which we mounted at the back of our proposed racing car. The arrangement worked perfectly and had the virtue of low cost—an important factor in those days, I may say.

From the start, everything was great. We didn't bother to think too much about where we were going to find some more Fiat 500 front ends for the second car—and the third. During World War II, the popular little Fiat 500, which the Italians had dubbed "Topolino," or "Little Mouse," had almost disappeared from the scene. To find any of those diminutive Fiat parts was hard enough, but the idea that we would be lucky enough to run into a succession of Topolinos with the front end intact and only the rear end pranged, was absurd. It took us very little time to comb all the breakers' yards (junkyards) within reach and to come up with exactly nothing.

Still, we had a lot of fun with our number one "production" test car. We used to get up early and test this machine along the Kingston Bypass, using dealer plates and some kind of a makeshift silencer (muffler) wired on. The muffler didn't always work, even so. Imagine trying on anything like that in this day and age with the local Gestapo! But in those days we seemed to make out pretty well and the constabulary was mostly on our side. It was ironical that my worst accident should occur on the very road where we used to do all this testing.

Of course, we very soon came to the conclusion that since no more Fiat 500 front ends were obtainable—or anyway almost none —we would have to fabricate those parts ourselves. We were not yet in the automotive designing business—not in a very serious sense, anyway—and the combination we had come up with seemed so exactly right that the quickest way around the hurdle was simply to copy the Italian parts we needed.

But that was by no means the end of our problems. Before long, since everything seemed to be getting bigger, we decided to build an 1100 cc version of the Cooper, which we ran in that class. The early 500 race car was used mainly for hillclimbing at Prescott and Shelseley, although it also took part in the Brighton Speed Trials.

I remember that on my first hillclimb at Prescott, we unfortunately blew up the engine during practice. The English term "blew up," by the way, which you often read about in race reports, does not mean that the engine literally explodes into a thousand bits and a rain of twisted parts showers down on the spectators or the nearest competitor. "Blew up" is a sort of convenient generic term used by the Press boys when they want to convey the idea that an engine has quit and there's simply no time to take it apart or fix it during a race. Anyway, what had happened to my engine was simply a bent valve due to hitting the piston top. We worked all night at Prescott with some makeshift tools and no spares and got the valve more or less straightened out, but on the day of the hillclimb we did the same thing all over again! It was time to invest in a revolution counter, or fit some kind of ignition-limiting device to prevent the engine from being over-revved!

My second event was at the Brighton Speed Trials, held yearly in September along the Esplanade, and here several of us had quite a lot of fun. Eric Brandon, an old school friend who helped me build our Cooper Prototype 500, and whose father ran a big London wholesale electrical business called Halsey's Electric, also had the racing bug. By then, we had cobbled together a pretty decent version of Number Two Cooper 500, which he drove, while I handled the original car in the 750 cc class. It was not an intentional thing, but just happened that way as the cars were started and timed in pairs. But my partner on the 750 cc run was none other than Alec Issigonis with a supercharged machine which he called the Lightweight Special. But Lightweight or not, I still beat him along that sea front run, using a straight 500 cc engine, and in fact set up the record for this class.

This in turn led us at Cooper to installing a 1000 cc twin-cylinder engine in the original 500 chassis, which made a marvelous hillclimb car. In fact, driving this little bomb, I held many records at Shelseley and Prescott in the 1100 cc class.

However, I seem to have jumped the gun just a bit. My very first racing involvement with our original 500 cc Cooper happened at Silverstone airfield, late in 1946. Several of us enthusiasts had received an invitation to come to Silverstone while it was still an airfield and before its conversion to a permanent race track. We were invited by Wing Commander Aitken, who was still an acting RAF officer and who owned a 500 cc race car called the Aitken Special. (By this time, although the Cooper design might be exclusive, the idea of designing and building a 500 in your own backyard certainly was not. In fact it was catching on like wildfire among the many impecunious racing bugs of the day.)

If my memory serves me right, there must have been eight of us who showed up at Silverstone on that momentous day. Wing Commander Aitken was fortunate in that, besides the 500 already mentioned, he had built another Aitken Special with a Triumph Speed Twin engine. Then, besides myself and Eric Brandon, there was Lord Strathcarron, who owned a Marwyn 500, Frank Bacon, a friend of mine who was a surveyor, and yet another of the "early 500 boys," Clive Lones with a Tiger Kitten of his own creation. There were, I know, a couple of other chaps whose names I have forgotten, so I hope they will forgive me. We were, I might say, about to share—all eight of us—in a very discouraging episode, from which not even Aitken's RAF rank could extricate us.

It began all right. We unloaded our cars off the trailers the moment we arrived, warmed up the engines and started belting up and down the main runway. But this blissful state of affairs didn't last long. Soon the police arrived, looking very disgruntled.

"I say, what are you fellows doing on Air Ministry property?" a scowling sergeant wanted to know.

"Well," Aitken intervened, "you know how it is, Sergeant. This place isn't being used by any aircraft. Hasn't been for some time. We're not really hurting anyone, are we?"

"I don't think that's the point, sir. What you're doing is trespassing on government property. And unless you can produce a special permit—which I doubt . . ."

"Oh, come off it, officer." Aitken grinned. "You know perfectly well what the score is. We're just having a bit of fun. The War's over, you know. Nobody's throwing any rank at you."

But the stolid sergeant was unimpressed. Perhaps he didn't like racing cars, anyway.

"Sorry, sir, but that's the law. You're trespassing on property that belongs to the government—and to no good purpose that I can see. Therefore, unless you get off these premises right away, we'll have to lock you up."

Wing Commander Aitken was furious but there was little he could do.

"Thank you, officer," he nodded coolly. "I hope you have a nice day, too." Then, turning his back on the Law he addressed us as a group. "Sorry, chaps. I thought the Law was a bit more flexible. It's not as though we were stealing anything. But there you are. Better load up and the sooner we're out of this useless place, the better!"

So, much disgusted, we did as our host told us and headed off to Towcester to the local pub, where we had some lunch and a pint of beer. We were pretty much disgusted at having traveled all that way for nothing, without even getting the chance to try out our cars.

But then the sun suddenly came up in the form of a young man who was probably about twenty-five at the time. He sauntered over to our group and asked, "What's the matter with you chaps? You don't look very happy."

We told him about Silverstone, how the police had chased us out and what the government could do with its surplus airfields and with Silverstone in particular. (It ended up by doing a great deal better than that!)

"Well," said the young man, "what do you want to do now?"

"We'd like to have a sprint, of course," we told him.

"Then why don't you come over to my place?" he asked. "No one will bother you there. It's private property."

All we had to do was cross the road to Towcester racecourse, for the man who had asked us that all-important question was the present Lord Hesketh's father! And that was our first sprint on the Hesketh family estate. The course was actually a horse racing track, on the grounds of which the present Lord Hesketh lives and not long ago built his world-famous Formula 1 racing cars.

Even though, as I have said, this story is not concerned with my personal racing exploits, it's hard to avoid any mention of what happened and the things I became involved in during those early postwar years. My first race abroad, driving the 1000 cc twin, was with Spike Rhiando, a former American dirt track car driver. The year was 1948 and I remember that we traveled up to Liverpool, towing a trailer, then crossed over to the Isle of Man. On the boat we met all the famous prewar race drivers who had returned to their favorite sport after various involvements with the War. They included Freddie Dixon, Tony Rolt (who had ended up in the dreaded Colditz castle, Duncan Hamilton, Bob Gerard and so forth. The cars were unloaded off the boat at Douglas, but these fellows weren't about to transport their cars on trailers to the local garage. They just drove them along the Madeira Drive to the Majestic Hotel, where most of them were staying. There was a two- or three-mile drive along the front and I recall that most of the entrants blew up their engines before they even got to the hotel! These prewar drivers who had survived the rigors of World War II were real characters. Some terrific parties went on there, as well as frolics. They had taken the fuses out of the hotel lights, planted trees around the bar and Freddie Dixon had even broken up the piano. I remember that the local police came to quieten things down a bit and everyone promised to go to bed. But then the chaps poured petrol and benzol into the swimming pool and set it alight, and that meant calling out the fire brigade. Later, this same lot got hold of a passkey and as there were other people staying at the hotel apart from race drivers, the practical jokers had a wonderful time of it. The hotel boasted quite a decent farmyard of its own, and before long hotel guests found geese, chickens and pigs in their bedrooms! At three o'clock in the morning the hotel was really a fun place to be in.

That was very much the way race drivers used to carry on before World War II. The prewar race driver in Europe was often a rich British playboy.

During the early fifties we built a few front-engined sports cars, using mainly the MG power unit in varying degrees of tweak. That was how the Cooper-MG came into being—quite a successful machine in sports car events. This in turn led to the single-seater Bristol-engined car, about which more later. Well-known drivers of these machines were the late Mike Hawthorn and Alan Brown. I drove one of those cars myself. And that was when I first realized that big-time racing was just not for me. My job was to concentrate on designing cars and running a team.

Even so, the story of how I got racing in my blood is not hard to trace. My father served his apprenticeship at Napier's, following the First World War, in which he had served in the Royal Army Service Corps. Later he actually worked on the great S. F. Edge's record-breaking car and ended up as chief mechanic to Kaye Don, who was involved with the famous "Silver Bullet," and with various Bugattis and Sunbeams. I spent a lot of my younger days, before I wore long trousers, in the paddocks at Brooklands and the Crystal Palace.

In 1934, my father started Cooper's Garage at Surbiton when he was still working for Kaye Don and a prewar race driver named "Ginger" Hamilton, whose Alfa Romeo had also been cared for by my father. Charles Cooper, my father, began by maintaining race cars; then, after World War II, by which time I had of course grown up, I suddenly decided I wanted to go motor racing.

It was in my father's garage, of course, that we produced our first 500 cc car after World War II, and so turned the premises into the Cooper race car factory.

One of the highlights of my postwar racing "career" was connected with the design of a streamlined race car body to fit onto the 500 chassis. With the help of Vivian Stanbury of Hawker Aircraft (who was directly under Sir Sidney Camm in charge of aerodynamics at Kingston), we designed a streamlined body. We first built a quarter-scale model which was tested in the wind tunnel. Then with Bill Aston, an apple farmer from Iver, Bucks, who was also one of our customers, we went to Montlhéry. There we set up various world records using JAP engines.

In its ordinary guise, the 500 was capable of about 105 mph, but the streamlined version could top 130 mph with a double-knocker (twin-cam) 500 cc Norton engine. The car was sitting in the garage after those very successful record attempts when I heard that a race was being held at the Avus, which I remembered before the War. It had a peculiar "flat-out" configuration with two long straights and a banking at either end. Just the place for sheer all-out speed. So we decided to have a look. Unfortunately, the Russian occupation of East Berlin had changed things quite a bit. The two long straights and one banking remained, but the other end of the circuit was truncated by a hairpin where the Russian Zone began. The straights were still three or four miles long, however, so we decided to take the Streamliner to the Avus and have a go. Seeing this track, even just after the War, was a great experience and one that I would not have missed.

When we arrived with our beautiful Streamliner, I remember that several teams were already on the spot and these included a big contingent from the Eastern Zone. Among them were the EMW people (the Eisenach Motoren Werke, which represented part of the BMW factory still left in the Eastern Zone after the War). This, in fact, was where the racing department had been located before Hitler cut loose, so the Russian occupying power inherited some very fine equipment which had been left behind. The EMW boys were, of course, under the watchful eye of several commissars and they lived in their own camp. Mixing with Westerners was forbidden, unless in the presence of a commissar. But I remember how interested those chaps were in my Streamliner, particularly because they had two machines of their own with bodies that strove to achieve the same effect.

Despite restrictions, they were able to invite us back to their camp for dinner, where we got into a discussion about my machine. These Eastern Germans thought it was a "wonderful car," which was of course very flattering. The evening went by all too quickly because we had such a pleasant time. As a matter of interest, several of the men I met that day later defected to the West.

One or two of them became very well-known drivers on the racecourses of our "decadent capitalistic world."

The next day, however, there was a certain amount of backlash from our own British Intelligence.

"What were you doing getting on such friendly terms with those people?" they wanted to know. "That's the Russian Zone, you seem to forget."

The day of the race at the Avus was another interesting occasion for us all. The Streamliner was, of course, quite a bit heavier than our normal Cooper 500, because of the extra bodywork involved to achieve the required streamlining effect. Also, we had to pull a very high gear due to the nature of the circuit, which was nearly all straights. I was hoping that way to obtain speeds of 135 mph or better. Since I had put up the fastest time in practice, they gave me pole position and I made use of it to get off to a fairly good start. However, some other cars went by me while I was building up speed. But when we arrived at the hairpin which terminated the first long straight, one of the drivers in front of me went sideways. I was forced to brake heavily but could not avoid him. It was only a light shunt, but my car spun and all those behind had to take violent evasive action to miss me. Luckily, they were able to get around without further collisions. I finished up in the sandbags at the hairpin and I remember thinking, "Well, that's the end of the ride for me!"

But the German crowd seemed wildly enthusiastic. They kept screaming at me to carry on, not realizing what this entailed. The Streamliner was a very difficult car to get into or out of once you were in. One reason was that you virtually had to lie on your back to drive the thing. Added to this I couldn't let anyone help me to push-start, for that would have meant automatic disqualification. There was nothing for it but to push the car, myself. It meant putting it into gear, pulling it back on compression, then jamming it into neutral, pushing like hell, scrambling aboard and shoving it once more in gear.

I made two exhausting attempts but failed both times. The engine just would not start. But the crowd continued to scream encouragement and, despite a feeling of total exhaustion, I had a third try. This time the engine started, but as I got going again the main bunch were coming down toward the hairpin at the end of their first lap. So that put me almost a lap behind. Well, I thought, now that I'm going again, might as well try to make a race of it. So I put my foot down and got up speed in a big hurry. I didn't see anyone at all for a long time—several laps, in fact—but the car was going like greased lightning, despite the shunt, which had only been superficial with no serious damage.

Then, suddenly, I began to see cars ahead of me, down the straight. When I overtook the first of them I realized I was going about 30 mph faster and had not only made up the lost lap but was back in the pack again. So it wasn't long before I overtook the whole lot, totally unlapped myself and began to pull ahead. From then on I eased off just enough to win the race without effort. It certainly was a wonderful feeling, especially when I remembered that on this very course many of the world's greatest drivers had won races before the War.

Some time after this event we went on to the Grenzlandring, which was then a German army depot with a very large perimeter road. It was located near Aachen. Once again, because my car was so much faster than anyone else's, I had pole position. This time I won with ease and there was no shunt to worry about—and no pushing! I think the race was about seventy-five miles long and I recall that my greatest kick was when I passed Stirling Moss as if he had been going backward! This, I need hardly say, was not the usual form!

In a normal 500 model of our little Cooper, I managed to win three years in a row at Rouen. The track was the same as it is today.

Another race I remember winning was at Monza in 1950, again with a normal 500 Cooper. This was a 100-mile event. Then there was the time when I led a 500 cc race at Luxemburg in 1949. It was a final heat and as I was dashing down the hill with three of my mates—Bill Whitehouse, a garage owner from Kent who was later killed in a Cooper at Reims, and Ken Carter, a real estate agent, also from Kent, and, of course, Eric Brandon—I suddenly lost it at the hairpin. All three of us were driving Coopers, and so were a couple of other chaps in the melée, whose names escape me now; but on this occasion there was absolutely no stopping! The sandbags were so light that the car pushed them out of the way. Luckily, this scrubbed off most of my speed, so that I ended up going about five miles an hour. I say luckily because there was an invisible wire drawn across the top of the sandbags, and this hooked me under the chin and lifted me out of the car! Had I been moving at any speed, I would have been decapitated. As it was, Whitehouse described the situation graphically.

"I remember coming around the hairpin, and there was Cooper flapping about like a chicken as he hung on the wire!"

Poor Alf Bottoms, the famous motorcyclist, was not so lucky. During practice that same day, he was killed when he shot down the escape road and hit a parked car. He had designed and built his own 500 cc machine, which was called the JBS, and very successful it was, too.

Last but not least, I remember in early 1949, testing a Cooper-MG chassis, once again along the Kingston Bypass. I was wearing a long garage man's coat and sitting next to an open drive shaft between the engine and rear axle. One of our mechanics was riding with me, but he couldn't help much. Suddenly, it was as if a giant hand had grabbed hold of me and was trying to pull me off and down toward the floor of the car. The thought flashed through my mind, "What on earth's happening?" But very little else. Everything happened so quickly that the truth hit me just as the emergency ended. The drive shaft had caught the corner of my coat, wrapped it around itself and of course ripped the coat off me. All that remained was the right-hand sleeve! How I avoided a very serious accident, I'll never know. If the stitches had been a bit stronger, I might not be here now. Anyway, that's one little interlude I'll never forget. I couldn't have been more surprised if the Man from Space had reached out and grabbed hold of me!

Well, that's about enough of my own racing adventures. I seem to have let my recollections of those early racing days run away with me, when what I really meant to talk about was that strange shunt in the twin-engine Mini—which I still believe would have made a wonderful road car for the sports-minded driver—and to hell with what the Army thought about it!

2

The First Racing Cooper

The Cooper which we built in 1946, immediately after World War II, and which was the first of a long line of race cars to come out of our Surbiton plant, was of course a 500 cc model. We had, in fact, built a couple of cars before the War, but they could hardly be called "production" models. Rather were they scaled-down versions suitable for a small boy. The first of these I have already mentioned. It had a miniature two-stroke engine. My father built it for me when I was eight years old. It was a beautifully detailed little machine which ran quite well under its own power. The second "prototype," my father completed when I was thirteen and its Austin Seven engine had considerably more power.

When the War finally ended, we were all very excited at the prospect of being able to get back once more to some form of motor sport. Unfortunately, at that time there was a very great shortage of any kind of car. Added to this problem, petrol was also in painfully short supply. But just about then the sun came out. The Motor Section (or Club) of the Bristol Aeroplane Company had, as I've said, written up a new Formula designed to enable enthusiasts (or firms) to produce a really cheap and simple race car. The power unit of this new machine was limited to a 500 cc motorcycle engine, using also a motorcycle gearbox. The complete car could weigh around 500 pounds but not less and the drive system, whether front or rear, was left to the discretion of the designer. The machine would of course be a single-seater, but the new Formula, for all its simplicity, was very interesting. For one thing, a motorcycle engine, air-cooled, of course, offered an excellent power–weight ratio. The whole idea appealed to us immediately and my father and I set to work designing a 500 cc Cooper which would embody all the new Formula requirements and could be produced in reasonable numbers. We also saw a way to keep the price well down so as to put the new car within reach of as many enthusiasts as possible.

In fact, we were not quite the first on the scene, and in all fairness I must put this on record. Early in 1946, the new 500 cc Class became reality when two ingenious fellows just beat us to the punch. One was Clive Lones, designer and builder of a machine called the Tiger Kitten; the other was Colin Strang with quite a nice little car to which he gave his name. Our first Cooper, as I have also explained, made extensive use of Fiat "Topolino" components, but here again we were not quite the first. Colin Strang, a garage owner from Harrow, had latched on to the same idea. Clive Lones, on the other hand, based his Tiger machine on parts from a veteran three-wheeler Morgan car of prewar vintage. He did copy the Morgan's unusual independent front suspension, but the rest of the machine was entirely his own brainchild.

There was a third independent designer-builder, Eric Brandon, whose competitive instinct in no way affected our friendship. On the contrary, if anything, it brought us closer together. Brandon was not actually an employee at my father's Surbiton (Surrey) Garage, but we allowed him the use of all our facilities to do his own constructing and basic designing, which, by the way, pretty closely followed the lines of our own first Cooper. Brandon, who almost invariably wore a bright red jersey, became quite a landmark at Surbiton and we liked having him around.

Anyway, several months after the War ended, motoring enthusiasts of all types were already involved in rallyes, hillclimbs and sprints—wherever this was possible. Again to digress a little, I remember attending my first sprint race, which was held at the Elstree ground (where the movie studios were located) just after the War, and seeing some really interesting prewar race cars that had just been taken out of their mothballs and hurriedly tuned up. They went zooming down the runway, two at a time, in the most impressive manner. And that was where I first saw Alec Issigonis and other interesting people, including George Monkhouse, who ran a race car business called Monaco Engineering, in Watford.

He owned a beautiful Bugatti. In fact, on this particular day, Monkhouse clocked the fastest time. There was also the late Reg Parnell, a well-known race driver in his own right, and later of Aston Martin fame. That day, Parnell appeared with two cars, no less—an ERA and a Delage.

As the result of this experience, Eric Brandon, who was really a close friend of mine, and I sat down to do some serious thinking. No doubt, if we really wanted to get into motor racing and not just fool around, we had better push ahead with building a machine that conformed with the new 500 Formula. The first thing we did, in fact, was to take a good look at Colin Strang's 500 and discuss some of the design details with members of the Bristol Aeroplane Club; but somehow Strang's car was not quite the way we saw this new design evolving, ingenious though it was.

However, since my father had a fully equipped garage and workshop at Surbiton, we were at least not faced with the usual problems of less fortunate "backyard" constructors. We had all the tools and facilities we needed; but what we required just as urgently was the right kind of parts to make a start. That's when we had our first inspiration. We happened to have in the yard a crashed Fiat 500 that had been badly damaged at the rear end. In fact it was a write-off from the insurance standpoint, even though the front was still in perfect order. This, we thought, would make an ideal front end for our first 500 cc Cooper. The wishbones, leaf spring and front assembly proved so suitable that we went on using this layout on our "production" Coopers until 1955. My father had learned a lot while working for the famous Kaye Don, a great prewar driver who had once held the British Championship with Bugattis and Sunbeams and had even attacked the World's Speed Record in his famous "Silver Bullet"—a Sunbeam-inspired machine. These two were still the greatest friends, while another of my father's close connections was J. A. Prestwich of JAP engines. The latter immediately grasped what we had in mind and let us have a JAP Speedway engine which, although it ran on alcohol, was just what we needed for our first car. It was very light, air-cooled, of course, and lubricated by a simple drip-feed system. Its output was about 45 bhp, and running on alcohol we didn't even have to worry about keeping the engine cool.

Our next step was to lay this engine on the garage floor, along with the Fiat chassis front end and try to figure out what we would have to do to put together a complete car. Then it came to me quite suddenly that things would be much simpler if we used the Fiat front assembly as the *rear* of our car, complete with built-in gearbox. But that still left the problem of the *front* end of the Cooper and I thought—why not again put in a Fiat unit? So I rushed off to a friend's shop at nearby Walton-on-Thames. His name was John Heath, he was then a Fiat agent and later acquired fame as the builder—or rather the co-builder—of the famous HWM British race car with George Abecassis, a wartime bomber pilot. My first request, I must say, left Heath a bit surprised.

"Do you happen to have a Fiat 500 with a wrecked *rear* end that you've no use for? I'd be happy to buy the car from you." (It had already occurred to me that such a wreck would be much easier to find than one that had been hit from the front, and it would actually make no difference. The salvaged Fiat front unit, if we found one, would suit our needs perfectly.)

"What on earth do you want a thing like that for, John?" Heath wanted to know.

I explained it all as briefly as possible.

"Oddly enough, I do have what you're looking for."

I was delighted. "Buy it right now."

I had already figured out a way of turning around the undamaged front end of the second Fiat so as to provide us with a perfect *front* end unit for our car. It would be just a matter of welding both ends, back to back, and that's exactly what we did. We cut both the wrecked cars in half and welded up the two undamaged assemblies into one complete chassis with independent suspension and transverse springs at either end. There was one problem which we quickly overcame and that was to replace the front swivel pins with a couple of welded uprights which carried the hubs. This prevented the little car from "steering" at the rear. Then we installed the JAP engine at the back of the new car, driving the rear wheels through a Burman motorcycle gearbox, suitably adapted. For the actual drive we used a sprocket, or gearwheel, with a chain which was located in the center of the gearbox. We also adapted the Fiat steering box in the middle of the front suspension unit.

Completing our Prototype 500 cc Cooper was a very light aluminum-paneled body which practically "wrapped" around the driver and main components and had a not very pretty but rather practical truncated nose.

The problem of feeding gas to the engine was easily solved. We installed a small gravity tank right above it, with a pipe leading down to the carburetor. The wheels and tires were Fiat 500, which gave us just about the required gear ratio, and I remember that by toiling day and night with a kind of devouring enthusiasm, we had the first test car ready in about five weeks. This included machining all the parts which we needed for adapting the various components and also fabricating the body.

Of course, as soon as we fired up the engine, I thought, "We've got to give this thing a try-out, just to see how it goes!"

So I put some dealer plates on it and drove off along the good old Kingston Bypass, an accessible, smooth and fast stretch of road with—in those days—moderate traffic and no ticket-hunting cops. Today, of course, you wouldn't even get on the Kingston Bypass with the kind of makeshift, noisy exhaust we then used, and as for trying out a race car, they would hand you a summons just as soon as you dared to stick your nose on the highway. But at that time we could still get away with "murder"—the kind of mayhem, anyhow, that hurt no one.

Our little Number One Cooper ran so well that we immediately entered it for its first competition event, the Prescott hillclimb I mentioned earlier, and the nemesis of so many hopeful contestants in a wide variety of machines, even for those days. This car-busting climb is located near the town of Cheltenham in Gloucestershire. At that time we were selling off surplus Chevrolet army trucks and one of these made an ideal carrier for our race car without the need of a trailer.

I remember that we got to the foot of Prescott early in the morning on practice day and unloaded our precious car. We gave everything a final checkup and I then charged up the hill on my first attempt to conquer it and find out its intricacies, which were many. Yes, this was it! I had the wonderful feeling that I was actually motor racing for the first time and the thrill was indescribable.

Eric Brandon, my mate, also had a go at the hill, but unfortunately an engine mount broke, due to excessive vibration. This was not surprising as the power unit was mounted solidly on a pair of tubes with no cushioning device at all. Undaunted, we took off for Hereford, about eighty miles away, where Eric Brandon's brother-in-law lived. Luckily, besides a farm he also had a usefully equipped garage which was just what we needed. The way we repaired that engine mount is really worth the telling. I remember walking around the orchard, at night, using a candle for lighting, as we didn't even carry a torch (flashlight) in those days. Suddenly, I found what I was looking for—a wooden plow handle of just the right diameter to slip inside the broken engine mount tube! So we liberated the handle, shoved it into the tube and, that same night, rewelded the engine mount.

We were back at Prescott the following morning, somewhat short on sleep but ready for the fray, once more. In fact, we even found time to eat a hearty breakfast before things started popping. As so often happens, all our work plus a sleepless night turned out to be for nothing. We had too low a gear ratio, which meant that the engine quickly over-revved, and before we could show our paces a valve bent. I know I've mentioned this before, but I thought I would save the really juicy bit about the broken frame tube till now. I don't believe I went into details about how we got that bent valve more or less straight, either. Our workbench was a log and our only tool a hammer! We didn't do too bad a job, all things considered, but of course the valve wasn't seating properly because it was the stem that had suffered damage and the valve guide refused to co-operate by so much as a fraction of a millimeter. So any record attempt was out of the question. Still, we figured that we had learned a lot and headed for home far from unhappy—especially as the little car handled as well as we could have wished.

So our next step was to sort out the engine-mounting problem and learn a bit more about suitable gear ratios for a given event.

Our second outing was only two weeks away and this was the famous Brighton Speed Trials, held each year (to this very day) along the sea front Esplanade. This time we entered the car in both the 500 cc and 750 cc classes so as to get some extra practice runs. Again, Eric Brandon and I shared the car as we had at Prescott and we made a good combination. (He had not yet begun work on his own car.)

Well, there's always a surprise around every corner! As I've already mentioned, who did I find myself paired with in the 750 cc Class but the great Alec Issigonis! Luckily, I managed to beat him in a pretty tough neck-and-neck sprint along that sea front drive—

a fact which he has never let me forget! This time we did not do too badly. We had solved the engine mount problem and could figure out the gear ratios needed for almost any course or hill. By then, unfortunately, the racing season was coming to a close, but that gave us the whole winter to think about what we would do next year!

At that point we decided to build a replica of the Number One Cooper for Eric Brandon. Although in no way employed by us, he had contributed much free time and all his considerable enthusiasm, so we thought it only right to offer him the same kind of assistance in building his own car. At the same time I managed to build a Triumph-engined sports car which also featured two Fiat chassis, back to back—the same sort of idea as we were using for the Cooper. However, the body of this new car was much prettier than that of the Cooper. Also, the engine was a two-cylinder job known as the Triumph Speed Twin. This overhead valve unit was extremely reliable—so much so that it was used by our speed cops from 1939 until well into the fifties.

By the end of that winter we thought we knew just about everything in the racing game—at any rate insofar as our cars were concerned. We had really put the spare time to good use in acquiring knowledge, but we didn't realize right then that there was still a lot for us to learn.

Back to Prescott again, we did very well as a beginning. We ran both in the Sports Car Class with the Triumph-powered Twin, and in the 500 cc Class with the two Coopers, Brandon's machine now being complete and fully prepared. During the 1947 season we also had a go at the redoubtable Shelseley Walsh climb and ran in sprints at Poole. Another hillclimb we tackled was Grandsdon Lodge in Essex. Adding it up, we won pretty well everything with the 500 Coopers and also several events with the sports car. As we had done earlier, we used the Kingston Bypass for our testing ground without getting any static from the cops. On the contrary, they seemed interested and willing to help us.

I remember that after the Poole Speed Trials near Bournemouth in Dorset, we were still using our Chevy truck, towing a trailer. The truck carried the heavier Triumph sports car while the Cooper was loaded on the trailer. We were on the Poole Bypass—a four-lane highway (or dual carriageway as we call them in England), when our truck ran out of gas. We had been going at a good clip so as to get home as quickly as possible, and the truck engine was getting hot. We did have a spare can of gas with us but that nearly proved our undoing! The idea was to put through enough gas into the truck's tank to get us to the nearest filling station; but we also had to prime the carburetor to get things going. They got started all right! The mechanic allowed some gas to drip on the hot exhaust manifold, and—vroom! Everything seemed to catch fire at once. My clothes were alight and the mechanic looked like a firebrand as he started running away in a panic. I caught up with him, threw him on the grass and rolled him over till the flames were out, at the same time beating out my own burning clothes. It was quite a party, but as it turned out I was the only casualty. I burned my hand badly enough so that they had to get me to Poole Hospital for treatment. I came out all bandaged up and looking like a mummy, but things were not quite as bad as they seemed at first glance.

Luckily, that was the end of our second season, in 1947, so we again had a long winter ahead of us to make preparations and digest what we had learned during the summer.

And now things really began to perk up in a commercial sense. A number of enthusiasts who had seen our cars perform so well, came by to ask if we could build them replicas of the Cooper 500. Naturally we said yes and took orders and deposits as fast as they came along, but we were really up against it in one major respect. We couldn't go round the country trying to ferret out wrecked Fiat 500's to convert for our purpose. How many would we have found, anyway? So we did the only thing possible. We sat down and designed a new racing chassis from scratch. I discussed the whole project with my father, and besides the chassis problem we did not even know whether we would be able to get our hands on a sufficient number of JAP engines. There was also a budgetary problem. Until we could get paid on delivery, building these cars would mean a considerable financial outlay.

It took two weeks of pretty heated discussions about going in hock, at least temporarily, but in the end we decided to build twelve brand-new 500 cc Coopers, designed entirely by ourselves, without the help of any Fiat parts. We didn't actually stray very far from the well-tried basic idea of the Fiat transverse spring suspension units, but now we had to make everything ourselves, right there at Surbiton, in my father's workshop and garage.

Yet fortune seemed to smile on us. Among our first customers were Sir Francis Samuelson, followed by Stirling Moss (destined to reach the pinnacle of fame in motor racing) and Peter Collins, a natural-born enthusiast whose father, Patrick, had a large automotive dealership in Kidderminster (Worcestershire), the carpet manufacturing center on the river Stour. Moss had got wind of the fact that we were building a production 500 cc race car, but he was at this time still at school. He was under sixteen years old and not really old enough to drive a four-wheeled motorcar legally; but he did have a three-wheeler Morgan which his father had bought him. This in itself was quite a "hairy" machine that demanded good handling and driving.

Stirling came to see us on a Friday, I remember, and took a look at our "production line" which was just then getting under way. He at once ordered a car from us and went off quite happily. Until Sunday, that was, when his father called us up and canceled the order.

"Stirling's still too young to go racing," he said, "no matter how enthusiastic he may be. What's more, this whole project is going to affect his school studies."

I don't know how Stirling got around his father, but on Monday morning Mr. Moss was back with a check and reinstated the order. So it came about that Stirling had one of the first production Coopers to come off the line. Upon its completion, we agreed to deliver the little car to his home at Bray, near Maidenhead. I well recall how eagerly the lad was waiting for us when we arrived. He already had his white coveralls on and was ready to go! So we towed the car to a local building site where they were putting up houses but there was no traffic since the project was located on a very large farm estate. We quickly unloaded the car and I drove it around the half-built houses a couple of times to get things warmed up. Then I handed over the machine to its youthful new owner for his first effort in a four-wheel race car. And I must say I realized right away that this boy was going to be somebody in motor racing. He was quite fantastic in the sure, easy way he handled the car. In fact I grew terrified just watching him. Within minutes of first getting into the car he was going at a tremendous speed and with complete self-confidence.

Unfortunately, or perhaps fortunately at the time, the terrific noise of the car's open exhaust brought the cops around and we had to load up at once and do a lot of fast talking. Then we went back to the Moss farm. I remember also that in those days Stirling was a great horseman—a sport at which his sister, Pat, also excelled. Anyway, they converted the horse box into a covered trailer for the Cooper, so that it could easily be transported to the next race meeting. Soon after, the whole outfit got a coat of white paint, which made it look very attractive and clean. They used a Jeep, I think, as a tow-car for the horse-box trailer, and this too was painted white.

As can be imagined, laying down a production line for a dozen similar machines was an entirely different proposition from building one or two "one-off" prototypes as we had done before. In the past we had always managed to find some junkyard that would sell us a motorcycle gearbox or some other needed part not necessarily connected with a Fiat. But getting a dozen items at one time was something else again. We had no alternative at this point but to arrange a meeting with the Burman people, who manufactured gearboxes in quantities for Norton and Triumph motorcycles, and to persuade them to build some extra gearboxes for us. This they agreed to do. Just after the War, it was very difficult to buy anything like that, at all. Motorcycle manufacturers naturally wanted to grab hold of every gearbox they could lay their hands on. But gentle persuasion paid off and our luck held. At the same time, Burman also agreed to produce our steering boxes, since these presented another supply problem. There were just no more wrecked Fiats around. Then the wheels gave us still another headache. On the earliest cars we had used the standard disc-type Fiat wheels, and in those days no manufacturer was producing a fifteen-inch wheel. So we decided to go for a cast wheel design of our own.

My cousin, Colin Darby, happened to be a draftsman with a firm called Celestion who manufactured loudspeakers in Kingston. So, on the off chance, we sat down with him one evening and designed a cast aluminum wheel to replace the Fiat product. We took out a patent on this design and the wheels were duly cast from aluminum, after which we ourselves machined them to the right tolerances on our old garage lathe. To say that this wheel was an instant success is merely to state the case. It was far better-looking than the Fiat product and, of course, lighter. So perhaps we can claim to have put into production the first of numerous designs of cast aluminum wheels for sports and racing cars which came along later. Incidentally, after a few years we decided to go to magnesium so as to save even more unsprung weight.

I've said nothing about our tribulations in fashioning wishbones and getting springs for the Cooper's suspension, but the result here again fully repaid our determination to push ahead with these projects.

The first completed "production" 500 cc Cooper was a very exciting car to drive. It had tremendous acceleration combined with excellent road manners. It was really what you might call a breakthrough in chassis design, despite its simplicity. It was not so much that we came up with anything startlingly new as the fact that, for the first time, or pretty much so, we combined a variety of known features into one car and made them work together very well.

Prior to this time I had mainly driven cars with solid axle beams, front and rear, and perhaps an occasional American sedan with the so-called "knee action" independent front suspension. But that was the extent of it. Now that the new Cooper also used a solid rear axle (a practicable idea because the car was so light), and we did away with a differential altogether, the machine became much more exciting to drive. You could really hang out the rear end on turns while keeping things under control. And the effect, too, was spectacular. Naturally, the idea at once appealed to some of the new drivers, who enjoyed pushing the rear end of the car where they wanted it on a turn.

Then there were our own vastly improved brakes, which could really stop a lightweight like the Cooper. When we abandoned the Fiat brakes we designed an eight-inch drum with two leading shoes which really did the job. The way we got around this new design problem was to press a cast-iron liner into each of the aluminum wheels. Bugatti had, of course, been using cast alloy combined wheels and drums, but I believe that in fact we were the very first manufacturers to use this particular technique.

The Cooper 500 had a top speed of 105 to 108 mph and could go from a standstill to 60 mph in eight seconds! For the day, this was really an outstanding performance, especially when measured against the simplicity and low cost of the car. Of course, the excellent power–weight ratio helped a lot. The engine at this time put out about 50 bhp with which to propel a road weight of 500 pounds—so that gave us a ratio of 10 pounds per bhp. By projecting this figure you got around 200 bhp per ton—quite outstanding for the time. The gratifying thing about all this was that we had reckoned our production run of twelve cars would probably "saturate" the market, and in this we were totally wrong. We hardly seemed to make a dent in the demand for Cooper 500's, and long before the twelfth car was built many more enthusiasts were practically standing in line to give us their orders. So we decided to procure parts for another dozen Coopers. Even so, we easily sold everything we built and still had to take more orders! Our product needed no advertising of any kind. Its performance backed by enthusiastic word-of-mouth comments and recommendations was all that we needed.

One of the attractions of our little car was, of course, the modest cost for a very well-finished and hand-built article. The price tag was £500 (at the time about $1,750) ready to go, which exactly matched in pounds sterling the number of cc's of our engine.

Nobody is going to pretend—least of all ourselves—that the Cooper 500 was a "thing of beauty." It certainly was not, at least from the front, but we were out to give the customer something good for his money—a small race car of new concept and design that would really do the job. Nobody sitting in the cockpit ever complained about what a Cooper 500 looked like on the outside!

The initial reaction we got from the driver was invariably, "My God, that thing can really go!"

It seems to me that's what race cars are all about. To start quickly, motor fast, and keep going that way with a minimum of trouble.

3

More Power, More Speed, More Everything

It wasn't long before I met an American named Spike Rhiando, a former speedway driver who had something very interesting to tell me about. During the War he had stored away a couple of Skirrow Speedway cars powered by 1000 cc V-twin JAP engines. In fact, they were simply two single-cylinder engines bolted onto a common crankcase specially cast for the job. Spike had already ordered a Cooper 500 from me, but he now suggested that we build a chassis a few inches longer to accept the big twin he had available. At that point an inspiration came to me. This twin put out approximately 100 bhp, or double the power we had been handling, with a very minor increase in weight. It was too good a thing to pass up.

"Tell you what," I bargained. "I'll build you the car you want and fit your JAP twin in it, but on one condition."

"What's that?" Rhiando asked.

"Something quite logical."

"Come on, out with it."

"That you sell me the other JAP twin you're holding in reserve."

"You've got a deal," he agreed without hesitation. "You just bought yourself an engine!"

"I think we might be going somewhere," I told him, and we were. That was the start of the 1000 cc—later the 1100 cc—hillclimbing Coopers. These machines, with their fantastic power—weight ratio, were ideal for hillclimbs and proved an immediate success. Virtually, we had double the former power with almost the same weight. This meant that each bhp was lugging along only about five pounds! Even today, only the most advanced Formula machine can beat that ratio, even with those fat, wide tires. And that was saying nothing of the torque, which was quite terrific for those days.

Now we were really in our element. We discovered a British-made V-twin which was used on the Vincent-HRD "Black Lightning" motorcycle and which had its own gearbox built in one unit with the engine. So our power supply problems were over.

And almost immediately, of course, the Cooper 1000 Twin brought new faces to our Surbiton works. Faces that all said, "I want one, too. How soon can I have it?"

Michael Christie, head of Alexander Engineering, a large business in Buckinghamshire, and Ken Wharton were among the first in line. At about this time, too (1952), circuit racing was just beginning again, albeit in a modest way, but costly race cars such as the ERA began to reappear as our competition, and this brought us more publicity. Our only problem with the early Cooper Twins was reliability, since at the start we depended on drip-feed lubrication rather than a pressure pump, and now the engine oil needed to go into the bearings under pressure. Still, we managed very well in short races while we tackled an improved lubrication system to cope with the heavier engine loads.

At this point the gates to success really began to open up. The J. A. Prestwich firm was so impressed by our successful adaptation of their old prewar twins that they decided to design and build a real racing engine especially for us.

This was to be an altogether novel power unit of 1097 cc, air-cooled, embodying the latest ideas in building high-efficiency competition engines and of course capable of a higher output. It really was a beautiful unit, which produced 95 reliable bhp at 6000 rpm on alcohol with a compression ratio of 14 to 1. We installed it in many of our Coopers right up until the late fifties. And during that time it repeatedly won the British Hillclimbing Championship with various drivers such as Ken Wharton, Tony Marsh, David Boshier Jones and David Good, to name a few. Michael Christie, by the way, later converted his factory to produce special cylinder heads, steering wheels and various other accessories for sports cars and is still in existence.

Ken Wharton owned a garage in Birmingham and was also a

very successful Trials driver. In fact he was British Trials Champion. He had just started getting involved in circuit racing when we, at Cooper, began using the new twin-cylinder power unit. Boshier Jones also ran a garage in Wales, while David Good—who had only one hand—was a fabulous driver on hillclimbs, despite his handicap. All these named people won the British Hillclimbing Championship at various times—Wharton in 1951; Tony Marsh during 1955, 1956 and 1957; and Boshier Jones in 1958 and 1959 as well as 1960. By this time we had become very much involved in all forms of competition.

Another of my early customers was Bill Aston, an apple farm owner who convinced me that now we had the powerful 1000 cc twin it would be a great thing to build a new chassis with a streamlined single-seat body to be designed by Vivian Stanbury of Hawker Aircraft. Stanbury was then second in command to Sir Sidney Camm, after whom a new type of aerodynamic truncated rear end for race cars was named. (Not, as many people have since believed, the German Professor Kamm.)

This car actually was produced to accept 350, 500, 750 and 1000 cc JAP twin engines and proved to be a highly successful machine used both for record-breaking attempts and outright racing. Without getting technical, the new JAP (Prestwich) engine, designed specially for us, featured some very significant improvements. These included dry-sump lubrication using pressure and scavenging pumps for the oil; a displacement raised to just under 1100 cc and the cylinder barrels, formerly of cast iron, now replaced by aluminum ones capable of much greater heat dissipation. There were other desirable features such as a camshaft with more lift and overlap and a reworked cylinder head that gave much better combustion.

During the three to four years it took us to become firmly established as race car manufacturers, and during which time we built and sold more than fifty hand-made cars, we also acquired a lot of new and good friends in the racing world. The nice thing was that everyone in our company—not the least, my late father, Charles Cooper—was tremendously enthusiastic about what we were doing. By this time our staff had grown to thirty people, but we still managed to carry on in the same Surbiton premises where, prewar, my father had worked on Kaye Don's famous cars and those of other drivers of that day such as Ginger Hamilton. The place was no longer big enough for our needs, but we kept adding to it and remodeling the interior to get more room. Unfortunately, but inevitably, the bread-and-butter side of my father's business, which had mainly been the servicing and repair of all kinds of cars, was allowed to run down. We simply no longer had the manpower or the time to cope with that kind of thing. On the other hand, our activities as race car builders were showing a nice profit which gave us all the incentive we needed, financially. We seemed to have hit on exactly the right design for the popular 500 and 1000 cc Formula competition of that day, and—compared with present times—our cars were very reasonably priced.

By about 1950, other firms had come to realize that we couldn't be allowed to get away with what was a virtual monopoly in the 500 cc race car field, so they too began to get into the act. One of our first serious competitors was Cyril Keith, a Birmingham industrialist, who built a 500 cc machine with the object of getting some of our trade. Then the JBS Engineering firm, headed by the famous motorcyclist Alf Bottoms, also produced a 500 cc race car. Naturally this Formula appealed to motorcyclists, since about half of each of these cars was built from motorcycle components; but if I were to express a view, I would say that the beautiful little Keith 500 was by far the more successful of this new pair of competitors and we really had to pull out all the stops to stay ahead of it. This is not to say, of course, that Alf Bottoms didn't do a cracking good job, too. Both these makes kept us on our toes.

By 1953 (I'm going ahead a bit), when we announced our Mark VI 500 Cooper, the JAP engine was still producing much the same horsepower as it had done in its Speedway form, so we began to look around for other motorcycle engines. Norton, for example, seemed like a pretty good prospect. They were racing their Manx Norton motorcycle very successfully in the Isle of Man, and one of our customers, Curly Dryden (so named because he was completely bald), came up with one of those Norton engines for us. To our pleasure we found it not only very reliable but capable of a higher output than the JAP—a useful five bhp more, or so. I got all charged up about this engine and went off to the Norton factory in Birmingham to ask them if they would supply us with engines. I could have spared myself the trouble. The answer was a flat no—at all events as far as the Manx Norton racing engine was concerned. And that had been exactly what we had been looking for. Just a few extra horses with the same reliability.

So we were obliged to do the next best thing. We bought complete motorbikes from Norton, removed the engines and sold the frames separately while the power units went into our cars!

After a while there must have been an awful lot of Norton motorcycles lying around without their engines—more so as some of our customers bought spare engines from us—just in case!

It was not until 1953, when we also got involved with Tony Vandervell, that I realized his father actually owned half the Norton Motorcycle Company! Tony Vandervell, as is well known, was the genius who first produced Thinwall bearing inserts for use with the connecting rods and main bearings of race car engines and eventually produced the Vanwall race car.

Most probably, the Bottoms 500 cc car would have given us a lot more competition than it actually did, but unfortunately, as I have told, Alf Bottoms was killed in a racing accident at Luxemburg during an event in which I, too, was competing. I think his brakes must have failed and the next thing was that he shot down an escape road and smashed into a parked car. The family tried to carry on the business, but with Alf gone the spirit of the enterprise was not there any more.

One night, I was taking a tub and doing some deep thinking—a lot of ideas often come to me in these circumstances!—when a thought suddenly struck me. The standard Cooper chassis design, with a leaf spring front and rear, was shaped rather like a coffin, tapering in a little at either end. This was not exactly a happy configuration, though no one had found it to be the least bit of a handicap. Still, by this time we had a regularly employed draftsman and it occurred to me that we should sketch out a new configuration which would also accept a front-mounted engine, probably of four cylinders. It would of course have a drive shaft and a differential located at the rear, where we normally mounted the chain-drive sprocket on the Cooper. The idea, at this point, was purely experimental—just to see how this design would shape out. The fact that we actually did use a four-cylinder, 1100 cc Vauxhall Viva engine was the result of chance. We just happened to have a spare engine in stock, together with its gearbox. No changes were made to this engine, which was dropped into the new chassis quite stock, but we did build rather a pleasant-looking body around the whole thing.

Oddly enough, although our regular garage business was, at the time, sadly neglected in favor of Cooper race cars, we were still Vauxhall agents (dealers). I raced this machine a couple of times at Goodwood Club sports car meetings and it went so well that the inevitable happened. We began to consider building a second car with a more powerful front-mounted engine. And that was how the famous Cooper-MG came into being. It, too, was a success when you consider how small our manufacturing facilities really were. We built and sold about twenty-five of these cars, which were raced very successfully by Cliff Davis and Lionel Leonard. Davis was a South London car dealer while Leonard grew, of all things, bulbs—Dutch flower bulbs!

The Cooper-Vauxhall got tied into a story which I think is worth the telling. A Major Barker showed up at our Surbiton factory one day, who turned out to be the right-hand man of Sir Bernard Docker, Chairman of the BSA Company, Daimler, Hooper Car Bodies and I can't recall what other enterprises. He was also the husband of the famous Lady Docker whose exploits appeared in the newspapers now and then. Lady Docker was perhaps best known for her Hooper-bodied Daimler cars with leopard skin upholstery. She always matched her dresses and outfits to the color of the car, or to that of its interior.

Anyway, Major Barker told me that Sir Bernard's son, Lance, who was then about twelve years old, wanted a small two-seater sports car to drive around the family estate at Poole in Dorset. Would we be interested in building something special for this young man?

"By all means," I said. "In fact, I think I have the very car he wants, right here."

This was the Vauxhall-engined Cooper we had built prior to the MG-powered machines. Barker agreed at once and the little car was immediately shipped off to Hooper's, the Royal coachbuilders, who built bodies for the Royal Family's Rolls-Royces and Daimlers. There I met a man named "Michelangelo" Fletcher, who probably styled bodywork for every country where there was still any royalty left. I must say he did a beautiful job, too. When I went to pick up the car from Hooper it was unrecognizable. They had built on a miniature Daimler radiator and done a super job of upholstering the interior. It must have cost the Dockers a fortune, but what their son got was a perfect outward miniature of a Daimler. I'm sure that Lance Docker had a lot of fun driving that little car around the family estate.

For our MG-engined Cooper we used the famous TC model engine as our power unit. I remember visiting John Thornley at the MG factory in Abingdon, where he was then managing director. He was very helpful in making available to us engines which we needed for our Cooper cars. In racing, our cars scored many victories and the association between ourselves and MG turned out to be an excellent one. This was probably one of the early financial contracts with what became the great British Leyland empire.

We did a lot of work on the TC engine to get it up to racing standards and so became involved, among others, with the great Harry Weslake, whose fantastic skill in improving the breathing of engines is a byword. Included among his equipment was a machine that drove air through the engine's intake ports to measure the increase in volume that was coming through.

Jokingly, during one of my visits to his interesting little works at Rye in Sussex, Weslake once said to me, "You know, John, I must be about the only man alive who's literally made a fortune out of hot air!" Weslake, by the way, also had a lot to do not only with the Jaguar XK engine, but with the power units of many famous race cars. At that time, his shop was a beautifully located building on the edge of a high cliff, overlooking the sea, and one of his hobbies was cultivating flowers, of which he had a profusion. But it had not begun that way. Weslake's original premises were not far from our own, on the Kingston Bypass.

One of Weslake's men, however, John Lucas, stayed behind and opened his own tuning shop in our area at Chessington. In this connection we found his dynamometer invaluable when trying to squeeze some extra horses out of our tuned MG engines.

It's really not difficult to figure out why the front-engine Cooper was so competitive. For instance, as compared with the standard MG-TC of that day (and later with the TD model too), it weighed at least 700 pounds less than the production job. And this, with the extra horses and independent suspension on all four wheels, just about did the trick. We must have been getting at least 20 per cent more power than the regular 60 bhp of the production engine, coupled with far superior handling on wet roads. Of course we kept the cast aluminum wheels with integral brake drums as on the Cooper 500, along with the transverse leaf spring suspension. The already excellent brakes we had evolved called for no improvement. Acceleration, too, was outstanding and the whole car could only be described as a joy to drive.

All Cooper-MG's were built to special order, some being sold complete with our own body while others went out in chassis form. Customers then had their own individual bodywork made for the car. Our original "production" model featured cycle-type fenders, but later we adopted an all-enveloping body which made the car look like a scaled-down version of the Farina-bodied Ferraris of that day. At the rear we installed a differential casing fabricated by the ENV company of automatic gearbox fame. Of course we retained the universal-jointed axles and wishbones of the original Cooper, as well. The whole combination had been tried and proven again and again. It still worked extremely well on a larger and heavier car than the Cooper 500.

From the Cooper-MG our next step was a Cooper-Bristol, which used the British version of the famous prewar BMW 328 transverse pushrod engine. This ingenious method of valve actuation made possible a hemispherical combustion chamber usually associated with outright overhead cam engines costing a lot more money. Moreover, the BMW six-cylinder, two-liter power unit had the great virtue of remaining seemingly unaffected by passing years and of always running well. It really was a remarkable compromise in design, far ahead of its day if one takes into consideration the practical economics of engine building. But here we come to a single-seat design, once again. In fact, this was the only single-seat, front-engine model we ever produced at Cooper. The car proved so interesting and successful in a variety of ways that I think it worth a chapter to itself, later on.

Eventually, in 1954, we came up with the Mark I Cooper-Jaguar, but this had to be beefed up considerably because of engine weight. And, once more, we were back to a two-seater. But although we didn't produce many of these cars—probably not more than eight in all—a description of the design would not be out of place here.

The first Cooper-Jaguar customer we had was that famous race driver Peter Whitehead of Cooper-Alta and Cooper-Bristol fame, who was also a factory driver for the Jaguar company. (In 1951, many readers will recall, Peter Whitehead and Peter Walker won the Le Mans 24-Hours in a C-Type Jaguar.)

Whitehead, in fact, came to see me at Surbiton and sketched out his idea without wasting a moment.

"How about building a tubular-frame Cooper with independent suspension strong enough to accept a Jaguar XK engine?" he asked.

"Well," I said. "That's what you might call big league stuff. I'm not saying we can't do it, but only that we've never had a go at anything this size before. But there's always a first time."

And so it was decided, following a talk with my draftsman-designer, Owen Maddocks. We roughed out a sketch which we showed to Peter Whitehead, who thought it a good idea.

"Let's go ahead with it," he said.

Naturally all suspension components had to be strengthened considerably on this car, although we retained the identical design characteristics of earlier models. That 3.4-liter Jaguar engine certainly was no lightweight! Then there was the problem of stopping this machine as well. It was just at the time when serious experiments were going on with disc brakes, especially on the Jaguar cars at Le Mans. In this case they were designed and manufactured by the Dunlop Company in Birmingham and they cost a lot of money—somewhere around £750 a set, or—in those days—more than $2,600!

But even so, that was not the whole story. We gave the car an unusual streamlined body which looked pretty good, we thought, but in fairness we got some help once again from the aerodynamic team at Hawker Aircraft. We kept the transverse wishbones front and rear, beefed up, of course, and also installed double wishbones to cope with the extra load. This was very much like the layout on the Ferraris built in the middle fifties.

Peter Whitehead thoroughly tested the prototype for us and found that it handled extremely well. We seemed to have hit on just about the right combination where it mattered.

Next, some orders came through for a similar car from some quite interesting people. One of them was Tommy Sopwith, son of the founder of Hawker Aircraft; but he had radically different ideas about the power unit of our new car. Sopwith wanted it set up to take the French Turbo-Mica turbine engine! This was a shaft-type turbine then being manufactured under license by

Blackburn Aircraft, one of the Hawker subsidiaries. Unfortunately, this rather sensational engine never turned up and we finished the car with an XK Jaguar unit instead. Sopwith raced that car himself, and in so doing became the turning point of our manufacturing experience. We were now in the business of building much larger and heavier cars and learning how to stop them efficiently as well as make them go fast and handle in a manner suitable to that performance. The first six Cooper-Jaguars were known as the Mark I and the remaining two as the Mark II. This version used improved spring rates and was fitted with dry-sump lubrication. We also modified the steering and the cooling system in the light of our practical experience.

We first started work on the Mark I Cooper-Jaguar in 1953 and completed the car the following year. The Mark II version made its appearance in 1955.

And that was about how we, at Cooper, from very small beginnings, got into "more power, more speed, more everything!"

4

It's an Ill Wind . . .

If the twin-engined Mini-Moke was not a success, this should be blamed on the Army's lack of foresight. In fact, Issigonis designed a machine that was absolutely unique. It was a new concept in capsuled motoring which was fated to revolutionize British transportation. And that is not even to speak of similar problems in other European countries. I am happy to have played a practical part in the development of this wonderful little car and to have at least given it a hearty shove in the direction of worldwide fame.

My first meeting with Alec Issigonis (who long ago became Sir Alec) was in 1946 at that unforgettable Brighton Speed Trial. I think I have already bragged more than enough about how I managed to beat him on acceleration during an event which annually attracts a great many true sports enthusiasts, some of whom one might call famous, rather than just well known. Certainly, Issigonis had every reasonable expectation of needing binoculars just to find out where I was and how far I would be trailing behind that famous 750 cc supercharged Lightweight Special of his. It was, in fact, a very advanced motorcar for its day, with a monocoque chassis, even though he had apparently kept it in mothballs during the War years.

The early stages of my racing career—fortunately for me—brought me into contact with Issigonis while he was involved with the design of what was then known as the Morris Mini Minor. This proved to be the basis of a fantastically sound design which, I understand, ended up by selling over two million copies of that amazing little car. At a later date (in the early fifties), when Formula Junior was first introduced—and I'll have a lot to say about that in the next chapter—the Formula called for a small race car powered by a production engine of which at least 1,000 per year would be marketed, with a limit of 1000 cc. The Continental boys would of course turn to the reliable Fiat engine, while it occurred to me that the "A"-type engine used in the Austin-Healey Sprite and Morris Minor might prove ideal for the new Formula.

So I went along to see another old friend of mine, Donald Healey, at Longbridge, near Birmingham in the Midlands, and once again Issigonis was brought into the discussion. It was decided there and then that we—and by that I mean my father's firm of Cooper— would be able to buy some of these "A"-type engines for use in the projected Formula Junior which we intended to build, and this was really the start of our long association with BMC. These engines were, at first, standard, but later were specially prepared for racing by Morris Engines of Coventry. This is another subsidiary of BMC.

I know I'm jumping ahead a bit at this point, but that's just the way things were fated to develop. By this time I was getting to know Issigonis pretty well, discussing with him the racing engines and the results of our budding Formula Junior efforts, which incidentally were doing very well at this time. In fact, our first prototype Formula Junior car, powered by an "A"-type BMC engine, we tested at the local Goodwood circuit and found its performance entirely fulfilled our expectations. So much so that it was decided to begin production with a batch of twenty-five of these cars.

But let's get back on track, historically at least! During one of my many visits to Longbridge, Alec showed me the prototype of his infant prodigy—the Mini, which is really what this chapter is about. I remember seeing it for the first time in mock-up form and I must admit that it looked rather unusual with its very small (ten-inch) wheels stuck out one at each corner of the car. The effect resembled nothing so much as a shoebox on wheels! I think Issigonis had a tough time convincing Sir Leonard Lord of BMC that such a design offered any serious hopes of a commercial future as the People's Car for Britain. However, providentially perhaps, one of the things that really helped to get the Mini going was the 1956 Suez Crisis, which flared up just about then, involving us and the French while the United States played the role of peacekeeper and persuaded us not to go on to Alexandria. The connection may seem a bit indirect, but the momentary lack of funds in Britain and the great uncertainty about petrol supplies at the time, turned motorists toward transportation of a more economical kind.

Anyway, Issigonis, helped by George Harriman (by then Chairman of the vast BMC combine) convinced Leonard Lord that the Mini *was* the car of the future. It was therefore agreed that after suitable testing the prototype would be put into production. However, the amount of money allocated for the production of this car was very small. That's why, in fact, you see to this very day how the Mini bodies are put together with external ribs and joints. This was a much cheaper method than the usual elaborate jigs to locate the body parts, and a change has yet to be made. I, myself, happen to like this form of styling and so have two million other enthusiasts, which would indicate that it's nothing much to worry about.

I well remember when the Press was invited to take a look at the first Mini and the reaction was very much predictable. Everyone remarked about the small wheels. Issigonis shut most reporters up by producing a photo of an older Morris and putting it alongside the Mini. The earlier car had nineteen-inch wheels and it was at once evident how ridiculous and ugly a Mini would have been, running along on wheels of that size! But the clincher was of course the test drives. The moment any motoring reporter got into a Mini and drove it, he quickly got the message and realized what the design concept was really all about.

Naturally I, too, was invited to drive one of the prototypes, and I must admit that once you sat in the car and drove away, you immediately became part of it. This was to be the basic philosophy of motoring in the future. The identification of the driver with the car in a close relationship. Then, too, front-wheel drive gave excellent directional stability; the wheel at each corner made for much superior handling to that of other cars. And on top of this the Mini was the shortest wheelbase car ever built, yet with a surprising amount of honest room inside for four people. There was none of this sitting with your head between your knees for the rear passengers. The car was also very easy to get in and out of—a point that scored well with the women in the family. Yet I must admit that even I, at this time, did not appreciate fully the extraordinary potential of this little car, nor what tremendous sales it was destined to achieve. But I knew it was good, all right, and I understood at once the objectives and ideals motivating this extremely ingenious yet simple design.

When you think that within a decade of the Mini's appearance, all the world's leading manufacturers began copying its transverse front-mounted engine (known in Britain as east-west and in the States as a sidewinder design), that was quite a compliment. Fiat, Datsun, Ford and Peugeot, to name a very few—and now even Volkswagen—are in the act.

Soon, there were quite a number of Prototype Minis on our roads, which was an excellent form of advertising and practical everyday testing. Issigonis lent one to me and another to Roy Salvadori to drive to the Italian Grand Prix at Monza in 1958, and I well recall zooming over the Alps as we followed Reg Parnell's stately and powerful Aston Martin; but this sequence didn't last long. Salvadori, with an engine of only 850 cc, got ahead of the three-liter Aston, and on the twisty mountain roads he completely lost Parnell. Finally, Roy and I both stopped at a little Alpine café and waited for Reg to show up with his very costly Aston Martin of infinitely greater power. Parnell simply could not believe that the Minis were so fast on twisting roads, where, of course, they were exactly in their element. I remember that when we finally reached Milan and continued to Monza track, we met Ing. Lampredi, who had left Ferrari and was then chief engineer at Fiat. (He later became Engineering Director of the huge Fiat plant and is now, I believe, in charge of all engineering for that firm.)

Anyway, his first words to me were, "What on earth have you got there, John?"

Smiling at his astonishment, I simply said, "Oh, that's the new BMC car. Why?"

Lampredi stared long and hard at the Mini and I could see what was going on in his mind. Something like, "Gosh, what a funny-looking little car, to say the least."

At what I hoped was the right psychological moment I casually offered, "Would you like to try it?"

"Why not?" Lampredi grinned. "I'll try anything once."

So he got in the car and drove it around the inner roads of Monza, but instead of coming back in a few minutes as we expected, he was gone for at least an hour. We were convinced, by then, that Lampredi had written off the borrowed Mini somewhere on the other side of the Monza circuit. But this was far from being the case. When he eventually reappeared he was grinning from ear to ear, quite obviously pleased and intrigued.

"I must confess," he told me, "that I've had tremendous fun driving this little machine. And I'll tell you one thing more, John. If it wasn't so damned ugly, I'd shoot myself!"

Coming from such an engineering genius, this really was a compliment.

On our return from Italy was the time when Issigonis really released the Mini to the Press boys, *en masse,* to drive where they liked and carry out any tests they wanted. This was really a top-notch advertising gimmick because the whole Mini concept was so totally new, and here was BMC telling the Motoring Press, "Okay, be our guests. That little car will do all you expect of it and quite a bit more."

In turn, we knew that the public would soon be swamped with superlatives and enthusiastic reports. We were not disappointed.

After the Press had had its fun—and many of them took their borrowed Minis to the Continent—BMC announced the start of full-scale production. And here again the timing was excellent. It wasn't long before the paddocks at racecourses were jammed with privately owned Minis purchased by racing enthusiasts and drivers. They could think of no better way of getting from here to there in ease and comfort—and quite fast, too. The general consensus, even among the most critical owners, was "It's a fun car to drive!"

At this point, with my type of mind, I began to ask myself, "Why don't we build an improved Mini? One with more power, better brakes, improved gearshift linkage and—why not?—a slightly less spartan interior finish?"

So once again I went to see Alec Issigonis and suggested the idea to him. He did not react with immense enthusiasm right away, however.

"You know, John," he pointed out, "this is only a People's Car. It never was intended for what you have in mind."

But I wasn't put off that easily.

"Wait a minute," I said. "A whole lot of rich people are buying these Minis by the truckload. Why at least don't we build something better suited to *their* taste and with an even more impressive performance? Why not?"

"Okay." Alec shrugged. "Let's go and talk to George Harriman." (He, too, was later knighted and became Sir George for valuable services rendered to the British motorcar industry.) He was then, of course, still the BMC Chairman and I wasted no time putting my proposal to him. It might well have shaken a less flexible man, because it amounted to this, "Why don't we put into production a thousand really improved Minis so that the car will automatically get inside the GT [Gran Turismo] production minimum, in case anyone contemplates racing or rallying it?"

"Go on," Harriman told me. "Be more specific."

"Well," I said, "a thousand special Minis with slightly larger engines, still of the 'A' Series but let's say 1000 cc's instead of 850 as at present. That's merely a boring job and fitting larger pistons. We should also include twin carburetors, a high compression ratio and a more radical camshaft, though one that will not detract from its smooth performance."

"Anything else you might have in mind?"

"Matter of fact, yes," I said. "We also need to rework the gear-change linkage to make it more positive and quicker. Then, of course, the logical thing would be better brakes to cope with the extra power and performance."

"How about dressing up the whole car?" Harriman half joked. "A little more luxury, perhaps?"

"Absolutely." My reply was in dead earnest. "I would suggest a more luxurious interior *and* a two-tone paint job outside, which would do wonders for that little car."

Harriman wavered for a moment, weighing up what I had said, then asked what was the real test question.

"Do you honestly think, John, that we can sell a thousand of those improved Minis you have in mind? A thousand, mind you!"

"I haven't the least doubt about it," I said. "In fact I'm confident the demand will be considerably greater."

From my point of view, of course, as I've just explained, I had set the figure at a thousand cars so as to get the Mini homologated by the FIA and out of the prototype class altogether. This was what the international rules called for, anyway.

At that point I got at least half a green light from Harriman. He did not share my unbridled enthusiasm but he was willing to have a try.

"Take a Mini with you," he said, "and do whatever you like to make it conform to what you have in mind. Then bring it back and show it to me. At that point we can really see what it's like."

Had we been in the States, I would have answered, "You've got yourself a deal." But in England something like "Right-o," is enough. So I took the car home and went to work on it at once. We dismantled the engine and bored the block out to 1000 cc. We fitted a new intake manifold to accommodate twin SU carburetors. We put in an improved camshaft with a higher lift and more dwell. The gearshift linkage came in for some redesigning. But even then I was not quite ready.

I knew Jack Emmott of Lockheed, who was one of the suppliers of parts for BMC brakes, and here I really struck it rich. Lockheed just then happened to be experimenting (as an engineering exercise) with fitting a disc brake inside a Mini ten-inch wheel. What luck! Lockheed's reasoning not only was quite simple but it happened to suit me perfectly. If they could make a disc brake work in a ten-inch wheel, then it could be fitted to almost anything.

These were the days, remember, when disc brakes were just becoming part of some production cars and were getting the recognition they deserved. I knew that Lockheed was quite advanced with this particular type of brake and that the automobile industry was just beginning to sit up and take notice. Obviously, discs were the only way to stop a car quickly and *keep on* stopping it without brake fade, which was inherent in the drum system.

Anyway, I managed to persuade Lockheed to let me have their prototype set of ten-inch disc brakes, pointing out what our intent was and how little they were risking by comparison with what they might gain by way of vast orders for the improved Mini. All this made good sense and Emmott realized it at once.

It took us just two weeks to transform a completely stock Mini into something approaching what we had in mind for our thousand-car run; and if I do say so, nobody could have done the job any quicker. Harriman didn't say much but took the car home. The outcome surpassed my wildest hopes. We never did get that car back from Harriman. He simply refused to part with it!

"It's fantastic!" he had to admit. "And I can well see, now, the tremendous potential, commercially, of a tuned Mini."

Soon after we held another meeting with Harriman and Issigonis and reached a decision there and then. We would go ahead and build 1,000 production models of my improved Mini. It was also decided on that day that the car should be called the Mini-Cooper, which meant a great deal to me, of course. There were to be two models: the Austin Mini-Cooper and the Morris Mini-Cooper, so that devotees of both makes could have their choice.

I well recall how excited I was when I left that meeting, secure in the knowledge that from now on Britain's largest car manufacturer would turn out a car with my own name on it. The decision produced waves at BMC, but they were very positive waves. Everyone in the Engineering Department wanted to get in the act and offer help. This naturally proved invaluable in getting the new model out much faster than might otherwise have been the case. Remember, we didn't have an abundance of time to get those 1,000 cars modified to suit the FIA so that they would be eligible to compete in events the following year.

Just to make things clear, I had better restate the plan that was evolved as the result of that fateful second meeting with Issigonis and Harriman. The modifications were mine. The cars would bear my name. But the various ideas I had suggested would be built directly into the production run at the Longbridge factory. This would not be a "backyard" job as we, at Surbiton, simply did not have anything like the required facilities. The engines were to be separately built at Morris Engines in Coventry, to my suggested specifications.

It was fantastic, really, how quickly the new Mini-Cooper went into full-scale production. Once again, the pre-production models were turned over to the Press for a good look and another tryout. This time, BMC leased a place called Chobham, in Surrey, which was an army vehicle testing ground, north of Guildford, and on Press Day that was where the new Austin- and Morris-Coopers were given their send-off. The Press had a field day around the army test track and came back full of superlatives and rave notices. We really were off to a great start.

Of course people asked, "Why have two kinds of Mini-Cooper, both Austin and Morris?" I think I've already hinted at the explanation. BMC was producing both makes, which were, in turn, serviced by independent dealers handling them. And that was the way they wanted things to go on. It really did no harm at all. We just used two slightly different radiator grilles adorned with different badges, but the cars were otherwise practically identical.

The Press Day at Chobham ended very successfully—so much so, in fact, that we had quite a job getting those Press people out of the cars. They were at it all afternoon. Believe it or not, by the end of Press Day most of the motoring correspondents had ordered new Mini-Coopers for themselves!

Thinking back, this was perhaps not too surprising. The little car would top 90 mph and run better than 30 miles on a gallon of gas. What was more, it handled virtually like a race car. During that memorable afternoon, also, there was a lot of hot air released by curious Press boys. The tenor of their questions was: "Why does BMC want to become involved with Formula 1 constructors like you Cooper people?"

Also, did we have any plans to race or rallye the Mini-Coopers?

"Naturally," we admitted. "That was the whole idea behind the production of this car, anyway."

The interest and enthusiasm generated by that Press outing made us naturally curious to read the road test reports which we knew would be coming along. On top of all this, the enthusiasts and actual race drivers who had been driving around in regular Minis at once put in orders for Mini-Coopers. And what was more, they got them fairly quickly, too.

The new Mini-Cooper cost about £100 ($350) more in those days than the standard Mini, but it was worth every penny of the extra price. I think the Mini-Coopers ended up costing between £500 and £600, which was then between $1,750 and $2,100, depending on the state of tune and the number of goodies ordered by the individual customer.

I am reasonably sure that what originally tilted the scales in our favor with BMC's Harriman was the fact that we had won the World's Formula 1 Grand Prix Championship for the two previous years, 1959 and 1960, with Jack Brabham and Bruce McLaren driving for us. Harriman figured we knew a little something about performance and how to get it. He also realized the benefits his huge firm would gain by tying in directly with race car manufacturers, and was quite aware that my request for a production run of 1,000 units was to get into legitimate GT racing.

However that might be, I believe that during the first year of their manufacture (1962), over 7,000 of these Mini-Coopers were sold! This compared with some 200,000 ordinary Minis. Five years later, a million Minis had rolled out of Longbridge. That was a long way from the original prototype we had driven to Italy and Monza, where we had met the great Lampredi. The first Mini had gone into production in 1958 and here we were, barely four years later, with more than a million of both types on the road.

As soon as the Press binge was over, we got down to the serious business of forming a team of three Mini-Coopers to run on the British Saloon (Sedan) Car circuits. These included such tracks as Silverstone and Goodwood. We thought it might be nice, by way of an ad, to have a separate Mini-trailer and tow-car for our racing Minis, and that was how we handled it. Our first team consisted of the Rhodesian driver John Love, Sir John Whitmore and Tony Maggs, another Rhodesian. On top of the factory team, many of our customers had acquired Mini-Coopers to go racing independently, so there were a lot of these little firecrackers scooting around racecourses all over the country and abroad. In fact, this particular Championship class was very quickly filled and no more entries could be accepted.

Our first year of racing Mini-Coopers turned out to be a great success for the marque. And as time went on, BMC became even more enthusiastic. That was when George Harriman invited me to join the official BMC Competition Committee. Naturally, I was very pleased, and readily accepted. I remember coming into contact with Stewart Turner, who, in later years, was responsible for the tremendous run of wins scored by Mini-Coopers in international rallyes. You might say, in fact, that we developed a close relationship, and I don't think I could praise Turner enough for the fantastic promotional and organizing job he did with those Mini-Coopers to boost them on their way to world success. He was the kind of guy you could call up in the middle of the night to do a job for you and he would get it done and never beef about it.

One question I've often been asked is why Issigonis produced the east-west (sidewinder) engine in the original Mini? What prompted him to adopt this design? Well, I think, to begin with, he had always had in mind the idea of grouping the engine, gearbox and transaxle in one unit. I also think he favored front drive because it gave good directional stability. And not the least, this layout permitted a vast amount of space for the passengers—especially legroom, since it took up so little of the front end. Another point overlooked by many people is that in the event of a head-on shunt with a Mini, you have the transverse engine acting as a protective "brick wall" in front of you. This is a lot better than having the engine slide up alongside you in a collision.

In terms of space, the Mini, which is only ten feet long, has it all over the competition to this day. It's also very easy to park, of course, and can slip into a tiny space.

I think Alec Issigonis' engineering philosophy behind the Mini was to produce a small car with all-independent suspension which would handle almost as well as a race car; to build an unusually maneuverable car because it was so short; and last but not least, to provide maximum passenger room combined with ease of entry and exit. Obviously, the east-west engine was the only layout that would give all these advantages for a moderate cost.

So far as I know, the Mini was the first real, practical, front-drive, transverse engine design. There may have been one or two mid-European models such as the Tatra, I think, with a sidewinder engine mounted far at the back and producing over-steer, but that was in any case before World War II.

5

Formula Junior

In 1959, a new Formula came into being which quickly gained international acceptance. This was called the Formula Junior, and although it's well known, a brief description of its original objectives and purposes might not here be out of place.

Formula Junior permitted the building of a race car which would be powered by a 1000 cc production engine, provided this came from a model of which at least 5,000 examples had been sold. Beyond any doubt, therefore, this would be a run-of-the-mill production unit. However, a number of modifications were allowed so as to give the engine more steam. These were clearly stated: you could change the camshaft for one of higher lift, increased overlap and greater dwell; you could modify or change the ignition and carburetion systems; and you could also polish the cylinder head and modify (enlarge and smooth out) the ports. Compression ratio could be raised by planing the cylinder head, but you could not use a different head or block. This also applied to the crankshaft, which had to be standard, though balancing was permitted. There was, of course, considerable leeway for the rest of the car, since its purpose was to be used for racing only. The general guidelines were that the Formula Junior had to be a single-seat, open-wheeled race car without the benefit of a streamlined sports body. Another restriction was a minimum weight of 750 pounds. You could go above this but not below, and a very careful watch was kept over this rule by weighing each car before a race.

I remember watching one of these early Formula Junior races in Monte Carlo—an event held (as it still is) prior to the Monaco Grand Prix Formula 1. Jack Brabham was with me and we both observed very carefully what was going on. The decision we came to was identical. This was going to be an ideal school for new drivers and it would undoubtedly replace the 500 cc brigade in providing the required training on the way to Formula 1 graduation by those who showed the required promise. In this we turned out to be quite right, for many of our present-day top-line drivers have come up via the Formula Junior route, gaining valuable experience in the process. Another point was that here was a truly international Formula, open to most countries since the majority had some good 1100 cc production engines in a variety of sedans.

A further advantage was that Formula Junior made available at modest cost a relatively cheap yet in every respect true version of Grand Prix, open-wheel racing.

That year at Monte, the predominant Formula Junior cars were of Italian manufacture and were called Stanguellinis, which used the reliable Fiat engine. There was also, I recall, a Renault-powered machine. Anyway, as soon as we got back to England I decided to lay out some sort of plan for producing a new Cooper Formula Junior car. Now was the time to act and get involved in what looked like a busy and almost certainly successful project. It was a great chance for Britain since our Cooper works could get the engines we wanted and we had, by then, considerable race car building experience at many levels. Obviously, the most important thing would be the engine: "Which one of several British products am I going to use?" I asked myself.

Naturally, because of my close association with BMC, they were the first people to come to mind. My old friend Alec Issigonis was still very much in the saddle, as was also Donald Healey. I therefore paid him a visit and quickly sold him on the idea of getting into this new Formula Junior with a British product.

"As I see it," I said, "the advantages are twofold. Not only will we be encouraging new drivers, many of whom are obviously Grand Prix material; but also your engines are going to get a lot of free publicity in competition, whether we build a Cooper-Morris or a Cooper-Austin, or what have you."

"Well," Healey agreed, "we certainly have the Austin A40 engine, which, as you know, is also being used in the MG Midget. In fact quite a lot of development has been done on this engine."

To cut a long story short, Healey at once caught on to my enthusiasm and took me along to see my old buddy Issigonis. Alec also was very responsive and offered to put at our disposal a couple of dozen of these engines, on which a lot of experimental work already had been done. I was then introduced to Eddie Maher, who was in charge of Morris Engines—a Coventry factory owned by BMC. Its purpose was precisely to produce special engines such as those for the MG Midget and taxicab engines as well as a number of diesel units.

I left Birmingham very happy in the knowledge that we at least had the engine problem solved for our Formula Junior project.

The next hurdle was the gearbox-rear axle unit. Since the gearbox also had to come from a production car, it was a little difficult obtaining one from an English car because we weren't bothering much about any production rear-engine layout at the time. So we had to settle for a Renault Dauphine transaxle as the most suitable component at that time. We therefore adapted a Renault Dauphine four-speed gearbox to the BMC engine and the combination worked very well. I set to with my designer, Owen Maddocks, and we designed a light tubular chassis which would easily cope with the engine and gearbox combination we had in mind. Everything was kept as simple as possible, so that only about six weeks after my return from Monte Carlo, we had a prototype Formula Junior ready to undergo tests. This was, of course, in 1959, so we wasted no time.

In fact, when it came to designing the Cooper Formula Junior in detail, we were able to tackle the job with no serious difficulty. By this time we had become much more sophisticated in the art and craft of building race cars, and in addition I now employed two draftsmen-designers. Yet, even though this new machine was territory we had not before specifically explored, something told me that many of my old design principles were still valid and could be applied to it. Mainly, we used our time-tried method of putting all the main components on the workshop floor—the engine, gearbox, suspension and front end—then taking a good look at the *ensemble* before we set about getting all these parts to fit together so that they would add up to a race car. My next step was to have a sketch roughed out, showing the basic idea, and when we felt we were on the right track, we hand-made mock-up pieces of some of the missing parts for a final tie-in before designing the actual tubular chassis.

This procedure was in fact not new. I was aware that Alec Issigonis, one of the finest production car designers ever, also made use of the layout technique before going into detail construction and design. I recall that Alec was pretty sold on the idea of mock-ups, sketches on the back of Gold Flake cigarette packs and even on tablecloths! At BMC, where his own section of the Experimental Department employed about fifty people, Alec would have these designers fashion small mock-ups of wishbones and suspension units, then come visiting each afternoon to see how things were progressing. On one memorable occasion when we got involved in a heated argument with Alex Moulton, the BMC suspension specialist, sitting in a restaurant, Alec allowed no inhibitions to stand in his way. He was a very good artist and began expressing his idea with a pencil on the tablecloth. By the time we finished that meal, there were so many drawings on the tablecloth that Issigonis sent for the restaurant manager.

"Sorry about all this"—he smiled—"but I'm taking the tablecloth with me. Just put it on my bill!"

Nor was this merely a gesture. The tablecloth duly ended up in the Experimental Department, where Issigonis pointed out the sketches he liked best to some of his designers and told them to go ahead and make some mock-ups.

For my money, Alec Issigonis, even today, is still one of the world's finest automotive designers. All the time he's talking to you his mind is on cars. He virtually lives motorcars, which are not only his vocation but his avocation as well. He does have one other consuming interest, though, and that is steam power. Steam trains seem to fascinate him completely.

As for myself, fortunately I was trained as a toolmaker during my apprenticeship and this came in very useful when we started making jigs for our tubular chassis, wishbones and other components which had to be fabricated on the spot. The routine was always pretty much the same. After Owen Maddocks and I had come up with a new chassis, my next step would be to design the jigs that would enable us to build it. I personally would machine the necessary jig and I remember how I enjoyed working our old shaper to fashion the metal into the required patterns. That was a lot of fun.

Condensing our basic design into a practical mock-up, then being able to produce the necessary tooling myself, naturally was a great help. It saved a lot of time and as a result cut down our costs and enabled us to build the prototype car that much quicker. We were able to do away with all the usual hoopla you have to go through when you depend on outsiders of differing temperaments, and that let us get on with the job.

I remember that when the first Cooper Formula Junior was nearing completion and we decided to fire it up for the first time, it was already about eight o'clock in the evening. Still, the car looked so attractive that on an impulse I decided to take it out.

"Just put some dealer plates on it," I told a mechanic. And once again my trial road was the Kingston Bypass, where comparative peace and a scarcity of cops were still the order of the day! Yes, those were indeed "the good old days" for driving on the highway.

When I came back after a brief run up and down along that nice concrete road, things looked rosy. The men didn't have to ask how I felt. They could see that, but in any case I told them.

"It's not a bad little car, at all! In fact it goes quite well. Handles, too. It's going to be a winner—no kidding!"

Our first "production" Formula Junior machines were supplied to Ken Tyrrell, today known to all racing enthusiasts as the manufacturer of the world famous Tyrrell Formula 1 car. It was with this machine that Jackie Stewart three times won the World's Championship.

It was a heartening feeling when the following year, in 1960, Tyrrell went to Monaco with three Cooper Formula Junior machines at the same time that we were fortunate enough to win the Formula 1 Grand Prix with our Cooper-Climax. We felt pretty good when the flag dropped for the main event, since one of the Cooper Formula Junior team managed by Ken Tyrrell and driven by Henry Taylor had just scooped the preceding Formula Junior Championship. Henry Taylor, by the way, later became competitions manager for the Ford Motor Company.

The Cooper Formula Junior was, without question, one of our most successful race cars, and for the next four years had things pretty much its own way. And even in 1964, when the Formula was slightly revised and tightened up, and re-emerged as Formula 3, we were still on top of the heap. Now it was Jackie Stewart who, with Tyrrell running the team, became Formula 3 World Champion.

The specifications of the Formula 3 Cooper (the main differences with Formula Junior) I shall talk about in a minute. Meantime, I think I am right in saying that Formula Junior provided many promising drivers with an opportunity to work their way up to Formula 2 and bigger sports cars, not to mention Formula 1. I have no doubt that Formula Junior helped produce some of the great name drivers of today by acting as an intermediate training step.

As I've said, the minimum weight permissible with Formula 3 machines was 750 pounds, but our car weighed about 45 pounds more than that.

Some of the early drivers of our Formula Junior cars—men such as Tony Maggs, the South African who later drove one of our Formula 1 cars, soon also joined our works Mini-Cooper team. John Love, who drove one of the Tyrrell Formula Junior cars followed the same route. He later joined our Mini-Cooper team. In fact Love won the British Saloon Championship in 1962. Warwick Banks, son of another industrialist and an ex-pilot in his own right, also won the European Saloon Car Championship for us in 1964.

Of course we were not alone in producing Formula Junior cars. Lotus quickly got into the act, as did Lola and Elva, so that the competition became very keen.

I believe that when we British car manufacturers eventually got down to producing a sensible rear-engine race car, we scared off most of the foreign competition. We did, however, find a good many customers in the United States and exported quite a few Formula Juniors over there. One of our American customers was the late Timmy Maher, brother of Eddie Maher, who is now a director of McLaren cars. Unfortunately, Timmy was killed in a Formula 1 Cooper out in Australia. Among our "Junior" customers were Briggs Cunningham, who gave us repeat orders, and various teams in the States.

Here are some names out of our order book for the 1960 Mark I Cooper Formula Junior. Lex Beels of Holland; Kurt Ahrens of Germany; Kurt Lincoln of Sweden, whose daughter married the late Jochen Rindt; Hubert Pathey, Switzerland; Andre Leikens, Belgium; and E. Agostini of Italy. There was also J. Nordell of Sweden, but the U.S. contingent was by far the largest. Included were Carol Smith, L. G. "Whacky" Arnold, T. P. Waring, A. O. Stearns and last but by no means least, the American Hap Sharp. After buying three of our cars, Hap gave us a repeat order in 1961, and so did Alfred Momo, who had already bought four Cooper Formula Junior machines. Probably our most interesting 1962 customer, however, was Steve McQueen. He came to see us at Surbiton and said he wanted to buy a Formula Junior car. But he also wanted to go to Brands Hatch to see how he got on with the car, while at the same time getting a few tips from the late Bruce McLaren.

So we loaded a car up on the transporter and Ken Tyrrell and I personally took McQueen to Brands Hatch. In fact, we spent a couple of days there and the time was well employed. Apart from being a real charmer, Steve McQueen turned out to be an outstanding driver. The way he got into his stride was something to watch. Anyway, he ordered a Formula Junior from us, with instructions to have it shipped out to the States, where he planned to race it. I think he got into a bit of trouble with the company that was insuring him during his film-making, but even they were finally convinced that he was a good risk.

While at Brands Hatch, McQueen hardly stopped asking questions, all of which made sense. He wanted to know exactly what the score was about driving a race car and he retained everything we told him. Had Steve not been such a successful actor, perhaps he might have become a world champion driver! An idea of his enthusiasm can be gained from the fact that he refuses to hire stunt men to do his acts, but goes through the whole routine himself.

I remember, coming home from Brands Hatch on one of those two days, we all pulled up at a roadside café for a cup of tea and a sausage roll. All of us were wearing racing coveralls which we hadn't bothered to remove, but there was a waitress who refused to be put off. She kept looking at Steve McQueen and finally came up and said, "Don't I know you?"

"I doubt it." McQueen grinned. "You shouldn't, anyway."

Still not satisfied, the waitress brought her girl friend along for another look. Then suddenly it dawned on them. "I know who you are. You're one of the Magnificent Seven!"

She was quite right, since Steve had only recently completed the picture and at that point couldn't very well deny his identity. As a result, all the local girls came flocking in to admire him.

The Brands Hatch interlude was the start of a long and friendly association with McQueen. He came to a party at my house in Surbiton and I was invited to a return party by Steve in London. I saw him again in the States in Los Angeles at various race meetings, and we later discussed the film he was about to produce, called *Le Mans*. In fact I built a special Mini-Cooper station wagon for Steve, which he planned to use on the film sets. It was equipped with a Stage III, Downton-modified engine and could really go. I think he had a lot of fun with it, zipping from one part of the course to another on location.

As I mentioned further back, at the end of 1963 Formula Junior was renamed Formula 3 and legalized with one major change. Only one carburetor could be used instead of two as formerly, and a restriction in the diameter of the intake manifold precluded the use of a larger carburetor. Naturally, this had an appreciable effect on performance, but otherwise things were pretty much as before. The block, cylinder head and crankshaft had to be standard, though balancing was allowed and all the finer points such as polished ports, higher compression and a different camshaft remained free. The displacement also was unchanged at 1000 cc. By this time (in late 1963) Ken Tyrrell was fully involved, running a team of three of our Formula Junior cars; so in 1964, with the advent of the new rules, he switched to Formula 3 Coopers.

This brings to mind an interesting recollection. I recall testing a Cooper Formula 1 car at Goodwood when the track manager, whose name was Robin MacKay, came by. He told me he had been watching a club race on that same track the week before and he had particularly noticed a young Scotsman driving for the Border Reevers private team.

"That chap's a real flyer," MacKay said. "Never seen anything like it. The way he got around corners—absolutely sure of himself like a real pro. He was heads above anyone else!"

"That so," I said, only mildly interested. "What was he driving?"

"Would you believe, one of your cars—a Cooper-Bristol? But it looked really old and tired. I expect a lot of beginners flogged it. Even so—"

"He was that good, huh?" Tyrrell chipped in, ever on the lookout for new talent. "Not just a show-off?"

"Show-off?" MacKay shook his head. "If that young man doesn't have the makings of a champion, I'll eat my hat! You mark my words. I can tell a real driver when I see one."

Ken and I looked at each other and I suppose the same thought crossed our minds. Suppose this young chap was as good as MacKay said and some other team got hold of him. We'd kick ourselves. Young drivers of top caliber potential don't grow on trees, even though a lot of those who *think* they're good do end up on trees, or in them!

"Why don't we give this fellow a trial?" I said.

"Indeed, why not?" Ken agreed.

And that was it. We found out from MacKay who this chap was and where he could be reached and he accepted an invitation to Goodwood for the following weekend, to try out one of our Formula 3 cars. As a matter of fact, come to think of it, this suited Tyrrell very well because, at the time, he happened to be scouting around for fresh driving talent.

Well, this young fellow's name was Jackie Stewart and he spoke with a marked but pleasant Scottish burr. His name meant nothing to us then, but he arrived at Goodwood on time and we had a car ready warmed up, waiting for him. Bruce McLaren had just taken it out for a few checkup laps to make sure everything was running right.

Tyrrell then gave Jackie a brief lecture on what to do and what not to do, since he himself admitted that his experience with single-seaters was very limited. Then we sent him off.

While Tyrrell stayed in the pits, manning the stopwatches, I walked over to Madgwick Corner, the first bend at Goodwood. I had only to see Jackie go by a couple of times to realize how quick he was. So I rushed back to the pits (by which time Stewart had done about six laps) and told Ken, "There's no need to look at the watches. He's quick, isn't he?"

"Quick?" Tyrrell gasped. "That boy's bloody quick! I think we may have found someone."

"Then you'd better sign him up," I said.

To which Tyrrell readily agreed. However, there was a problem.

Stewart at that moment faced a rather tricky situation. He was entirely agreeable to joining our team for the coming Formula 3 season, but he was already under contract to Esso, who were then backing the Border Reevers team as a whole. They were on to a good thing, anyway, since the future World Champion, the late Jim Clark, had also been a member of Border Reevers.

These canny Scottish people might easily come up with another winner, but the main obstacle was that Ken Tyrrell was running on Shell gas.

"How do I solve this problem?" Stewart asked, quite reasonably.

The solution came to me in a flash. "What you have to do," I told him, "is go back to Geoffrey Murdock [Esso's Competition Manager] and tell him John Cooper says he should buy you a car, trailer and transporter, plus give you some money for spare engines. Under those conditions you'll race a Formula 3 car for him this season, and of course you'll use Esso!"

"I can tell you right now what his answer will be," Jackie said. "I'll be told to just take off and forget the whole thing!"

"That's precisely the idea," I said. "You'll then be free to negotiate with Shell and join us!"

"It's just possible you might be right." Jackie nodded.

As it turned out, things happened in exactly that manner and Jackie Stewart found himself free to join Ken Tyrrell's Formula 3 team. From then on, he won practically every race he entered and by the end of the 1964 season he was the Formula 3 World Champion!

To say we were delighted is to put it mildly, but we were not the only ones to feel that way. BMC took great pride in the fact that their little engine had carried Jackie to his lofty pinnacle in one short season, beating all the rival manufacturers with practically no mechanical trouble that I can recall.

6

Enter Coventry Climax

Whoever called the Coventry Climax power unit "the fire pump that won motor races," spoke no more than the simple if astonishing truth. The origins of this famous racing engine that went on to win two successive Formula 1 World Championships for Cooper cars (as well as countless sports car races) were precisely as described. A light, compact fire pump driven by an extremely modern overhead camshaft all-aluminum engine. The firm of Coventry Climax was no stranger to fine automotive engines and had, in fact, been supplying them in various forms to British car manufacturers for nearly three decades when, in 1937, the momentous decision was made to discontinue this activity. Two years before the outbreak of World War II, Coventry Climax switched to the manufacture of lightweight trailer fire pumps as a defense measure in a war that then seemed almost inevitable.

Even for those readers who may not be familiar with British-built, prewar "component" cars, I think a brief list of the makes which over a period of twenty-six years used various Coventry Climax engines would not be out of place. The first British firm to adopt this power unit was the 1911 friction-drive GWK roadster. It was followed in 1913 by another make called the Foy-Steele. In 1921, the Bayliss-Thomas roadster began using a Coventry Climax engine, and was followed a year later by the Waverley touring car. Then came the 1924 Armstrong Siddeley Stoneleigh, the 1927 Clyno, the 1930 AJS, the 1932 Crossley, the 1933 Triumph Gloria, the 1934 Standard 9 and finally the 1937 Standard V-8.

From the 1930 AJS onward, manufacturers who became Coventry Climax customers installed these engines in saloon cars or sedans.

When, in May 1941, the defenseless city of Coventry was devastated by a rain of Nazi fire bombs and high explosives, Coventry Climax trailer pumps did a stalwart job of helping to contain fires that threatened to engulf the whole city. But the Godiva portable fire pump, forebear of one of the world's greatest racing engines, had not yet made its appearance. The important role played by highly mobile trailer fire pumps during the War led to the demand, in 1950, for a lighter, more powerful and truly portable unit. In fact, the British Home Office issued specifications for such a pump to be used by a newly formed body which was called Civil Defense.

Requirements were extremely tough. The new pump must weigh half what its trailer counterpart did during the War, yet be twice as powerful, completely self-contained and so light that four men could easily carry it. Coventry Climax went to work immediately, Walter Hassan, the technical director (one of the original designers of the famous Jaguar twin-cam engine), was joined by Harry Mundy, an ex-Bentley-ERA man, now chief engine designer for Jaguar. Together, these two outstanding engineers working under Leonard Lee, then Chairman of Coventry Climax engines, evolved a complete set of blueprints. Peter Windsor-Smith, a skilled engineer, was at the time in charge of the Coventry Climax drawing office and design of the FWP (Featherweight Pump) began in September 1950. By April the following year the prototype was undergoing tests.

Without going into a maze of technical details, I think this diminutive yet great fire pump (which went on to win countless Grands Prix and GT races the world over) deserves a brief description. The entire FWP unit—engine and pump—was contained within a very slight framework with two horizontal shafts at either end for easy lifting. The all-aluminum Coventry Climax engine was a four-cylinder, chain-driven, overhead camshaft unit of 1020 cc displacement with magneto ignition which gave the pump an astonishing output of 300 gallons of water per minute at a pressure of 100 pounds per square inch. The single-stage pump, with a light alloy casing and a Francis-type impeller, was driven directly by the engine crankshaft via a flexible coupling. Priming was achieved by a simple exhaust gas ejector system which had been well tried on wartime pumps. The engine, which had wedge-shaped combustion chambers, put out 35 bhp at 3,500 rpm, yet the whole unit, fully fueled, weighed only 365 pounds.

The dimensions of the complete Coventry Climax FWP fire pump were so remarkably compact that the main ones are certainly worth quoting. Overall length (with electric starter), 47 inches; width, 19.75 inches; and height, 34.5 inches. I doubt if anyone realized at the time that the first of an entirely new breed of racing engines had been born.

Once again, Coventry Climax was awarded large government contracts as the Godiva Fire Pump (such was its name!) became standard equipment for civil defense, fire-fighting authorities and the armed forces. It is still being manufactured today (twenty-five years later) and in many cases has retained its regular equipment.

In 1954, only three years after government acceptance of the FWP fire-fighting unit, the first Coventry Climax racing engine, known as the FWA, Stage I, made its appearance. Enlarged cylinder bores (from 70 to 73 mm) gave it a capacity of 1098 cc, which kept it within the 1100 cc class (an important one in racing), while the output, with a suitable camshaft, higher compression ratio and twin SU carburetors, jumped to 71 bhp at 6,000 rpm. This engine was first tried out in the 1954 Le Mans 24-Hour Race, installed in a Kieft sports car, and the retirement of this entry had nothing to do with Coventry Climax or the power unit. The rear axle failed after ten and a half hours and some pretty good motoring.

It was the following year that the firm of Cooper came into the picture and we began ordering Stage II FWA Coventry Climax engines, which by then had reached an output of 84 bhp at 6,900 rpm. Elsewhere in this book, the progress of this wonderful engine to Grand Prix status and finally World Championship, can easily be traced. I like to think that we, the small Cooper firm from Surbiton, more than anyone else, were responsible for "discovering" and pushing into world prominence an entirely British mechanical masterpiece. Anyway, I went up to see Leonard Lee and Wally Hassan at Coventry Climax in Coventry and immediately thought, "Gosh! What a lovely engine that could be to put in the back of one of our Coopers!"

Until then, we had been dealing with an air-cooled engine of single- or twin-cylinder type, and to install a water-cooled four in the same position would be quite an achievement, despite its very modest weight. There was no doubt, however, that the lightness of the Coventry Climax, due to its all-aluminum construction, made it ideal for rear-location mounting. So, after a discussion with these two engineers, things looked even brighter when they conceded that it would not be too difficult to extract still more power out of the engine. In fact, Leonard Lee made the gesture grand: "Take a couple of these engines back with you and see how you get along," he suggested.

To this I readily agreed, but the next problem was to find a suitable gearbox. Unfortunately, because at the time no one in England was producing a rear-engined car, we again had to improvise. It so happened that my old friend John Heath at Walton-on-Thames—the designer of the famous HWM race car and also a Citroën dealer—was able to locate a spare gearbox for me. Of course this was intended for a front-drive (not a rear-drive) car, and even so it had only three speeds. But we figured out a way to graft this gearbox onto the rear of the Climax engine and bolt the whole thing together as one complete unit. It immediately became apparent, however, that we needed a fourth speed. Here, another friend, Jack Knight (an engineer who still machines race car parts for McLaren cars) came to our aid. He not only converted that gearbox to four speeds but two years later built an entirely new box which we, ourselves, had designed. The actual manufacturers of the four-speed conversion were the ERSA firm, in Paris. They still supply goodies for bolting on to Citroëns.

We then had a very nice aluminum gearbox and transaxle unit which was quite suitable for the Climax engine, and around this combination we set about designing our rear-engined two-seater sports car. At that time, the regulations still allowed us to use a central seat with room for the passenger on a sort of outrigger arrangement which was very minimal. So what we really had was a single-seat race car with an aerodynamic body just wide enough to allow for the passenger seat to one side of the centerline. Here, we had further friends to help us, this time at Hawker Aircraft, where Vivian Stanbury gave us a very useful hand. It was decided that rather than have a long, streamlined tail, we would chop the tail off and make it concave. This turned out to be quite a startling improvement—not only in maximum speed but also in directional stability. Professor Kamm, the German aerodynamicist, seems to have had the same idea and he got a lot more publicity than we did.

Anyway, that was how it came about that we were probably the first automobile manufacturer to feature a sawed-off rear end, and this caused a lot of comment. At the car's first race meeting at Goodwood, late in 1954, people crowded around it as we unloaded the truck and asked, "What's the matter? Did you have to saw the tail off your car?"

"Yes," I said with a straight face. "It was too long for this truck, so we just cut it off and saved ourselves the expense of buying a new truck!"

I don't know how many people believed us, but it didn't leave them very much to argue about. So the Cooper-Climax with its central seat and rear engine turned out to be the first of many sports racing cars of this type which we were to produce. The very first of these machines took us about two months to design and build, and quite a lot of thought went into the gear linkage, bearing in mind that the Citroën gearbox was really designed to be located at the front end of a front-drive setup. However, as with other problems, we eventually sorted this one out, too, using parts from other production cars. For example, the gearshift lever came from a Ford Zephyr and we also used Ford Prefect front axle stubs. And of course, as usual, before even we had fitted the body panels I was rarin' to go out and test the car. So the boys slipped on some dealer plates and off I went. But this time, for a change, I used the Chessington Bypass and it didn't take me long to realize the potential of this car. It had speed, acceleration, stability—in fact, all the required attributes. Just to make sure I was not being carried away by my enthusiasm, I asked Ivor Bueb, who at the time was preparing his Cooper 500 in our garage, also to try the car. He came back equally sold on this new design and our next job was to finish off the body panels in time to rush the car down to Goodwood for its first competition.

Fortunately, when it came right down to the wire, we were very impressed with our lap times, which compared more than favorably with the other 1100 cc cars. We obviously had a fast little car with a promising future. The only thing was that we did not have a monopoly on the Coventry Climax engine. Colin Chapman had also become involved and produced a front-engined Lotus sports car which went very well. Kieft in Wolverhampton, too, were turning out a sports car designed around this converted fire pump unit.

Anyway, after we completed our testing, we rushed back to the Coventry Climax plant and told them we wanted to order a dozen engines. We also asked them to get still more power out of the unit and this is where we first came into contact with Harry Spears. He was in charge of the Coventry Climax experimental department and test house and a very useful man to know. Spears was of medium build, with thick dark hair and he enjoyed his pint of beer as much as the next man, if not more. Luckily he took everything in his stride and was never seriously upset.

At a later date, Spears was another of those destined to leave Climax and become involved in the Jaguar test program.

I must say that when I first asked Leonard Lee for at least twelve and preferably two dozen of his engines, he raised a slightly skeptical eyebrow and his query was pretty much the expected one.

"Are you sure you're going to sell that many cars?"

"No question about it," I told him. "Your engine is the best thing of its kind that ever happened. In fact it's the first time anyone's produced a real four-cylinder race engine since the war!"

So our order went through and we began to hustle, trying to meet a backlog of orders that was already building up. We ran a couple of "factory" Coopers, one of which was built for Jim Russell and the other for Ivor Bueb. Oddly enough, that was how Jack Brabham first came to drive for us. He was working in the Garage, where we kept a special space for his Cooper-Alta—a one-off model of ours which he had bought from Peter Whitehead soon after arriving from Australia. The interesting thing about the Alta engine was its very advanced twin overhead cam design, although less than twenty of these fine power units were ever built. The designer was Geoffrey Taylor, an engineer who had a workshop of his own on the Kingston Bypass.

Anyway, at the next Silverstone meeting, which was sponsored by the *Daily Express* and took place in July, as I recall, we had two factory sports cars entered for Russell and Bueb respectively, but Russell couldn't make it at the last moment so I offered the car to Brabham. He did so well and was so pleased with the car that from then on we increased our factory team to three Cooper-Climaxes.

You have to be in the race business to realize that enthusiasm alone doesn't make up for a lack of cubic inches (or centimeters). If you want to go faster you have to use a larger engine, especially if you're faced with minimum weight limitations. So we got after Climax once again and this time asked them to convert their 1100 cc into a 1250, then to a 1500 cc engine. This proved to be a very successful power unit for our cars, which won a whole lot of races from the time we began using them in 1956 for our Mark I, Formula 2 machines and our sports cars.

At the same time that the 1460 cc Coventry Climax engine went into quantity production, International Formula 2 was announced, which would go into effect the following year, 1957; so we promptly reversed our body design to meet the new demand. Instead of a somewhat dubious two-seater body, we started building single-seat, open-wheeled cars for Formula 2 buyers. And that was how we had the prototype completed well ahead of time, in July 1956.

I remember that when we first fitted the 1500 unit to our cars, we ran into a lot of trouble with the engine suddenly cutting out at high speed during tests. This was especially true of the production Formula 2 model and since we were building many more of those it became quite a bother. Finally, I loaded a car on our truck and took it to Coventry Climax for a demonstration of the problem. While the test went on I stayed for three days at the Leafrick Hotel in Coventry. Each day we tested the car on the Coventry Bypass, which was quite handy, and various remedies were tried, such as putting an air cowl over the carburetors and changing the mixture. None of this really helped until we discovered that by reversing the air intake so that it faced to the rear instead of the front, our problem was cured. It's difficult to see why what amounted to a modest ram-type air intake should have caused the engine to cut out, instead of helping it along, but it did and the engineering side of cars seems to be full of imponderables of this sort—unless of course you're a specialist of great experience.

During those days, anyhow, things really moved in a hurry. I remember that the fault was discovered and cured on a Thursday, and by Friday we were at Oulton Park, practicing for the Gold Cup! And on the Saturday we won the 1956 Gold Cup with the first 1500 cc Formula 2 car. This time we had different drivers allocated to the three cars. One was for Roy Salvadori; another for

Jack Brabham; and a third (which by then had been acquired by Rob Walker) for Tony Brooks.

In dealing with this particular period, I've jumped ahead a bit. To get things in their proper context, I should hark back to 1954 for a moment, which was when we ran our first 1100 central-seat sports car at Le Mans. By 1956 we had redesigned this model "over a pint of beer" as someone put it, and come up with a regular two-seater. Dividing the two seats was a horizontal tube under tension. During the two previous years, King Hussein of Jordan, who was interested in all forms of motor sport, had been following our progress with great enthusiasm. The upshot was that his adjutant, Colonel Hunt, got in touch with me and said that the King would like to come over to England and try out some of our sports cars. Naturally, our response was that we would be honored and we at once made arrangements to use Goodwood for testing. So, when King Hussein arrived with his entourage in October 1955, we were able to head straight for the racecourse without wasting any time.

First Hussein tried out our center-seat 1100 cc sports car and drove it surprisingly well. It seemed to me, though, that those closest to him were greatly relieved when the demonstration was over. They were obviously scared that the King might hit something or flip the car, but their fears were entirely without foundation. The upshot was that Hussein ordered a car from us with the object of running it at Le Mans, but since for 1956 the rules had been tightened up to the above requirement of two parallel seats, one either side of the centerline, that was when we did our redesigning. It was never the King's intention to drive the car himself; he was going to nominate two drivers for his entry. But unfortunately, because of the political crisis at that moment, his entry was turned down by the French. The reason was that France was having some trouble with Jordan, which was supporting Algeria, so the French didn't feel too kindly toward that part of the globe.

However, while we're still in 1955, I'd like to mention another incident which occurred at Goodwood while we were running Ivor Bueb and Jim Russell in the Nine-Hour race. This was of course with the central-seat Climax sports car. I remember that while we were practicing we had a visit from Anthony Marsh, who was then working for the BBC. I had virtually introduced him to motor racing in the early days by taking him to the Grenzlandring in Germany and giving him a ride and a thorough briefing on what motor racing was all about. Anyway, that day Marsh arrived at our pit to find it loaded down with bottles of a Vitamin C black currant drink called Rybena. It so happened that Ivor Bueb was under contract to this firm, the idea being the Rybena would slake the thirst of our entire pit during the rigors of racing, and that perhaps other firms might want to copy the idea. In fact we had far more of the stuff than we needed, good as it was, and I suddenly conceived a brilliant idea. Since what Marsh obviously wanted from us was some kind of a newsy reporter's statement, I went one better and gave him a visual interlude which was too good to miss. I poured a bottle of Rybena into the radiator of one of our cars!

Immediately, eyebrows raised in astonishment, Marsh inquired, "What on earth are you doing there?"

"Nothing," I said, keeping my voice down. "Nothing at all. You haven't seen me do it, Tony, and you know nothing about it."

"Wait a minute," he insisted. "I *want* to know!"

"All right, then. Firstly we pour this stuff into the cooling system because the Vitamin C gives it a higher boiling point. At the same time it does a good job of lubricating the water pump."

Marsh fell for the gag, hook, line and sinker. He announced the incident over the radio that evening and received letters from all over the world, asking what it was all about!

The Chairman of Beecham's, who was responsible for producing this drink, actually phoned me. He didn't sound pleased at all.

"I'd lay off, if I were you," he warned. "The joke's over, and I must say it wasn't exactly in good taste."

Good taste or not, we got a load of laughs out of the whole thing and the repercussions were more extensive than I had thought likely.

For us, the withdrawal of King Hussein's entry presented no great problem. We immediately found two American drivers—Ed Hugus and John Bentley—who decided to drive the car themselves. John (who is helping me write this book) is, in fact, an Englishman by birth who had been living in the States since the War. And I must say that these two (at the time) relatively unknown drivers did an astonishingly good job with our car. They finished seventh overall out of forty-nine starters of all displacements and were second in class. Very possibly, but for an error which landed Hugus well and truly in the sand at Mulsanne, we might have won the class, too. It was a very close thing with Lotus.

Of course, when you have a team of men like Wally Hassan, Harry Mundy and Peter Windsor-Smith under the chairmanship of Leonard Lee, with a fire pump engine doing fantastic things in sports car racing, it's hard not to expect them to get the bug themselves.

The upshot of all this successful activity was that they decided to design a new 2.5-liter V-8 power unit in addition to their four-cylinder, twin overhead camshaft, 1.5-liter engine—both of them for racing, of course. The V-8 2.5-liter somehow never turned out to be much of a success, but the four-cylinder 1500 was a fantastic engine. This unit was run in sports car and Formula 2 single-seat machines with outstanding success. Of course, it wasn't long before we talked Mr. Lee into boring this unit out to 1750 cc, using the time-worn but still valid argument: "There's no real substitute for capacity."

Then we really got into the act with lightweight, rear-engine Coopers and began to get involved in the Grand Prix scene, albeit in Formula 2 to begin with. The first race was at Monaco in 1958 with Brabham driving, but this story appears later in the book. Of course, it wasn't long before Climax bored out their engine to two liters and later to 2.2 liters. (All this took place between 1958 and 1959.) Finally came the 2.5-liter, four-cylinder version of this engine, which enabled us to win the Formula 1 Grand Prix Championship in 1959 and again in 1960. These engines were so good that in some later Grands Prix (such as Reims, Spa and Portugal) Coopers finished first and second or even took the first three places and in one case the first four! Such an occurrence can be called extremely rare in full-fledged Grand Prix racing and to the best of my knowledge was pulled off only by Mercedes-Benz during the British Grand Prix at Aintree in 1955. It certainly was the highest possible tribute to Leonard Lee and his team of engineers.

Perhaps the reader will forgive me if I once again break the chronology of this chapter to include a rather humorous incident that occurred during the 1965 Motor Show in London. This certainly is jumping ahead a bit, but I feel it rightly belongs in the Coventry Climax part of my story. The Motor Show, that year, was a critical moment from the Grand Prix standpoint since it coincided with an announcement that the 1966 GP Formula was about to undergo a drastic change. The FIA had just decreed that for the next three years the piston displacement limit for Grand Prix cars would be increased by 50 per cent—that is, from 1.5 to 3 liters. This opened up complicated vistas not only for the engine department, but also in the drive train. Power would go rocketing up with the probable advent of multi-valve, sixteen-cylinder engines, while to translate something like a probable 500 bhp into practical road use—to provide adequate adhesion on the road surface—would likely usher in an era of four-wheel drive. What other alternative was there? Completely new designs would now be needed both for engines and chassis.

During the Motor Show, numerous component manufacturers such as Girling brakes and Dunlop tires, together with the fuel companies and so forth, were as usual fully represented. And as usual they hosted dinners and banquets for people of note in the car industry, and of course the Press. This was not just good public relations, but "keeping an ear to the ground" in trying to anticipate what Formula 1 designers might have in mind for the coming season.

This particular anecdote occurred at a Girling dinner which drew a pretty wide cross section of guests (including, of course, newsmen) who might provide and report pieces of the coming Grand Prix jigsaw puzzle. I happened to be invited, as were Jack Brabham, Colin Chapman, various other race drivers, an interesting assortment of designers and engineers involved in the racing scene, and of course the usual bevy of motoring journalists.

During dinner, I got into one of those moods where you have an irresistible urge to "sort somebody out," or as the Americans say, "put them on." And as it turned out I could not have found a better target than a member of the Press sitting at our table. He was Dennis Holmes, then the *Daily Mail* motoring correspondent. Previous to this he had been political correspondent to the same newspaper and he prided himself on the kind of alertness that missed very little. He was a presentable chap who went around in a pinstripe suit and bowler hat and, of course, when out of doors carried the traditional furled umbrella inseparable from "city people." Especially those with a respectable public school background. It was all part of a convincing picture intended to disarm the unguarded and loosen their tongues prematurely about information which was still "under wraps."

Since Holmes had switched to the motoring business, he had shown a commendable insistence on "getting the facts straight," and so providing readers with hard information of a reliable kind. Incidentally, I think he was on his way up to something bigger in the *Daily Mail* and needed to prove his versatility. Anyway, sitting next to me was Keith Challen, an old friend of mine from the *News of the World,* who had been that paper's motoring correspondent for many years. During lunch I thought up a really good one and began talking to Keith just loud enough so that Dennis Holmes could overhear me.

"Look," I said, "this is completely off the record, you understand, and I know you're not going to betray my confidence, but something's brewing in relation to the new Formula which I'm sure you would like to know—even if you have to keep it to yourself for the time being."

Keith looked at me sideways and when he felt a slight nudge from my elbow he at once got the message.

"Of course you can trust me," he said with a straight face. "You know that."

"Well," I said, "here's the gen. After the Show I'm off to Leningrad to visit the Moskvitch firm and discuss a fantastic new engine they're developing. It's really something!"

"That so?" Keith's eyebrows went up. "How interesting. What sort of an engine is it?"

"Ha," I said. "Hold on to your seat, Keith. It's a sixteen-cylinder job, no less, with four valves per cylinder and fuel injection. It's intended for the new Three-Liter Formula, of course."

"My God!" Keith said. "That's certainly news. You mean you're planning to use that engine in your Grand Prix Coopers?"

"If it's what Moskvitch claim," I said, acutely aware that Holmes was almost flapping his ears trying to catch our conversation. "And they seem pretty confident. In that case we've really got a winner for the coming season. The test bench results are terrific but they haven't yet developed a chassis and it looks as though ours was made for it!"

"You're really serious about that?" Keith went along, playing his part to perfection. "Fantastic!"

"That's exactly what I think, but as I've said, this thing is strictly off the record. So just forget it—there's a good chap. At least for the time being."

"Not to worry." Keith nodded. "Until you give the go-ahead, not a word!" He had been a motoring correspondent for a long time and of course knew I was joking; but not so Dennis Holmes. We had made it possible for him to overhear enough of our conversation to put the pieces together. Then, by common consent we abruptly changed the subject and carried on with the dinner as if I had not "revealed" anything.

After the meal, however, Holmes could no longer contain himself. "John, I'm very sorry," he confessed, "but I overheard what you were telling Keith Challen. About the Moskvitch Grand Prix engine, I mean . . ."

Doing my best to keep a straight face and succeeding rather well, I said, "Dennis—whatever you overheard, please forget it. I really mean that. For the record you heard nothing. The subject doesn't even exist. Okay?"

"You mean it's not true?"

"I mean forget it. Do me a favor."

Holmes gave a helpless shrug but I could almost read his thoughts. "If Cooper came out with that bit of news, it really must be true. Boy, what a scoop!"

And sure enough, in next morning's *Daily Mail* there was a big article carrying the Dennis Holmes by-line. Something about "John Cooper of the World Championship cars is on a visit to Leningrad to discuss with the Moskvitch people a new sixteen-cylinder, four-valve racing engine which will go into next year's Formula 1 Coopers."

Unfortunately, what I had intended as nothing more than a joke didn't end there. Within three or four hours of the paper appearing on the newsstands, I had the Russian Trade Delegation on the phone to me.

"What's all this about your going to Russia to discuss a new racing engine?" they wanted to know. "*We* haven't heard anything about it. Where did the story originate?"

"You know as much about that as I do," I told them. "The whole thing is a complete misunderstanding, of course. I haven't even seen the paper, yet."

The Russians hung up, mystified and far from happy and I'm afraid Dennis Holmes never forgave me for that leg-pull, but after all I *had* warned him to keep quiet about it, hadn't I?

7

Invitation to Nassau

I first met Red Crise at the 1959 Italian Grand Prix, where he was disporting himself in the newest Studebaker product—an exotic machine called the Avanti. Crise, who was nothing if not an entrepreneur of the first magnitude, had come up a long way in the world and by his untiring efforts had not only built up the so-called Nassau Speed Week into an all-time glamorous promotion, but had also made a bundle out of it.

We had scarcely been ten minutes in conversation when Crise—a ginger-haired former midget race car promoter—invited Jack Brabham and myself to compete at Nassau.

"Bring along one of those good-looking two-liter Cooper Monaco sports cars of yours," he said. "It should be the right kind of car for our circuit. All expenses paid, of course."

"Sounds tempting," we chorused.

"It is," Crise grinned. "There's a cocktail party at a different Nassau hotel every night, with drinks and snacks free for the first hour. How does that grab you?"

We didn't hesitate much about accepting the invitation, and I recall Jack Brabham later saying to me, "We're having such a wonderful week here it's a pity we have to find time to motor race as well!"

He was about right, but let's take things in their proper order.

When Crise told us "all expenses paid," he really meant it. The Cooper Monaco we shipped to Nassau at his expense while Jack and I each got a free round-trip air ticket. In addition, our hotel room, breakfast included, also was paid for. All in all this fitted in perfectly with our plans. We had not been to Nassau before, and two weeks later we were scheduled to run in the American Grand Prix at Sebring, Florida.

I remember that we flew the Atlantic in a Bristol-Britannia propjet and were two and a half hours late reaching New York because of stiff headwinds. I don't recall exactly how long that flight took, but it seemed to stretch on endlessly. However, we had a great time on the plane and on arrival at Nassau were driven to our hotel. It was the same thing with the other teams as they came in. Each was allocated a different hotel to stay at. Places like the British Colonial, Emerald Beach, Gleneagles, Halcyon Balmoral and so on. From the first I thought Nassau was a pretty fantastic spot—a sort of dreamland place with a perfect climate and incredibly smooth, beautiful beaches. One thing that stuck in my mind as Jack and I strolled down the main street was the dozens, if not hundreds, of lawyers' offices with registered company names. Obviously, this was the place to register your company and escape the tax grind!

The morning after our arrival, following a restful night's sleep and with a good breakfast under our belts, we decided to find out what was going on. First we took a quick look at the course, which was really an old wartime airfield converted for motor racing. Jack and I both thought it a fairly easy course, although the perimeter roads built into the main circuit (as at Sebring) could have been wider and the concrete surface in better condition. Another snag was the thick undergrowth which sprouted high on either side and extended far and deep. In fact it seemed to us as if a search party would be needed to locate any car that went off course! It would be completely invisible from the track itself.

The car we had shipped over was basically a standard Cooper Monaco sports two-seater with a four-cylinder, twin overhead cam Coventry Climax engine built of aluminum. Top speed was about 170 mph—fully as much as anyone could attain on that course, and we had the further advantage that the car was highly maneuverable. In fact, that particular model was doing very well in Europe at the time.

Our next stop was Red Crise's office, where we tried to find out something about practice times and what the general schedule was; but the only real thing we found out was that races of some sort would take place every day, in between practice periods. I had always thought that England held the monopoly for lack of organization, but for sheer confusion Nassau Race Week had it all over us.

On our second day there we did get in a little practice with Jack at the wheel. We were finally given some kind of a Speed Week program, but soon discovered that racing was secondary to partying. The hors d'oeuvres served with the free drinks were so abundant that after dining out once and paying for our meal we decided this would not be necessary. Breakfast at our hotel was sufficient to keep us going until party time, when we stuffed ourselves with all those goodies which were certainly enough to last us until the next morning. We also learned something. After spending a week eating things like chicken and ham, standing up and using only a fork, we discovered how Americans got along without knives! The drill was to hold your plate with one hand and cut up your food with the edge of the fork.

Of course there was a wonderful swimming pool at our hotel and I took a quick dive at the first opportunity. That was where I met Lloyd Bridges, the movie star, who was in Nassau making one of his diving pictures. He turned out to be quite an interesting guy to talk to, and the fact that he was also a motor sports enthusiast helped a lot.

Then, during that practice session on the second day, we met a couple of kindred spirits. One was Bill Mitchell, Vice-president in charge of Styling at General Motors and a great racing enthusiast. The other was our old friend Roy Salvadori, whom we usually ran into at most race meets. So let's take Bill Mitchell first. (For the record, I eventually sold him a Cooper Monaco chassis—he was that interested in our car!) Anyway, he invited us out to dinner that night, following the usual lavish cocktail party, and it turned out to be a great evening. Included in Mitchell's group was a whole bunch of General Motors engineers who had come over to see whether they could learn anything. Naturally, the subject that came up foremost was the then new Chevy Corvair. Already, many enthusiasts were calling it "the working man's Porsche." Certainly, if you count the flat six-cylinder, rear-mounted, aluminum engine, it qualified as such. Another interesting point was that no U.S. auto manufacturer had produced an air-cooled engine for about a quarter of a century—since the demise of the famous Franklin.

I remember asking all kinds of technical questions during that dinner—such as how they designed the swing axles and sorted out the rear-end geometry of the Corvair. In fact, I later found out, until the rear end was redesigned in 1960, it did not present anything new in that type of car. (If the truth be told, it was more successful on the Volkswagen Beetle than on the heavier Corvair; but in fairness, with the redesigning of the rear end all the bugs were gotten rid of.)

"You know," I told Mitchell at the time, "it's really interesting that the U.S. has actually put into production a layout of this type. You know how I feel about it."

"Tell you what," he said. "Since you're going to Sebring anyway after this show is over, I'll have a Corvair waiting for you at the airport. Use it as long as you like and let me know what you think."

"Thanks," I said. "That sounds like a great idea."

Nassau Speed Week sped by all too quickly, but not without my seeing my old friend Donald Healey once again. And that was where Salvadori came into the picture. Donald had a beautiful house overlooking the Bay and, as it happened, Roy turned out to be his driver in a three-liter Austin-Healey which was entered in the Production Sports Car events. Roy, as it turned out, was staying at our hotel, so we saw a lot of each other. We also had some good fun in the evenings. I remember going with him to a Limbo dance at a place called Over the Hill in the nightclub area of Nassau. There, to a rather barbaric rhythm, native dancers wriggled under horizontal poles held only three feet up, parallel with the ground. There was, of course, someone at each end grasping the poles.

Looking back over the Nassau Speed Week interlude, I would sum up our various social activities (not all of which by any means had economic implications) as follows: besides the visit to Donald Healey's place and the extremely interesting dinner with Bill Mitchell and his General Motors people, we also paid a call on David Brown of Aston Martin and his newly acquired wife, Angela, who graciously taught us to water-ski. Roy Salvadori, who rarely missed any bets in those days, "sloped off" with Lady Oakes—wife of the Governor's son—during that hectic evening at the Over the Hill nightclub and was not seen again that side of midnight. We never did ask him when he got back to the hotel.

As for the racing itself, our Cooper Monaco, which had been shipped to Nassau in December and had arrived in good shape, acquitted itself quite honorably. Of course our mechanic, Tim Wall, was there to keep a wary eye on things and that helped a lot. It had originally been Brabham's intention to arrive in Nassau in plenty of time to get in at least two practice sessions. But this was not to be. The Esso Petroleum Company decided to make him a presentation of a silver model of a Cooper in London and this took place during December—actually on what should have been Jack's first day of practice at Nassau! Since I intended being at the presentation, Jack and I did not fly out of London until midnight on December 2.

By the time we had driven to the circuit, several miles out of town, and Jack had been checked over by the medical officer and completed the processing of the required paperwork, official practice was over. Still, the race people were nothing if not co-operative. They extended practice time by half an hour especially for Jack's benefit! Needless to say he took immediate advantage of this and set off to learn the circuit at once—actually the first racecourse of any kind he had driven around on the other side of the Atlantic. It took him a little time to discover that all was not well with the car, but when he did he came in quickly. Nor did it take us long to spot the trouble. Prior to Jack's car leaving England it had been stripped down and gone over thoroughly, so that on arrival in Nassau no more than a routine check would be required.

John Coombs, a garage owner, race entrant and former race driver from Guildford (in whose garage the car had been prepared with the help of Tim Wall), had told Jack that the gear ratios had been changed to suit the long 3.4-mile Nassau circuit. The reduction gears, it seemed, were 25 and 28 teeth respectively, but the trouble was that they had been installed upside down. Thus, instead of being overgeared, the car was way undergeared and far better suited to a slow circuit like Brands Hatch. In fact, Nassau was even faster than Silverstone.

There was no time for any post mortems, so Jack went out again with the car way undergeared and tried to learn the course. As usual he was very quick to find his way round, but obviously could not put up any worthwhile times without the risk of bursting the engine. That night, we took the gearbox apart and changed the gears around, and the next day Jack found himself in the sixth row of the grid. The only driver he knew from our side of "the pond" was an Englishman named Michael Taylor. All the others were American. The race was a five-lap sprint for sports cars under two liters.

Jack found that the opposition was not tough and on the first lap he had already moved up into third place. Next time around he was second and started closing the gap on Taylor, who led. About halfway round the third lap, Jack was getting ready to go around Michael on a curve when a stone thrown up by the leader's wheels smashed his goggles. These were seemingly made of safety glass, but they were pretty ancient and the worst happened. The glass splintered away either side of the Celluloid center, temporarily blinding Jack. Hardly able to see at all, he slowed almost to a stop, tore off the goggles and tried to drive with one eye while the other stung like blazes. He was able to finish fourth, which in the circumstances was pretty good, but his injured eye was full of glass splinters.

Back in the pits, a doctor took one look at Jack's eye and rushed him to the medical center, where they took out as much glass debris as possible, but our doctor still looked worried.

"I don't think I'm competent to do any more," he honestly admitted. "What's left is too deeply embedded. But I'll send you along to someone who *can* help."

Our next stop was an English eye specialist living in Nassau, who had the equipment and skills to do the job. The doctor who had referred us to him was in fact the medical officer of the Nassau leper colony, the existence of which we were not even aware. This man was donating his services during Nassau Speed Week, in support of the medical team. Jack's eye remained sore for the next twenty-four hours, and even on race day he was not entirely free from pain; but his real worry was that the eye might not heal before the next Championship race a week later. However, he decided that if it was at all possible he would start anyway, and on the Saturday he rested as much as possible in readiness for the International Nassau Trophy—the main event scheduled for Sunday. This was originally to have been a 56-lap (250-mile) race but it ended at 5:30 P.M. because of the waning light. There were 65 starters, including such famous names as Stirling Moss and George Constantine in 4.2-liter Aston Martins, Phil Hill with a 3-liter Ferrari, Carroll Shelby in a new 2.8-liter Maserati and Jo Bonnier driving a Porsche.

When 49 of the 56 laps were completed, Constantine got the checkered flag, winning at an average of 87.2 mph. Hill was second, Bonnier third and Jack fourth. It had been our intention to leave Nassau immediately after the race and go directly to Sebring, but the specialist was still far from happy with Jack's eye and persuaded us to stay on another two days while he made further examinations. There was apparently still a chance that a splinter had lodged deep in Jack's eye, but it was so bloodshot that the doctor could not be certain. So while we lingered on at Nassau for another forty-eight hours, I'll hark back to that other interesting character who joined us—Roy Salvadori. Roy was down to drive for my old friend Donald Healey, whose house had a marvelous sea view. Donald had entered a three-liter Austin-Healey in the Production Sports Car events, but I believe Roy's interest was equally divided between racing and the two very charming lady companions who were Healey's guests at his wonderful beach home. Apparently Roy's thinking went somewhat along these lines: "This is all right for me! Not only am I here, being paid to drive in a race, but there's even a bird thrown in as well!"

I very much doubt that Donald Healey shared this view, but he was a wonderful host and we had a very good time as his guests. Unfortunately, Salvadori didn't do so well in the race. He somehow managed to shunt the Austin-Healey and put it out of action. However, before doing so he put up fastest time in the touring car event. When it came to the prize giving, Salvadori wasn't there and neither was Healey. I therefore collected Roy's cup for Fastest Lap from the Club and held it until next morning, when Donald had arranged to meet him for breakfast. They planned to settle up their financial affairs, but as Salvadori again failed to show I walked up to Healey's table and set down the cup.

"I think this really ought to be yours, Donald," I said. "You've paid Roy; he's shunted your car and even pinched some of your crumpet. So you're at least entitled to the trophy!"

I've already mentioned David Brown (or Sir David, as he is today) and his delightful bride, Angela, but I forgot to mention that the party during which she taught us to ski included Salvadori and Reg Parnell besides Jack and myself. Reg, I recall, was not too adept at this sport. He spent most of the time on his back with his skis sticking out of the water at an extraordinary angle.

While I'm at it, perhaps I should elaborate just a bit more on the evening we spent at the Over the Hill nightclub. This was after the usual round of cocktail parties and our particular gang included the irrepressible Salvadori and Lady Oakes, the spouse of the Governor's son. She was a very lovely Danish girl, quite concerned about our having a good time and missing nothing on the island.

"I think you'd better see the Latin quarter here," she smiled. "It's known in Nassau as Over the Hill. Really, it's a black town where you hear a lot of steel guitars and bands."

We were happy to go along and learn the Limbo, while Salvadori, of course, was in the thick of things in more senses than one, and as I mentioned earlier he took off with our hostess. If the truth be told, though, the atmosphere in Nassau is irresistibly romantic and it would be a cold fish, indeed, who didn't react to it!

Stirling Moss was another fortunate one who had built himself a house in Nassau and insisted on our visiting him. He was then with his first wife, Katie Molson, of the Canadian brewery family, a very beautiful and pleasant girl. It was a pity those two didn't hit it off.

All good things seem to have a habit of coming to an end too soon, but when we eventually left Nassau on Tuesday evening, Jack's eye was still a disturbing query. On arrival at Sebring there was the usual medical exam and scrutineering of the cars, Wednesday afternoon, following which Jack took his first look at the Sebring course. Back in London, John Bullock, the Rootes public relations officer, had arranged for Jack to pick up a Rapier from the local dealer which he could use as he pleased. So what with the Corvair we were not short of private transportation, although as will be seen, the latter car involved us in something of a dilemma.

8

Sebring and Sequel

When Jack Brabham and I landed in Tampa, Florida, after the short flight from Nassau, we found that Bill Mitchell had kept his promise. Awaiting us at the airport was a gleaming new Chevy Corvair, ours to use as we pleased during our stay in Florida. After going through the usual customs formalities, we loaded our luggage into the generous-sized trunk in front and headed for Sebring. This was my first experience with an American rear-engine, air-cooled car and I must say I was impressed. The car offered a lot more room than the Volkswagen and the general standard of finish was far better than I had expected, while for a compact the performance fully came up to expectations.

"I can see what General Motors are trying to do," I said to Jack. "It looks to me like a pretty fair try."

"Agreed," he smiled. "But they're going to have a lot of catching up to do with Wolfsburg. Volkswagen are selling something like 600,000 cars a year in this country alone."

"Nobody can really compete with Americans when it comes to mass production," I reminded Jack. "I just hope the car gains general acceptance and does so quickly. It deserves the buying public's support."

How we ever got out of Tampa, I don't know. If you can find your way around that town you're never going to get lost. Neither South London nor even Brooklyn, New York, can really compete with it. Anyway, so it seemed to us, but we made it and duly arrived at Harder Hall, our Sebring headquarters, in good shape after a pleasant drive. One thing I found surprisingly easy in the Corvair was the gear shifting. With the necessary long linkage from the rear-mounted gearbox, it crossed my mind that the lever might have a "spongy" feel. But it did not. Considering the air-cooled engine the noise level, too, was very acceptable.

Harder Hall is Sebring's largest hotel and during the "season" houses a lot of elderly guests who dislike noise of any kind. There's a beautiful golf course nearby, too, but as it happened the holiday season was nearly over by March. We had the place to ourselves—and when I say "ourselves" I am talking about the majority of drivers competing in the Grand Prix. The lounge in that hotel is so vast you can almost lose yourself! High ceilings help to keep the place pleasantly cool at all times.

There was one drawback, however. That evening when we headed for the bar we found to our surprise that you couldn't buy any alcoholic drinks "over the counter." I never did find out whether this was a Florida law or a local ordinance, but the only way you could get a drink was to buy a bottle of whatever you fancied. They would just put a label on it with your name and keep it in the bar. If you wanted something to drink, it came out of your personal bottle. Not such a bad idea if you think about it.

Going down to dinner that first evening, we ran into Bruce McLaren, who had just arrived from England. Naturally, he was very interested to know how Jack and I had made out at Nassau. The best way we could sum up that experience was that while the racing just made it, the parties were out of this world! I suppose we should have acquired little more than a "nightclub tan" in Nassau, but in fact we looked deeply suntanned and fit as fiddles.

Dinner over, we headed for the bar once again, asked for our personal bottles and started up a little party. About the first personality we ran into was the American Indy driver, Rodger Ward, who had won the grueling 500 the previous year—1959. What was more, he had done it in a time-honored, Offy-powered "roadster" (the so-called funny cars with rear engines hadn't reached Indy yet) and set a new speed record for the race of better than 135 mph. In fact Ward, although we didn't know it at the time, hadn't yet reached the peak of his career by any means. It's interesting to recall that after finishing second in that year's Indy and third in 1961, he won again in 1962, took third in 1963 and finally was second in 1964 with a rear-engined Ford-powered car. Rodger was the first driver ever to average better than 140 mph in the famous 500 and in six years put up some of the outstanding performances in Speedway history. So this man really had something on the ball besides a pleasant personality. At the time, Ward was only a casual acquaintance but he soon joined our party and we found out what he was doing at Sebring.

"I'm driving a 1750 Midget," he said confidently. "A dirt track car."

"In the Grand Prix?" Jack asked with astonishment.

"Sure." Ward grinned. "And have you guys got a surprise waiting for you! Why, on every turn I'll blow you right off the road!"

Jack tried to explain the situation to him; then Bruce McLaren also put in some pretty persuasive arguments, but to no avail. I was the last to make the attempt but realized it was just a waste of time.

"Look, Rodger," I said, "you haven't really seen anything yet. I'm sure you haven't been out there. Just wait till practice time tomorrow and maybe you'll have your eyes opened!"

"No use trying those tactics with me," Ward kidded. "I know what a Midget can do and I know it can take a corner faster than any of those sports cars you have in Europe. You might be faster on the straights, but when it comes to turns you just won't have a chance. Sebring's a lot of turns, isn't it?"

At that point, all of us with several drinks under our belts, we just gave up. There were no hard feelings at all. I suppose we just felt a bit sorry for Rodger and wondered how a driver of his caliber could be kidding himself so royally. What surprised us about as much, next day, was how Ward's car ever got through the technical scrutineering. It was an out-and-out dirt track car, totally unrelated to any form of Grand Prix racing. I guess Rodger's tremendous Indianapolis reputation helped him to get through, but things soon developed just as we figured they would.

During the first practice lap, Bruce McLaren and Jack Brabham, each driving one of our Grand Prix Coopers, arrived at the first turn at about the same time as Rodger did. The main difference was that while they streaked through he almost came to a standstill. It must have been a bitter pill to swallow. Both my drivers left him cold and disappeared.

To Ward's credit he took it pretty well. I sought him out after practice and asked, "Well, Rodger? What do you plan to do now? Set up your car differently, maybe?"

Smiling a bit ruefully, Rodger shook his head no. "Boy," he said, "I've got to hand it to you. Those European buggies sure take corners fast!"

"Tough luck," I said, but he soon recovered.

"Tell you what," he said, "a car like yours would become a feature at Indy. No doubt about that."

Ward was to prove entirely right, as we shall soon see.

Our garage, if it could be called that, was in one of the giant airplane hangars that Briggs Cunningham had rented from whoever owned them. I suppose they belonged to the town of Sebring. Anyway, everything was laid on, including hot and cold water, and it was really pleasant to work in these conditions. We had Cunningham to thank for this—a great American sportsman and a wonderful character. The way he enthused over our cars, too, was a morale booster that made us feel pretty good.

The end of the first practice session saw us with first and third fastest times. Jack was quickest with only a small margin over Bruce—this on one of the toughest "road" circuits in the world, both for the car and the driver. Sebring is too well known to need any detailed account of the many problems it poses, but with eleven turns on each lap, varying from the four-wheel drift variety to tight hairpins and right-angled corners, and with something like nineteen gearshifts per lap and at least seven brake applications, what it can do to a car's transmission, clutch and brake system over twelve hours is not hard to imagine. Old perimeter roads of this former military airfield are skillfully blended with runways to produce all the true road racing hazards.

On the second day's practice, things were much the same, with, I think, two exceptions. Rodger Ward quickly learned his lesson and Jack Brabham thought he might be able to lap the course a bit faster, given the right gear ratio.

That night, during dinner at Harder Hall, he was quite emphatic about this.

"Look, John, I definitely want to go back to our hangar to see what the mechanics are doing about changing the rear end. If they don't run into any problems, I'm pretty sure I can turn in some better lap times tomorrow. We might also be able to save a little gas."

1. John Cooper in the Prototype 500 bearing his name, on his first hillclimb at Prescott in 1946. This diminutive machine, powered by a motorcycle engine, was very fast until an engine mount broke from vibration. Note lack of helmet, rollbar, seat belt or any safety precaution!

2. "Cat on a hot tin roof?" This 500 Cooper, driven by Major Braid at Blandford, Dorset (an army camp road course), in 1948, finished up in strange position atop the guardroom roof. Braid's car apparently hit a tree which bent, then catapulted him upward as it straightened. Driver was unhurt.

3. Batch of early Cooper 500 race cars taken (with some customers) in 1948. *Left to right:* John Cooper, George Saunders, Charles Cooper, Stirling Moss, Eric Brandon, Stan Coldham, Stirling's German mechanic, "Kraut."

4. Early Cooper 500 (1950 model) with a rear-mounted Norton twin-cam motorcycle engine. This highly competitive machine reflected simplicity and strength. Note megaphone exhaust and rear-view mirror mounting.

5. John Cooper winning one of the early 500 cc races at Monza in 1950 with a car of his own manufacture.

6. The late Mike Hawthorn (who performed wonders with the Cooper-Bristol) on his way to winning the *Daily Express* International Trophy at Boreham in August 1952.

7. Another Cooper enthusiast—singer and actress Petula Clark with the Cooper Central Seat 1500 cc sports car in 1956.

8. First of the 1.57-liter Coventry Climax-powered Formula 2 Coopers at the *Daily Herald* Gold Cup Meeting, Oulton Park, in September 1956. Brabham leads in a works car, followed by Tony Brooks with Rob Walker's private Cooper entry.

9. The 1956 Cooper-Climax 1100 cc rear-engine sports car under construction. This was the actual Le Mans version with a central tube chassis designed by John Cooper "over a pint of beer," and successfully driven by John Bentley and Ed Hugus.

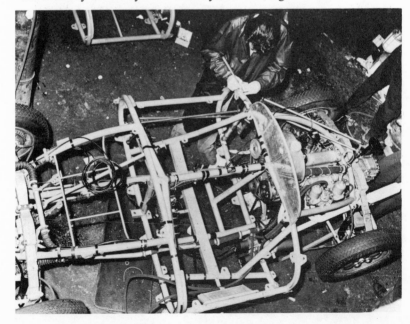

10. "This is what *could* happen!" John Cooper, *right,* in characteristic pose, briefs author-driver John Bentley in the garden of the Hippodrome Café during practice for the 1956 Le Mans 24-Hours. The Hugus-Bentley Cooper-Climax, a "semi" works entry, finished seventh overall, creditable first try with an 1100 cc car.

11. Le Mans 1956—drive to the Winner's Circle after a grueling race. Visible, *left to right:* Squad Leader Lamb, RAF, the team's timekeeper; John Cooper (instrumented top hat) behind; and co-driver John Bentley (blazer). Hugus is hidden behind rearview mirror. This 1100 Cooper-Climax, one of forty-nine starters, finished strongly despite stricter regulations.

12. Roy Salvadori (helmet) and team manager John Cooper at Oulton Park in 1957. Car is a Formula 2 Cooper powered by a 1500 cc twin-cam Climax engine. Salvadori won the event. That year, in fact, he scored an impressive total of ten wins, mainly with the Formula 2 Coopers.

13. Maurice Trintignant's Cooper-Borgward winning the Pau Formula 2 race in 1958.

14. Dinner at Nassau in 1959 during the famous Speed Week, which was mostly parties. *Left to right:* unidentified lady guest; the dashing Roy Salvadori; second unidentified guest; Mrs. Taylor (wife of race driver Michael Taylor); Lady Oakes; Jack Brabham; mechanic Tim Wall; and (of course) John Cooper.

Missourian Masten Gregory, Cooper team's "charger," was en entrusted with the difficult risky job of setting the pace forcing the opposition to ex- d. Here he is at the Avus in 59, where the German Grand x was held for the last time.

16. Stirling Moss and his first wife, Katie Molson, at Nassau in 1959.

17. Corner of the Cooper works at Ewell Road, Surbiton, in 1960. In construction are a pair of Formula 1 Coopers that clinched the Manufacturers' World Championship for Cooper two years running.

18. A study in concentration: Jack Brabham on his way to victory in a Formula 1 Cooper-Climax at Spa in 1960. This was the second year that Brabham won the Drivers' World Championship and Cooper the Manufacturers' World Championship.

So it was decided we would drive the ten miles back to the airfield when the excellent meal was over. It was raining a little when we started out in the Corvair, which Jack was driving. Normally, he doesn't press very hard on ordinary highways, but I guess that night he felt in a bit of a hurry. So he leaned on the throttle more than he should have done. For the first few miles we had no problems as it was mostly straight road, but about halfway there we arrived at a bend going a bit too fast and hit some leaves on the wet road. That was enough. The Corvair suddenly let go with complete abandon. Sensing what was about to happen, I ducked under the dashboard while Jack lost it in the biggest way, ever! We spun and spun and spun till I thought it would never end, or else end with a terrific crash. But as it happened we didn't hit anything. The Corvair finished up on the shoulder of the road, just missing a fence, and came to a stop feeling perhaps a bit ashamed of itself.

"Good God!" I said. "That was a pretty near thing, Jack! I didn't think we'd make it . . ."

Brabham, cool as ever, merely looked at me with slight distaste. "What are you talking about?" he asked. "It was just one of those things, but nothing to get excited about. I lost it for a moment—so what?"

To me, however, this was a frightening experience, and being a bit of a big-mouth I had to tell someone about it when we got to the circuit. No one seemed greatly impressed, I must say. Our two mechanics, Mike Barney and Noddy Grohman were working on the cars and getting on with the job while Briggs Cunningham was busy sweeping the floor and cleaning out the toilets. This seemed a bit unusual for a multimillionaire in the States, but Briggs harbored no pretensions at all.

I poured out my story of our multiple spin, ending up with "and we only just, just missed it!" But the effect was not what I expected. Briggs wore his usual worried expression, though not on account of my story. He nodded several times and agreed he knew the exact spot where it had happened, but beyond that he didn't seem greatly concerned.

The night before the race, Jack and I had a long session with Rodger Ward in the bar and he came up with an interesting idea. "I'm sure," he said, "that if you took one of your cars just as it is and ran it at Indy, you'd qualify without any trouble and with a bit of luck I'd say your chances of taking home some prize money would be mighty good."

"You seem pretty convinced," I told him. "Thanks for the compliment."

"It's no compliment, John. It's a fact. What's more, I'd be really tickled to see a rear-engined 'funny car'—a lightweight job like yours—showing the old roadsters the way round corners!"

Jack and I looked at each other, but Rodger didn't even give us a chance to catch our breath.

"Why the hell don't you try it?" he insisted. "Why don't you come to Indy as soon as you can? I'll get things organized so that you can use the track for a time. That's all you need. My pleasure's going to be the looks on a lot of those guys' faces at the track. Boy, are they ever in for a surprise!"

With so much enthusiasm going for us we could hardly refuse.

"Tell you what we'll do," I said. "We'll fly a car over from England direct to Indy. We're entered for the Watkins Glen Grand Prix in October, so the car will have to be set up for road racing— not for Indy. But we'll give it a whirl anyway. Then we can rent a trailer at Indy and drive to Watkins Glen in good time for the race. How does that sound to you?"

"Just great," Rodger grinned. "Just fine. I knew you'd see the light. Whatever else happens, you've got to try out your car round the Oval. Indy's waiting for you!"

By then, another personality had joined our session. He was an old friend of ours, Dr. Frank Faulkner, an Englishman who had migrated to the States twenty years before and acquired a professorship that had put him in charge of the Louisville Hospital. He was also a dedicated race car bug.

"I'm all for it," he said. "Get yourselves and your car over to Indy whenever you're ready!"

"Well," I said, "if we're going to make that long trip to Indy and then rent a trailer-transporter, you're the one who's going to organize the logistics of that operation!"

"Leave it to me," Faulkner agreed at once. "I'll take care of all that for you."

I think at this point we should talk a bit about race day at the Sebring Grand Prix. Jack was on the pole, having made fastest time, and Bruce was still third fastest. These were good grid positions to start from and Jack was especially pleased as he happened to be leading on points for the World Championship. So you can imagine how eager I was to see Jack win this race.

"Better start with full tanks," I said, "just to be safe."

But Brabham wouldn't have it. "I don't need full tanks. We know exactly what the car's gas consumption works out at. So we need just that number of gallons plus a small margin."

"Hell," I said, "all it would need to fill the car up would be another four gallons!"

But I couldn't budge him. He didn't want the tanks filled. I shouldn't have listened to him, but rather than get in a hassle and upset my driver, I let it go. Jack led from the start and was still leading about three laps from the finish, when he ran out of gas. I don't think he ever forgot that experience, which cost him the Grand Prix of the United States. Still, we made it all right. Bruce McLaren came through to win the race, which was, incidentally, his first Grand Prix victory for the Cooper Car Company. I remember how pleased I was, not only about the result but because Jack managed to limp home in fourth place, I think, which was enough to cinch the World's Championship for him.

With the Sebring Grand Prix behind us, we all went back to Harder Hall, where we had one of the best parties ever, to celebrate the occasion. Winning the World Championship really means something and Jack Brabham was the hero on that occasion—no mistake about it.

Bruce McLaren did pretty well, too, with his win. He not only collected prize money but also won several acres of land adjoining the Sebring Lake. To the best of my knowledge, his widow, Pat, still owns the land. The next time I go over to the States I must take a look at that piece of land and see what's happened to it.

Following the post-race celebration (next morning, that was) we had another long chat with Rodger Ward and also thanked Dr. Frank Faulkner for his offer to help. Everything was set up for the Indy trip and Rodger promised that the track would be available. Following our win, he was more convinced than ever that the future at Indy lay in our type of car; yet oddly enough he was one of the last Brickyard drivers to give up the front-engined Roadster which was a joint product of Offenhauser and Kurtis-Kraft and which held a virtual monopoly (with minor variations) at Indy.

When we did eventually run in the 500 in 1961, ours was the first rear-engined British car to appear at the track; yet by 1974 virtually all qualifiers—that is, the entire field of thirty-three cars—were using that configuration and at least half the entries featured British-made or British-designed cars. It's interesting to think about.

Going back to the Corvair for a moment, I never realized how badly I had goofed by telling with dramatic detail the story of that nighttime spin on our way to the course. Soon, the story made the entire round of Sebring, as usual in motor-racing circles, and what was even worse, a lot of people carried it home with them. Much later—several years, in fact—when a somewhat misguided character named Ralph Nader decided to reorganize the American Motor Industry, he seized on that story for propaganda purposes to convince the public that the Corvair was an "unsafe" car. Each time some scatterbrained driver ran into trouble with a Corvair, he was only too glad to write to Nader, blaming the car instead of himself. As a result of all this foolishness a lot of people really began to believe that the Corvair was unsafe—even after the rear-end geometry had been completely redesigned to make it as good as that of the Porsche. Nader unfortunately had his way and ruined one of the most interesting and promising automobiles ever put out by General Motors, forcing them to discontinue production. Yet the car had performed brilliantly, time and again, in many grueling sports car events run by the Sports Car Club of America. However, the negative impetus was too great; sales slumped and an excellent machine was phased out of manufacture.

The sequel to this was that one day, while I was in my office at Surbiton, a long-distance phone call came through from an American named Paul O'Shea. He was an ex-car salesman who had talked his way into several successful rides with Mercedes-Benz in U.S. sports car events and had benefited from factory backing. Anyway, he immediately asked me whether I remembered the incident near Sebring, years earlier, when Jack Brabham had "lost" a Corvair on a rain-slicked road?

"Now you mention it," I said, "I do remember something about it. But it didn't really mean anything. We all liked the Corvair very much."

O'Shea, however, was not to be put off so easily.

"The World Champion, Jack Brabham, completely lost control of the car and nearly killed you both and you say it didn't mean anything? I don't get it."

"Neither do I," I said, immediately on the defensive.

"No problem," O'Shea told me. "How would you like to come over to the States to testify about that incident? We'll pay all your expenses, first-class, plus a fee of a thousand dollars a day. Fair enough?"

"Phone me tomorrow," I said. "I'll think about it in the meantime."

And on that I hung up. It so happened at the time that I was very much involved with BMC over the Mini-Cooper. I therefore phoned George Harriman and told him what had happened. His reaction was prompt and definitive.

"For God's sake lay off, will you, John? Just forget the whole thing."

So that was exactly what I did and I never regretted it. Bill Mitchell was still a good friend of mine and he had shown us nothing but kindness. To condemn the Corvair just because it had spun on a rainy road now seemed pretty absurd—not to say disloyal. In fact, I met Mitchell again at the London Motor Show only last year, and we had quite a long chat about old times.

What I had not realized at the time was that Stirling Moss was acting on behalf of General Motors during the Corvair investigation, and with his superior knowledge he had "shot down" Nader "in flames" more than once! It's really a pity that the auto industries both of Britain and the United States have to suffer people like Nader. With his mania for "safety" carried to absurd—not to say hysterical—extremes, Nader made it very difficult for a number of small British firms to carry on their export business. These firms built cars by hand and depended on hard currency to keep going. Sure, Ralph Nader built up a huge new industry with snowballing "safety" standards, but all he really did was get people busy building a mountain out of a molehill—or very efficiently doing something that didn't need to be done. As if motorists in both our countries hadn't suffered enough from "legal" harassment already! It's my personal and privileged opinion that the sooner we forget about Nader, the better off we'll be.

Following the Harder Hall party, Bill Mitchell again caught up with us before we left Sebring and made a suggestion that we gladly accepted.

"Before you-all go back to England," he said, "why don't you stop off in Detroit and visit our Styling Department? We'd be happy to have you and you might see some interesting things."

I was all for it. "It's only going to take a couple of extra days," I told Jack. "Let's go up there and take a look."

"By all means," Brabham agreed, and so it was decided.

"The air tickets are on us," Mitchell said, "and I'll have a car waiting for you at the airport. During your stop-over, you're welcome to stay at my house."

Sure enough, tickets were waiting for us at Tampa Airport and when we touched down in Detroit a huge black Cadillac limousine with a black chauffeur was parked in readiness to whisk us off to General Motors.

Bill Mitchell's office was so luxurious that it brought to mind a gin palace with every conceivable luxury and gadget. We had lunch in the dining room reserved for top executives of the company, and more surprises awaited us. One of them was a revolving center to our table, controlled by individual electric push buttons. If you wanted salt, for example, and it happened to be on the side away from you, a push of the button would set the revolving center going without your having to reach for anything.

After lunch, Bill Mitchell took us all over the Styling Department of General Motors. This was divided up into several sections: one for Pontiac, another for Oldsmobile, a third for Buick and so on. While the stylist from each Division didn't mix with the others—at all events, during work—Bill Mitchell as the overall boss could go wherever he wanted. There were moments when Jack and I thought ourselves in some kind of fairyland. Imagine stairways made of glass, beautiful water fountains where tropical fish basked happily; doors of different colors; clever indirect lighting—you name it.

As we strolled along one of the seemingly endless corridors, I asked Bill Mitchell, "Why are these doors each painted a different color? Does it have any special meaning?"

"Well, in a way it does," Mitchell smiled. "You see, when the day's work is done, these guys go off to their various homes and at once get involved with the domestic scene. This isn't always the best kind of scene, so we have to get them out of it and back into a creative mood the next day. This is the sort of atmosphere they need. It helps them."

The next stage of our visit took us down to the basement—a very unusual and rare kind of basement—where Bill Mitchell kept all his special cars. Some of them were creations out of this world, never seen by the public at all. Idea treatments and so forth which were unlikely ever to go into production, but which sparked off more practical notions.

Another thing Bill Mitchell liked was motorcycles, especially English ones, and he kept quite a collection of our best-known bikes as well, each in immaculate condition.

Among the Ideas Cars was one that specially caught our eye. It had no steering wheel but a simple remote control lever which made the car turn in whatever direction the lever was pointed. A second control took care of the motion by a simple forward or backward push, as required.

That night, at dinner, we met the chief engineer of Buick, who told us about a new sealed engine operating like a refrigeration unit. It had transistorized ignition and everything required to set the ignition timing as wanted was printed on the flywheel. This did away with the need for a strobe light.

"When the engine wears out," we were told, "you just throw it away. Dump it in the trash can."

Probably due to the economics of production, this amazing engine never reached the assembly line, which was a pity. Meantime, our visit to Detroit lasted three days and besides a dinner party with all the engineers from Buick and Chevrolet Divisions, it was then that I met Zora Duntov, the technical genius who parleyed the timid, underpowered and originally useless Corvette into America's greatest sports car, the Stingray. To do this, Duntov, who was a dedicated enthusiast, had to brave all kinds of obstacles and political booby traps within General Motors. But he made it.

Some years earlier, Zora Duntov had been working for my old friend Sidney Allard in England; and even before that he had designed the Ardun cylinder head, which converted the production L-head Ford V-8 engine into an overhead valve unit of much greater power.

So ended our incursion to Sebring and our excursion to Detroit, both of them episodes I will never forget. In Detroit, certainly, every moment of our time brought some interesting surprise and gave us a new insight into the philosophy of automobile production. I suppose that in every country a car is some kind of a status symbol; but in the United States the auto industry did things on a scale unsurpassed anywhere else and catered to an extraordinary variety of people, climatic conditions, income levels and environment. Still, the tiny firm of Cooper had one or two ideas of its own which, before too long, were widely copied—at all events in the world of racing and sports cars.

9

Invitation to Indy

Following Rodger Ward's invitation for us to bring a Cooper to Indianapolis, we flew the car over in October 1960, which gave us about a month before the Watkins Glen Formula 1 race. At this time, Watkins Glen did not count toward the World Championship. I remember the car arriving at Indianapolis airport and how, with the help of some of the Speedway boys and Dr. Frank Faulkner, we drove over in a rented trailer and picked up the Cooper.

I must say that the first time you see that "Brickyard," as the Americans call it, the whole thing is a fantastic experience. I had been reading about Indy since my schoolboy days, and what an awe-inspiring circuit it was and all the marvelous and sensational things that happened there, so I was well primed.

Anyway, when we pulled up in Gasoline Alley with our little Cooper resting on its trailer behind a Ford station wagon, I must say the moment left a deep impression on me.

Although Indy is busy for the whole of May, prior to the 500, a lot of people still rent the lock-ups and workshops in Gasoline Alley to build and prepare their cars. This, remember, was almost five months after the great event, yet there were still many interested drivers, constructors and racing personalities around, waiting apparently to see how our small rear-engined Cooper was going to perform. Evidently, the word had gotten around and we were soon treated to questions and personal opinions, not all of them flattering. It would be unfair to say we sensed any hostility, but the prevailing mood was one of amused tolerance, mixed with obvious curiosity.

"Gosh, look at that little itty-bitty car! Say, what's the engine doin' in the back?" Or, "D'you reckon that little thing's really going to get around in a hurry?" That more often than not was the kind of approach.

It really didn't bother us at all and we had no trouble fielding questions as we prepared the car and set up the required gear ratios for an estimated top speed of 155 to 160 mph. That night we put up at the Speedway Inn, just outside the Speedway itself, where we met some more of the Indy boys. Drivers such as Eddie Sachs and, of course, that great Indy sponsor Agajanian, who always strutted around in a cowboy hat although he didn't look anything like a cowboy. If the truth be told, our more serious visitors were definitely curious to find out how an independently sprung car, powered by a rear engine, was going to measure up against the time-honored Offy-Kurtis roadsters.

The next morning we woke up to a beautiful day (as it usually is at Indy, except on occasions when it rains on race day!) and we got the Cooper ready for its first run. Meantime, Harlan Fengler, the track manager, put his observers at strategic points around the course, just to watch our progress. Things were a bit different here from European circuits—you had to abide by a different set of rules altogether. So Jack Brabham gave the word that he was going out to do a few "warming-up" laps, and without further ado he set off. This was apparently not according to the rules. When on his second lap Jack was timed at 144.8 mph (fast enough to have qualified for third row on the previous year's grid), Harlan Fengler nearly lost his mind! He came out on the starting line and flagged Jack down with a sort of outraged vigor that could hardly be ignored. So the next time Brabham came round he eased off as cool as a cucumber, came to an easy stop at the exact spot indicated and asked casually, "What's the matter?"

"What's the matter!" Fengler spluttered. "This is your first time out at Indy and you can't just go bombing around at that sort of speed. It's insane. You've got to pass the Rookie Test, first!"

Innocently, Jack inquired, "What's the Rookie Test?"

"My God—haven't you heard of that?"

Fengler then carefully explained that every "new" driver must complete two or three laps at 100 mph, then two or three more at

110 and gradually build up his speed. "This is a very dangerous circuit," he concluded, "and there's a lot of things you have to learn, first."

Jack was not impressed. "As far as I'm concerned," he smiled, "it's just four left-hand corners. And you try to take them flat out. Period."

Fengler was not to be put off, however, and Jack had to obey the rules and go through his "Rookie Test," which to him was quite farcical. Very quickly he began to lap at better than 144 mph without the slightest trouble or any sign of "losing" it. All the onlookers could do was shake their heads in wonderment. But not so Rodger Ward. He was so enthusiastic that he asked us if we would let him drive the car, to which we of course agreed.

We couldn't see Ward's face as he whizzed around, but we could tell by his grin and his relaxed attitude that this was, to him, quite an experience. Used as he was to the hard, unyielding suspension of the old roadsters, which gave the driver a hell of a ride and nearly shook his teeth loose, Rodger found it hard to believe that the same speed could be achieved in relative comfort and with virtually no handling problems.

"Boy," he said when he came in, "this little car's got a future. No doubt about it. Darned shame it doesn't have more steam!"

"We're working on that in England," I said. "Give us a little more time."

As for Jack, the more practice laps he put in, the better he liked the Brickyard. It held absolutely no fears for him and he enjoyed himself more than he had done for a long time.

When the day was over, Frank Faulkner introduced us to Jim Kimberly of the Kleenex fortune. In the past he not only had sponsored Ferraris but had actually driven them with considerable success in Strategic Air Command races put on by the Sports Car Club of America. For some reason, Kimberly was fond of red and his cars, coveralls, helmet, gloves, socks and shoes had always been red—a combination that had set him apart at race meets. Anyway, the upshot of this meeting was that Kimberly told us he would be very interested in sponsoring a Cooper for the Indy 500 the following May.

"Could you build a special car for the job?" he asked us.

"Well, as you know," I said, "this is only a 2.5 engine, but I'm pretty sure we can persuade Coventry Climax to bore it out to 2.7

liters and besides that run on alcohol instead of regular gasoline. That'll certainly give us a bit more steam."

"Great," Kimberly said. "Any other ideas?"

"We can fit larger tanks," Jack told him, "and also build an offset into the car, since it has to keep turning left all the time!"

Thus it was agreed and there and then we decided to fly back to Chicago with Jim Kimberly and set up the financial arrangements. And I must say that in those days, when sponsorship in Britain was far from being what it is now, we were very impressed with Jim's offer. He wrote us a check for a lump sum to build the car and make the trip the following year and also picked up the tab for all our expenses both at Indy and Chicago. We did explain to him that despite those endless practice and qualifying sessions which absorbed most of the month of May in race preparation, Jack would have to be elsewhere a lot of the time. He was scheduled to run in all the major Grands Prix for the World's Championship and it so happened that one of those events—the Monaco Grand Prix—would take place in the middle of May. This was going to involve quite a bit of flying across the Atlantic.

"Naturally, Jack will have to be in Indy on a Saturday morning to qualify for the 500," I said, "but he'll have to leave immediately afterward so as to get some practice at Monaco for the following Sunday's Grand Prix. And after that, back to Indy again for the Big Event itself."

Kimberly could hardly have been more co-operative. "I'll lay on a private plane for you," he told us, "to get you back from Indy to Chicago airport, and the reverse when you get back. So that'll be one problem less."

On that note we returned to Indy, picked up the Cooper and its trailer, hitched up the tow-car and took off for Watkins Glen. Of course we had to change our gear ratio back to suit the lower top speed and greater acceleration required on a road circuit, but this was no problem. Jack finished second after a trouble-free run.

By this time, all the American boys had heard about our visit to Indy and Colin Chapman came up and asked, "What's it like?" Bruce McLaren, too, was very interested and we spent most of our time talking about Indy. I must say I had it at the back of my mind that it was a pity we didn't have a more powerful engine for our first try at the Brickyard. But now, on our return to England, we would have the means and the time to build the right kind of car and "have a go."

Almost the first people I contacted when we got back to England were Leonard Lee and Wally Hassan of Coventry Climax engines.

"Our problem is simple," I said. "We'd like to run at Indy next year and in fact we've contracted to do so. I think we have a very good chance of finishing in the money."

"But of course you're short on power?" Hassan guessed.

"That's the rub. Could you enlarge the 2.5 engine to, say, 2.7 liters and make it run on alcohol?"

"I don't really see why not."

"We for our part intend to build a special car for the race," I told them.

Both men agreed to have a try and the estimate we got was that the engine could be made to produce an extra 40 bhp. This was about what we had in mind, anyway, so we told them to go ahead. With nearly 300 bhp our Cooper would still be about 25 per cent down on power as compared with the Offy roadsters, but it weighed a lot less and its handling was far superior in every respect.

So we got to work and designed a special car for the job. We offset the engine and driver two and a half inches from the centerline. Dunlop, who were to supply us with tires, said they would be very interested to come with us, because they had never been to Indy. At that time the tire supply situation was virtually a Firestone monopoly at the 500, but Dunlop produced some special offset tires with more tread on the inside of the left front and rear wheels and more on the outside of the right front and rear wheels. We also installed large fuel tanks with most of the fuel on the inside (or left side) of the car to help weight distribution. Dunlop supplied us with some special center-lock aluminum wheels with spinners that had extra large ears for easy hammering.

When the car was finally completed, we tested it at Silverstone, and although driving conditions were in no way comparable, we could feel the impact of those additional horses and Jack was confident we would do well at Indy.

At the beginning of the 1961 season we were also working on our Formula 1 Grand Prix cars, getting them ready for a whole string of events. By this time, however, the International Formula

1 had been reduced to 1.5 liters and this was one of our deciding factors in preparing for Indy. Compared with the new Ferraris of that year, our 1500 cc engines were down on power and during the first part of the season less competitive, where the 2.5-liter version was thoroughly well tried and had already won us two World Championships in 1959 and 1960.

Early the following May (1961) we set off for Indianapolis again. This time my father came over too, as did Mr. Lee from Climax and the Dunlop technicians. Mike "Noddy" Grohman, Jack Brabham's favorite mechanic, also accompanied us. As a precaution we took along three other highly skilled men—Alf Francis, Bill James and Tim Wall. I remember that when we arrived at the track we were given a terrific reception. This time, everybody was there. I doubt if any other visitors have ever been given such a royal welcome. Of course, during the whole of May, everyone who's interested in motor racing in the United States drifts over to Indy. We stayed at the same Motor Inn as before, which seemed to be the favored spot for many of the drivers. At first I drank scotch but soon got to liking Jack Daniel's Bourbon with ginger ale, and pretty soon everyone was calling me "Old Jack Daniel's."

I recall that every time we returned from the track to our motel, we found it impossible to proceed directly to our rooms. Invariably, someone would grab us when we came past and say, "Have a drink!" People like Agajanian, Andy Granatelli, Parnelli Jones and Eddie Sachs, not to mention of course Rodger Ward, were unbelievably lavish with their hospitality.

When we first found our quarters in Gasoline Alley, we discovered that Jim Kimberly had knocked two garages into one and ordered everything repainted. The effect not only was incredibly smart but it seemed as if the very air was as clean as that of an operating room. Kimberly had also sent along his mechanics to help and they were dressed in spotless white coveralls with KIMBERLY-COOPER embroidered on the back. Of course there were several Kleenex tissue dispensers around the workshop, but the business end had also been thoroughly catered for. Electric tools, a grinder and a power-driven lathe were only part of the lavish equipment. This was a real home away from home, only of course where we in England did things within a budget, Kimberly was not bothered by any such consideration.

I remember how Noddy Grohman's cussed streak came out when he decided to pull the legs of the American mechanics. He just dumped a somewhat soiled tool-kit all over the spotless floor, and without a backward look set to work on the car. This was not the way he really worked, but all those gleaming American tool-kits, arranged like drill squads, were just a bit too much for him. He wanted to show his independence, I guess.

"After practice," one of Kimberly's mechanics asked him, "are you gonna strip the engine down?"

"What for?" Noddy asked. "It's only another race. Look, you people only race once a year here. We race every other weekend. Our engines are built to stand up to that kind of thing!"

There was a pained silence and a shaking of heads.

Soon after, our Cooper was wheeled onto the course, Jack climbed in and joined other drivers in practice. In what seemed like no time at all he was lapping around the 145 or 146 mph mark without trouble. That year, it was Parnelli Jones who held the fastest lap at Indy. This was not yet 150 mph but 149 and a few decimals. Everyone was looking for that magic 150 mph. Jack didn't try for it, nor did he have any trouble. He was keeping something in hand and after practice we were very pleased with the car, particularly because we figured we might be able to get away with fewer pit stops than the American roadsters. Not only was our engine much more economical on fuel, but Dunlop seemed to have hit on the right compound and treads and we thought our tires would last longer, too. Unfortunately, during the actual 500 we were proved wrong in one respect, although it was not the fault of the tires. We had intended to make one less pit stop than the others, but one of our wheels overheated—at least the bearing did—and we had the devil of a job hammering off the dog-eared hubcap. It wouldn't budge for the longest time. The best Indy pit crews could refuel a car and change all four tires in less than twenty seconds, but we took four times as long, at least.

On the whole, though, we had every reason to be pleased and the car certainly was competitive, despite the fact that we were still 100 hp down on the rest of the field. As I've said, the lightness of our car and its superior roadability made up pretty much for that handicap.

Anyway, after several days' practice Jack flew back to Monaco, where other mechanics were waiting for him with our "regular"

Grand Prix Cooper. He now faced some very strenuous qualification laps on a round-the-houses course that was vastly different from Indy and much more difficult. I stayed on at the Brickyard to look after our Kimberly entry, but that didn't phase Jack at all. He qualified on the Thursday as planned, and made the starting grid. Our 1.5-liter Climax engine, however, was still no match for the "little Ferraris" and on the International Formula 1 Grand Prix merry-go-round 1961 was to prove a very lean year for us. This was in no sense the fault of our drivers, of course.

Having qualified at Monaco despite the odds, Jack Brabham winged his way on the return trip to the United States and reappeared at Indy as scheduled. Needless to say, we had gone over every inch of the car during his brief absence and were ready for him. Qualification runs at Indy are exploited to the maximum and on each qualifying day as many as 100,000 spectators may show up. The management have really built up this qualification business into a three-ringed circus that brings a lot of money to the Speedway. As is well known, cars can only qualify one at a time and you are given four laps from the moment you signify with your hand that you're ready to be timed. The fastest of those four laps is the one that determines your grid position, but even then you are still not necessarily a starter. A qualifying driver may think he's made it, only to find that a later qualifier has gone faster and bumped him out of the grid, which is limited to thirty-three starters anyway. In any event, you have to get in line to take your turn qualifying, and while the car is in line, waiting, you are not allowed to work on it. So that Jack wouldn't have a long wait to qualify, we stayed up all night with the car and found ourselves at the head of the line, which was a nice place to be.

As luck would have it, our starter went sour but we found this out during the night. By a little careful wangling we were able to sneak in a new starter motor without getting caught. We were not the only ones playing that game, but it seems that the more rules they pile on at Indy, the greater the incentive to "bend" them.

The morning broke beautiful and clear, and sure enough, tens of thousands of car buffs—many more than would attend an actual Grand Prix in Europe—began to fill the stands, just to watch the qualification runs. The rule at Indy is that when a qualifying driver has done a couple of laps or so he puts up his hand as he goes past the starter, to indicate he's ready for timing. Jack did put up his arm to indicate readiness, but the starter failed to see it, perhaps because Brabham was sitting so low in the car. At any rate he was soon flagged off the course after five laps and would have had to go back to the tail end of the line for a later try, but for Agajanian's intervention on our behalf. Agajanian was then a pretty powerful man at Indy and what he said was accepted mostly without argument. So, when he told the starting line official loud and clear, "I *saw* Brabham's hand go up," that was the end of the argument. They had been timing Jack anyway and his best lap was 145.144 mph without the least trouble. That put him in the fifth row of the starting grid. A year earlier, his speed would have been good enough for the third row!

However, what focused a lot of attention on us, both from drivers and spectators, was that we had unwittingly broken some deep-rooted Indy "taboos." For example, our Cooper was British racing green, and *green* of any shade is considered bad luck in Gasoline Alley. Another no-no was having women anywhere near your car until *after* the race was over; and thirdly eating peanuts— a very popular American commodity anywhere else—was considered bad luck. We did comply with the no-woman and peanut-eating taboos, but we were not about to change the color of our car. So, seemingly, we went to the starting grid with two strikes against us: a "funny car" as it had become known because of its rear engine and all-independent suspension, and a *green* car at that! People shrugged pityingly, or else looked us over with tolerant amusement—forgetting, it seemed, that Jack was in the fifth of the eleven starting rows which make up the thirty-three-car grid. Not bad for a first try.

Now Jack and I had to rush back to Monaco for the Grand Prix. A car was waiting for us at the Speedway entrance and we hopped in and drove to a private airfield where a special plane laid on by Jim Kimberly stood ready to take off. His own pilot was at the controls and we made a beeline for Chicago airport, there to catch the Paris plane on a regular commercial airline. We just caught the connection from Orly to Nice, landing there about an hour before the race at Monte Carlo. Jack was pretty tired by then, but as far as we were concerned Monaco that year would have been a bust anyway. We could have saved ourselves the trouble. It was at least some consolation that Stirling Moss, after a brilliant drive in an underpowered Lotus 18, managed to beat the

1.5-liter Ferraris at their own game and win the Monaco Grand Prix.

After that show was over, we couldn't get back to Indy quick enough, because we both felt that our car had an excellent chance of showing those dinosaur roadsters a thing or two.

Our return was the signal for more parties with the boys and the Speedway Inn fairly hummed prior to the actual 500. One long session that we had with Andy Granatelli proved very instructive. Andy is a rather short, stocky American who then weighed about 240 pounds! He was a real character and very interesting to talk to. His Indy entry happened to be a front-engined, front-drive Novi, driven by an immensely powerful V-8 engine. This was built up from two four-cylinder Offys, offset at an angle from a specially designed common crankcase. The Novi was certainly a big step forward from the then common roadster and much more sophisticated. The engine of the Novi put out something like 700 bhp, which gave it a far superior performance to anything else at Indy in those days, but as Granatelli succinctly put it, "The damn thing's still full of bugs, so you can't rely on it to keep going."

Both Jack and I made commiserating noises, until Granatelli came up with what he thought was a brilliant idea.

"How's about we put one of our engines in the back of *your* car?"

"You must be kidding," we said. "We'd have to redesign the entire chassis and suspension to cope with that monster!"

This didn't seem to bother Andy at all and he kept insisting that it would be a "great idea." Nor was he the only one, oddly enough. Several other sponsors came to talk to us about our "funny" car and the questions were pretty much the same. Would it be possible to put an Offy in the back of our Cooper, or say a modified Ford or Chevy V-8 engine? To get all these well-intentioned people off our backs, Jack and I evolved a simple formula in reply to their queries.

"Let's see how we get on in the race, first! Then we can talk some more."

Of course these people weren't stupid. They had latched on to our problem immediately and also knew where we had it all over the roadsters. On the straights the lack of power slowed us down, but around the turns we were much faster and steadier. Our car also had a far superior evasive capability because of its light weight. If a roadster ran into trouble at speed while committed to a certain course, it would keep right on going that way, no matter what the driver did. Jack, on the other hand, could get around sudden obstacles with no more than a quick flick of the steering wheel.

By race day, a lot of our friends and customers had arrived at Indy, besides Jim Kimberly. Hap Sharp and Jim Hall were there from Texas. Briggs Cunningham and Walt Hansgen also put in an appearance. I remember that Hap Sharp had a problem getting a cab to take him to the Speedway, so he offered to buy up the next driver who came along, cab and all, for the duration of the 500!

That famous World War I pilot Eddie Rickenbacker also joined us. In between the two Wars he had designed and built an interesting car powered by a straight-eight engine, but that had not been a success. Later, he was destined to become president of American Airlines. His stories about the old times at Indy were fascinating, I must say. Then we had a special dinner invitation, Jack and I, from the owner of the Speedway, Tony Hulman, Jr., and that, too, was quite an experience. It showed at all events not only the courtesy of Americans but also their awareness of us and our "funny car."

I am not going to describe the Indianapolis Speedway on race day—that's already been done several thousand times in every conceivable magazine and through every publicity medium the world over. The fairground atmosphere, film stars driven around the course, and myriads of multicolored balloons drifting into the sky as tension built up, produced the greatest and most impressive hullabaloo I have ever experienced. And it kept right on through the traditional singing of "On the Banks of the Wabash" by a famous vocalist of local origin, the last-minute driver interviews from each cockpit and the "Gentlemen, start your engines!" intoned by Harlan Fengler with great emotion. From there I had better take it on by giving both Jack's impressions from the cockpit of our little Cooper and my own from the pit wall.

Following the usual pace lap by a fleeing Detroit automobile, which reminded me of a rabbit chased by a pack of baying hounds, the flag fell, the race was on and the snarl and thunder of thirty-three engines suddenly unleashed to maximum throttle was absolutely deafening. On the first lap, Jack came by in about thirteenth place, seemingly quite at ease, and some four laps later he side-stepped a nasty incident which involved several cars and got through without a dent or a scratch. It all looked quite effortless and although Jack has always been what Americans call a cool cat —on that day he was far less nervous than I—yet he saw things differently from the cockpit.

"To be truthful," he told me later, "the whole show was a bit overpowering at the start, especially having all those front-engine monsters surrounding me on every side. For a while I felt boxed in and it wasn't until I started passing cars on the turns that I was able to relax a bit. On the two main straights, of course, I just lacked the speed to keep up with the leaders."

Still, Jack had worked himself up to sixth place when, at quarter distance, the first roadsters began coming in for fuel. We were sticking to our plan of making only two pit stops, so that Jack just kept on going. Unlike other drivers, he did not try to improve his position when the yellow caution light came on. Officially, this is not allowed, but any driver who can take advantage to sneak up a few places does so.

Jack signaled he was coming in for his second pit stop about fifteen laps short of scheduled time, but he had seen the white breaker strip beginning to show through his tire treads and it would have been foolish to take that kind of risk. Unfortunately, what did set us back was the frantic haste of the mechanic who had charge of changing the right rear tire. He slammed the wheel home in a desperate hurry, put the spinner back on cross-threaded and began hitting it with a hammer! While this problem was being sorted out, Jack dropped back several places, but even so he finished ninth after a completely trouble-free run as far as the car's mechanism was concerned. He probably could have crossed the line sixth but for this bit of bad luck, yet even so we collected some worthwhile prize money (around $9,000) and gained a lot of experience. Our trusty 2.5-liter Coventry Climax engine could take it—no doubt about that. What we still needed was a few more horses.

However, with the lump sum we had received in advance from Jim Kimberly and the great time we had at Indy for the best part of a month, we did pretty well. It was an experience that I wouldn't have missed for the world.

The partying that went on after the 500 was something else again. It never seemed to stop and people found themselves in the swimming pool, both clothed and unclothed. Dancing went on all night. There seemed to be barbecues everywhere—a wonderful setup.

Another fall-out benefit of the Indy race was the amount of flying both Jack and I were treated to. Rodger Ward had mentioned to one or two of his buddies who owned airplanes, that we were both learning to fly. In fact, Jack had just obtained his pilot's license while I was still three months away from getting mine. Immediately, Rodger's friends got the notion that we might be interested in buying a light American plane. Since the prewar days of the Tiger Moth and the Auster, there had been no British light planes in production suitable for private flying. Jack, as it happened, had already put his name down for a Cessna 180, while I was very interested in a Piper Tri-Pacer or Commanche. So each of Rodger Ward's friends showed up in turn with invitations for us to fly.

"Look," they said, "there's an airport just down the road. I've got a Beechcraft Bonanza laid on for you to try." Or, "How would you like to take a Cessna 150 up for a trip?"

We gratefully accepted all offers and must have tried out, between us, about ten different types of light American aircraft, yet I don't believe any of those boys knew that I didn't have a license at the time! Still, it was a wonderful experience and we had great fun flying over and around the golf course in the center of the Indianapolis Oval, where drivers and entrants played golf regularly between practice sessions. I surely acquired a lot of light aircraft flying experience in a hurry! Flying in the States was so easy.

To close this particular episode, I'm sure that without the foresight and confidence of Jim Kimberly, Indianapolis would not be the place it is today. Thanks to him, because we were able to run our rear-engine "funny" car in the 500, the character of the race changed entirely. Within three years, rear-engine cars were lapping the circuit 10 mph faster than we did on our first try, and people were ordering rear-engine Lotuses as well as our cars. In fact, Jim Clark won the 500 in 1965, setting up a new record average of 151.388 mph in a Ford V-8-powered Lotus; then Graham Hill won it in a Lola-Ford T90 in 1966 and two years later a McLaren-designed car powered by a rear-mounted 2.8-liter turbo-charged Offy made a lot of ripples at Indy. Unfortunately, it was sidelined with ignition failure after qualifying sixteenth with the late Peter Revson at the wheel. Nor were American designers and entrants slow to get in the act. At one stroke, almost, the roadster became outdated and the so-called "funny" car was "in" to stay.

10

The Cooper-Bristol

I have decided to give due space to the Cooper-Bristol in my story for some very good reasons. This car was a complete change from our traditional rear-engined cars and I suppose the idea came from more conventional sports cars which were then widely in favor. We had already built a few predecessors to this model—the Cooper-Vauxhall and the Cooper-MG. The prewar BMW engine was taken over after the collapse of Germany by the Bristol Aeroplane Company and was manufactured by them pretty much unchanged. Before the War, the BMW 328 was considered a very potent sports car and became famous in 1938 and 1939. When the War ended, the American and British governments rushed around with the tooling and plans, ready to offer them to anyone who wanted to take over the manufacture of the BMW and the Volkswagen. That was how the Bristol Aeroplane Company came into the picture. They took up the offer to go ahead and build the BMW engine and put it into an entirely new chassis. However, what they started out with turned out to be strikingly similar to the prewar BMW chassis as well.

Anyway, by 1948, when the FIA (International Automobile Federation, which controls motor racing) introduced a new Formula 2, this edict attracted a great deal of attention in Great Britain. The Formula called for cars up to 2000 cc unsupercharged or up to 500 cc supercharged. Needless to say, no one bothered with the second alternative; but the first triggered off some very competitive efforts which, within a couple of years, were whizzing around racecourses the world over. The pioneers in this field were small British firms such as Alta (who also built their own engine, as I have mentioned elsewhere), HWM (who borrowed the Alta twin-cam engine), ERA and Frazer Nash (who used the two-liter Bristol-built engine) and ourselves, who did the same.

But first a word as to what prompted our choice, besides of course availability. Dr. Fiedler, the original designer of the BMW engine as fitted to the Type 328 sports two-seater before the War, was a very ingenious man. He had adopted a unique compromise in order to make use of efficient hemispherical combustion chambers without the expense of dual overhead camshafts. What he had done was to use vertical pushrods for the intake valves and short transverse pushrods for the exhaust valves. One would have thought that with valve actuation moving in two directions at once, the result at high rpm would have been some kind of freaked-out Heath Robinson (Rube Goldberg) idea. But this was far from being the case. The BMW 328 engine ran so reliably that when Bristol Aeroplane took it over and put it into production, the only improvement they made was the addition of a front-mounted oil cooler. Eventually, the BMW two-liter unit found itself in the production chassis of one of Britain's oldest car firms—AC Cars Ltd. at Thames Ditton, which to this day is producing cars, though of a very different character.

Anyway, we decided to go along to the Bristol people and saw George White, the managing director, and asked for one of their engines to put in the front of a Cooper. They agreed to let us have an engine to try out and we quickly built a prototype Cooper-Bristol with box section side members for the frame. We also fabricated an ENV rear axle and after testing the assembled chassis we were very enthusiastic. The power–weight ratio was quite good, despite the relatively low power output of the engine. In this respect we had no illusions. The 1971 cc Bristol (ex-BMW) engine gave only 127 bhp at 5,800 rpm, which put it about 35 to 40 hp below contemporary engines such as those of Ferrari and Maserati. Furthermore, in itself it was by no means a lightweight and its considerable overall height posed some serious problems in trying to stuff it into a car with a low bonnet (hood).

Despite the lack-of-power problem, with which we were already quite familiar, we decided to enter the Formula 2 fray and see how we stacked up against some far more costly and exotic machinery.

For more reasons than one, this was to prove a sound decision and a far-reaching one. As things turned out, the Cooper-Bristol became the one vehicle in which some of the world's future top-ranking drivers and Grand Prix winners cut their teeth quite successfully, and learned a lot in the process. Two names that jump to mind are Jack Brabham (who was very successful with the car in Australia before coming to England, where he joined us) and the famous tow-headed Mike Hawthorn, who, in 1958, while driving for Ferrari, beat Stirling Moss to the World Grand Prix Championship by a single point! There were several other famous drivers who took to our Cooper-Bristol, but these two will suffice to illustrate what I mean, and in any case I'm jumping ahead a little.

We'll come back shortly and take a closer look at this brilliant but impetuous young driver and his association with our Cooper-Bristol. Having made the decision to "have a go" at Formula 2 racing and put this new car into limited production, we went back to Bristol's and they agreed to let us have some more engines. As a result, we laid down a batch of prototypes (three in all) and Eric Brandon and Alan Brown, who were virtually running our works 500 cc Cooper team, switched to Cooper-Bristols. My father, always an ingenious and far-seeing man, advocated that we choose a different and less costly route from that employed by other Formula 2 builders using this engine. (For example, the G-Type ERA cut down engine weight by scrapping the crankcase and going to dry-sump lubrication with all its attendant complications and added expense.) My father did not think this necessary and he proved right. He was not even sold on the idea of canting the engine to one side to lower the bonnet line.

"The way we can nullify or largely overcome the handicap from which this engine now suffers—undue height and weight and relatively low power—is to build a very light chassis," he said. "In this connection we've learned some useful lessons with our Cooper 500. Let's apply them." And we did.

The Cooper-Bristol had an extremely light basic box section frame with the side members extensively drilled to get rid of every surplus ounce. Yet the car was very rigid because of its ingenious tubular subassembly welded to the box frame. This too weighed very little but did the job so well that it could resist even the violent impact of a high-speed crash. Another contributory factor to

19. Famous group—famous occasion! *Left to right:* the late Bruce McLaren, World Champion Jack Brabham, John Cooper and father, Charles, on the occasion of the opening of Brabham's Garage at Chessington in 1960.

20. Jack Brabham wins the 1961 New Zealand Grand Prix and John Cooper is justifiably happy with the result.

21. John Cooper and sponsor Jim Kimberly at Indy in 1961. Cooper works driver Jack Brabham finished ninth at first attempt with what the old Roadster devotees called a "funny" car, but the Cooper rear-engine layout completely revolutionized race car design in the United States and the world over.

22. Formula 1 Cooper (2.7-liter Climax engine) specially adapted for the Indianapolis 500, where it finished ninth in 1961. *Left to right:* mechanic Mike Grohman, two American mechanics, Jim Kimberly's personal pilot, Jim Kimberly (sponsor) and another U.S. mechanic. *Foreground:* John Cooper and Jack Brabham at the wheel.

23. Production Mini-Cooper after its record-breaking run at Montlhery in 1961. Carrying four people all the time, this diminutive car averaged over 80 mph for twelve continuous hours.

24. The late Charles Cooper, who, with the help of this son, John, parlayed a small car tuning and repair shop into an internationally famous enterprise which designed and built winning World Championship Formula 1 cars. Photo was taken in 1962, two years before his death.

25. Steve McQueen with John Cooper during Formula 2 trials held at Brand's Hatch in 1962. McQueen quickly developed into a top-caliber race driver who could easily have made the big league but for his career as an actor.

26. Startling finish of saloon car race at Spa in 1962. Prearranged triple dead-heat Mini win came unstuck when Bill Blydenstein's Mini-Cooper (2) lost all but third gear. Jimmy Blumer (860 MW) and Sir John Whitmore were "jumped" at the checker by Holvoet's DKW, *extreme right,* a non-contender.

27. John Love, *left,* winner of the 1962 British Saloon Car Championship in a Mini-Cooper, brought home to BMC its third consecutive title. Here, at Oulton Park, John Cooper turns the trophy into a loving cup with the best of vintage champagne.

28. Rear engine of the fantastic twin-engine Mini-Cooper that nearly killed John Cooper on the Kingston Bypass in 1962.

29. The late Dave McDonald's Cooper-built King Cobra at Turn 6 during the October 1963 Riverside Grand Prix, which he won easily. A week later he repeated the performance at the Laguna Seca Pacific Grand Prix. The King Cobra was a redesigned Cooper Monaco built to accept the powerful 4.7-liter Ford V-8 engine. Carroll Shelby ordered twenty-five of these cars.

30. John Cooper, Lord Snowdon, *in profile,* with Paddy Hopkirk, winner of the 1964 Monte Carlo Rallye in a Mini-Cooper, and Alec Issigonis, *back to camera.* Occasion was the British Racing Car Show organized by the British Racing and Sports Car Club.

31. Phil Hill (1961 World Champion) takes to the air in a 1.57-liter Cooper-Climax at the Nürburgring in August 1964. Ferrari opposition proved too strong while this Formula 1 ceiling remained in effect.

32. The wreckage of Phil Hill's Formula 1 Cooper burning furiously after a first-lap shunt during the Austrian Grand Prix at Zeltweg in August 1964. Hill was unhurt but the accident caused a "major disagreement" between him and John Cooper which led to the former's retirement from the team at the end of the season.

33. Loading up the Cooper, BRM and Lotus team cars at Heath Row in 1964, on their way to be flown to New York for the U.S. Grand Prix at Watkins Glen. This was probably the most valuable cargo of racing machinery ever flown across the Atlantic.

34. John Rhodes (Mini-Cooper) leads Steve Neal at Brands Hatch in 1965.

35. Cooper-Maserati Formula 1 Grand Prix cars under construction. Six examples of this handsome T81 twelve-cylinder machine were built in 1966. Beefed-up suspension and chassis are easily discerned, along with meticulous Cooper workmanship, but the car was variously described as "clumsy" and "tail-heavy." Its 300 bhp-plus at 8,500 rpm was not enough for the added weight.

the light weight was our use of a scaled-up version of the Cooper 500 suspension with transverse springs front and rear, using only lower wishbones. The independent rear suspension, which did away with a massive pressed steel casing to enclose a "live" axle, also meant a weight saving. Production costs were kept down by using a standard four-speed Bristol-built gearbox, a Borg and Beck clutch and of course ready-made Lockheed hydraulic brakes.

As can be seen from the photo, our Cooper-Bristol was hardly a thing of beauty, but from its first outing it showed a clean pair of heels to many of the opposition. By 1952 we had three cars ready to make their debut at the Easter Goodwood meeting—the first important race of the season. Two of these machines were for the *Écurie Richmond* drivers, Brandon and Brown, who had done so well with Cooper 500's on various occasions. The third entry was by Bob Chase, an ex-naval commander and an engineer from Brighton who then handled GM industrial diesels. His driver was to be Mike Hawthorn, a young driver who had till then been racing a 1.5-liter Riley. Mike came into the picture more or less as follows. When our new model was announced in *The Autocar* with an attractive cutaway drawing which gave all the details, we received a phone call from Chase. He came straight to the point.

"Will you sell me a Cooper-Bristol?"

"Well," I stalled, "we're only building three of them at this moment and all are spoken for already." (I took this line, which was not strictly true, because I wanted to make sure that a good driver would be in the third works car.)

"I've got a good driver," Chase insisted, sensing my hesitation. "If that's what's bothering you."

"You're not driving the car yourself, then?"

"Lord no! But the driver I've picked is a pretty talented young man."

"Oh?"

"He's from Farnham and his name is Mike Hawthorn."

At that time nobody had even heard of Mike Hawthorn, but I was a fortunate exception because, when I had raced my Cooper-MG sports car in small events at Goodwood, I'd met Hawthorn, who was then running an ancient prewar Riley Imp that his father had tuned for him. I well recalled the way he drove and that was enough for me. Chase had not overstated the facts. Hawthorn was good; no question about it.

"Fair enough," I agreed. "If Mike Hawthorn's going to drive, you can have the third car."

When I mentioned this conversation to Brandon and Brown, however, the reception I got was pretty chilly.

"Who's Mike Hawthorn?" they wanted to know.

"You wait and see," I said. "It would be a good idea to run a three-car team if Mike joined us and that's the present intention."

I already knew by then that Hawthorn was interested in driving for Chase, but both the *Écurie Richmond* drivers remained adamant.

"Whoever heard of this character?" they asked. "We want to win races, don't we? Taking on some unknown chap is no way to do it."

At that I gave up the argument. "Okay. If that's the way you feel about it, we'll just run a two-car team."

By the time Goodwood came round, however, we not only had three cars ready, but four. I had one. Brandon and Brown, the other two and young Mike Hawthorn drove the Chase car as an "independent."

I'll never forget that race. Hawthorn was so quick that he blew everyone off the course, including the *Écurie Richmond* drivers, whose opinion of him, all along, had been less than complimentary. It was simply no contest and those who had so underrated Hawthorn were made to eat their words.

Incidentally, at this same Goodwood meet, the great Fangio was due to drive one of those temperamental, overcomplicated and illfated sixteen-cylinder BRM's, but as usual the car was not ready and didn't even show up. Fangio expressed great interest in our cars, though, and was even enthusiastic about Hawthorn's performance. I therefore asked him if he would like to try my car and he readily agreed to do a few practice laps. He came in smiling and I then offered him the car for the race. Fangio was delighted, but unfortunately this was the original prototype on which we had done all the testing and the engine went sour during the race. Looking back, however, I must be the only manufacturer who ever had Fangio driving for him with no starting money!

Since all our cars were new, at least in the design sense, and were making their first appearance in a race of any importance, they attracted quite a lot of interest; but even those who were rooting for us hardly expected that we would put up a great show on our initial outing. They were, as it happened, dead wrong. In the first event, the Lavant Cup, a fourteen-mile Formula 2 Sprint at Goodwood, Hawthorn ran away from the field, followed by Brown and Brandon, who took second and third places. Hawthorn's car ran on alcohol and had a much higher compression ratio than the other two Coopers, but that was not what carried him to victory, though it helped. What did it was simply Hawthorn's superior driving.

Next came the Chichester Formula Libre race, also of fourteen miles, and here Hawthorn repeated his win with ease. The main opposition consisted of Tony Rolt in an ERA-Delage and a 4.5-liter Talbot driven by Johnny Claes. As I've already mentioned, BRM didn't show up and Fangio, no less, drove my personal Cooper-Bristol, but due to carburetion trouble the best he could do was finish sixth. The day was not over yet. We sorted out my problems, or rather those of my car, and Brown next won a handicap race with it. Then Hawthorn came out again, this time in the Formula Libre Richmond Trophy, and took on the formidable Froilan Gonzalez, who was driving a 4.5-liter Thinwall Special. From start to finish, Hawthorn kept Gonzalez in sight and though he hadn't the speed to get by, nor anything like the power, his second-place finish really captivated the crowd.

So, in a single day's' racing, our Cooper-Bristol (along with Mike Hawthorn) became headline news. Hawthorn was now up and running and at the next meet—an airfield course at Ibsley in Hampshire—he won both the Formula 2 and Formula Libre races. Then came the *Daily Express* Trophy at Silverstone, which, following custom, was run in two heats followed by a final. Hawthorn won the first heat, beating Behra's hot Gordini by almost two and a half seconds; but that day was not a happy one for our cars. Hawthorn also took the lead from Behra in the second heat, but on the third lap had to pull into the pits. A broken gear lever held him up for five laps, putting him out of contention, though he eventually finished eighteenth. Both the other Cooper-Bristols also ran into trouble. Brown's *Écurie Richmond* machine had engine bothers and our prototype car, driven by Reg Parnell, was sidelined in its heat while running fourth.

I could go on like this for pages, but a few more examples will suffice. During Whitsun weekend, Hawthorn won a forty-lap Formula Libre race at Charterhall on Saturday, then on Monday, having moved to Goodwood, he scored another win in the Formula Libre Sussex Trophy. A week later we entered our prototype works car in the Ulster Trophy at Dundrod. This was, in fact, a Formula 1 race and once again Hawthorn found himself up against the big Thinwall Special with more than double his engine capacity. Furthermore it was now driven by that wily fox Taruffi. For once the Italian stalled on the line and Hawthorn jumped into the lead, where he stayed for five laps. Taruffi then caught him, but later had to pit for tires and fuel. Then Mike also had to make a pit stop, which relegated him to second place.

By that time, Hawthorn was regularly driving one of our cars for Chase, while Brown and Brandon stayed with *Écurie Richmond*. A week after Dundrod, the Gran Prèmio dell'Autodromo was held at Monza, where Brown and Brandon were entered, but not Hawthorn. They finished fifth and sixth in a race that was marred by Juan Fangio's only crash in his fantastic professional career. He had flown from Dundrod to Paris, expecting to make a plane connection to Milan, but the weather had closed in completely and all flights were canceled. Undaunted, Fangio borrowed a car and after a night-long drive got to Monza just in time to make the race. Having missed practice, he found himself in the back row of the grid, but when he climbed into his A6GCM Maserati, which was making its debut, he should have been climbing into bed.

The inevitable happened and Fangio crashed on the second lap, breaking his neck. He was lucky not to be killed or paralyzed but remained out of action for a year. It was his one and only accident in five World Championship seasons, all of which he won.

Team Richmond stayed on the Continent and ran in the Belgian Grand Prix at Spa in June that year. They were joined by Hawthorn, and this time encountered strong opposition from Stirling Moss in one of the new G-Type ERA's. Formula 2 had now become big league international racing and I felt we were taking on a bit too much with a car powered by an engine designed thirteen years earlier. My judgment proved right, but even so, Hawthorn performed wonders in finishing fourth, while Brown and Brandon were sixth and ninth.

A week later there was a Formula 2 race at Reims, which again found Hawthorn on the starting line with our prototype car. It made no difference that we had in the meantime sold this machine to A. H. Bryde, a wealthy farmer whose XK120 we had taken in trade. He was just as enthusiastic an owner as we had been, despite the fact that we were completely outclassed in a Cooper-Bristol with a maximum speed of 130 mph, which was much slower than the Ferraris and Gordinis. We had no business running a Formula 2 car against Formula 1 machines that were infinitely costlier, faster and more complex, not to mention power, but Hawthorn wanted to "have a go" just for the hell of it and because he loved racing, no matter what the odds.

The result was predictable, of course. The best that Mike could do was finish seventh in the Bryde car, while Brandon (due to several pit stops and obstinate carburetor trouble) took eleventh place. Brown had to retire with a bad oil leak.

Hawthorn caught one more race on the Continent during that 1952 season—the French Grand Prix at Rouen, but a split header tank in his radiator put him out of business.

By this time, production of our Cooper-Bristols was well under way and we were learning as we went. Cars had already been supplied to John Barber, a wealthy enthusiast, *Écurie Écosse* (a Scottish financed group) and the Frazer-Hartwell Syndicate, whose driver was the Frenchman, André Loens. So five Cooper-Bristols were entered in the British Grand Prix at Silverstone. Hawthorn was driving for Bob Chase; Reg Parnell, for A. H. Bryde; Brown, Brandon and David Murray all for *Écurie Écosse*. This race was totally dominated by Ferraris, but after the great Farina quit with engine trouble, Hawthorn actually moved up to third place and stayed there. Not even Harry Schell in a Maserati-Platé could get past him. A truly remarkable performance by a driver as dedicated as his car was outclassed. Hawthorn had now earned seven points toward the World Championship and held fifth place jointly with Manzon, who drove a Gordini.

On August Bank Holiday Monday of 1952, Hawthorn added to his laurels with another incredible performance. In the *Daily Express* International Trophy meet at Boreham, under the worst possible weather conditions, he won the Formula 2 Trophy at 82.21 mph. The Formula 1 and 2 races were run concurrently and it was this fact which added sparkle to Mike's performance. For many laps he led Villoresi's 4.5-liter Ferrari and the six other Cooper-Bristols in this event. Two weeks later, in the Dutch Grand Prix at Zandvoort, Hawthorn made such good use of his

Cooper-Bristol's excellent handling qualities on this relatively slow circuit that his practice time was good enough to put him in the front row of the grid, ahead of one of the Ferraris and the entire Gordini team. In the race, Hawthorn finished fourth behind three Ferraris and earned himself another three points toward the Championship for a total score of ten. For the Italian Grand Prix at Monza—a course where the Cooper-Bristol was about 30 mph down in top speed as compared with the Ferraris—Hawthorn tried again. This time a sheared magneto drive put him out of the running, but Ken Wharton in an *Écurie Écosse* car finished ninth while the two Team Richmond cars were thirteenth and fourteenth.

At this point, Enzo Ferrari, who seemingly had been watching Hawthorn for a long time, offered him a ride in a Ferrari for the Grand Prix at Modena. Mike accepted and handed over his Cooper-Bristol entry to Roy Salvadori. However, he decided to try out the car anyway and because of the sudden changeover from the faster and much more powerful Ferrari, he shunted the Cooper-Bristol so badly that it could not be repaired. He also injured his ribs seriously enough to prevent him driving. So neither Hawthorn nor Salvadori got a ride that time.

The rest of the 1952 season consisted of minor events unrelated to the World Championship, in which Hawthorn did not participate. He probably would have run in the Formula 2 Madgwick Cup at Goodwood, but for the fact that meantime Duncan Hamilton had blown the engine of the Bob Chase Cooper-Bristol skyhigh, even breaking the crankshaft. This engine, which had the highest output to date of any Cooper-Bristol, had been prepared by Mike's father, Leslie Hawthorn, and put out 150 bhp at 5,750 rpm. This was the result of raising the compression ratio from 8.5 to 10:1 and various other tricks. By October 1952, we were so far ahead with development work on this now famous car that the 1953 model was ready for testing. But its greatest driver, Mike Hawthorn, the boy wonder from Yorkshire, no longer was available. He had accepted an offer to join the Ferrari team for the following season.

There was not a great deal we could do with the completely outdated Bristol engine while still retaining any degree of reliability, so we made some radical changes to the chassis and running gear. These reduced the weight still further and gave the car greater rigidity. The box-section frame was discarded for a new tubular configuration which ran throughout the chassis. This was made of sixteen-gauge, inch-and-a-half-diameter steel tubes welded up to form a lightweight, functional structure of enormous strength. The lines of the car, although still high in silhouette, were greatly improved. The entire configuration rested on two parallel tubes which were the mainstay for the front and rear transverse spring suspension units. The pressed steel casing for the hypoid rear drive was replaced by one of magnesium alloy, which saved a lot of weight. New Alfin brake drums, separate from the light alloy wheels, were now fitted and their diameter was increased to eleven inches. Cast magnesium also was used for the brake back plates and stub axle carriers. And finally the oil and coolant radiators were redesigned and given a different shape. This permitted a direct flow of air from the frontal intake to the carburetors. The rather ugly humped air intake of the 1952 car, sitting astride the top of the hood, was scrapped entirely.

We put a great deal of careful thought and much time into building the new Cooper-Bristol, yet we should have known that with the existing engine we were at the end of the line. There was simply not enough steam available, no matter how light the chassis or how excellent the handling.

For the 1953 season, Ken Wharton, an experienced Formula 2 driver who had been running Frazer Nashes the previous year, entered the fray on our team. New cars were ordered by Bob Gerard, Rodney Nuckey, son of the man whose tool manufacturing company was known worldwide, and the Ferrari driver Tom Cole, son of the famous shipping magnate. Other sales followed and we received an invitation to take part in the Argentine and Buenos Aires Grands Prix. My father went along as team manager for the two private entries made under our banner. These were a Team Richmond car driven by Alan Brown and the Frazer-Hartwell entry with John Barber at the wheel. Only one of these two was a top-caliber driver and as we still suffered from the chronic handicap of insufficient power, we didn't expect too much. In fact, these two finished eighth and ninth in the Argentine Grand Prix, while in the Buenos Aires event Alan Brown wrecked his engine and Barber took twelfth place.

There would be no point in wearying the reader with a detailed account of all the events we ran in during 1953. Sufficient to say that in nineteen starts we did not score a single win of importance and our best showing was a sixth place by Stirling Moss in the German Grand Prix. And even then he did not use a Bristol engine but converted our Mark II chassis to take an Alta twin-cam power unit with fuel injection. This engine ran on nitromethane, an oxygen-bearing fuel which raised the output of the engine from 150 to 200 bhp at 6,000 rpm. Immediately, maximum speed rose from 130 to 165 mph and Moss then had a competitive car—all except for the tires, which wouldn't stand up.

Had we chosen to go to a new engine which would have put us somewhere in the Ferrari league, there is no doubt that we would have become involved in further chassis development. But we decided at the end of 1953 to leave well enough alone. Not so, individual owners such as Bob Gerard, who by prodigious efforts increased the piston displacement of the Bristol engine from 1971 to 2157 cc and finally to 2246 cc. But it was a losing battle. The odd valve actuation of the Bristol engine (which by then dated back sixteen years) gave it an absolute ceiling of 6,000 rpm if any reliability was to be achieved. And even then the maximum output was way down on that of other engines with overhead camshafts. We were in a dead-end street and we knew it, yet we had given the "big boys" quite a run for their money and acquired a worldwide reputation in the process.

In 1954, the ruling Formula 2 was superseded by a new Formula 1, which permitted unsupercharged engines up to 2500 cc. But Cooper-Bristol owners of open-wheeled cars were a faithful and stubborn tribe and they continued racing despite the enormous handicap now imposed on them. Notable English drivers who pursued this lost cause were Horace Gould, a garage owner from Bristol who later went to a 250F Maserati; Keith Hall, who became a works Lotus driver; and of course Bob Gerard with his forlorn 2246 cc engine, who, in 1956, managed to finish eleventh in the British Grand Prix.

By then we had converted many of our twenty Formula 2 Cooper-Bristols into sports cars, giving them different and much more attractive bodywork, undershields and other goodies. We had returned to the original box-section frame, using undrilled side members and longitudinal upper tubes to support the body, which was given added cross bracing for stiffness. The complete Cooper-Bristol two-seater sports car weighed 225 pounds more than its

Formula 2 predecessor, but it now ran in a class where it was far more competitive. Our original schedule for sports car production (begun in 1953) called for us to build about twenty-five of these machines, but in fact we only completed six, besides the conversions.

In 1953, the famous Bob Chase Cooper-Bristol was totally rebuilt as a sports car, but we didn't do the body. That was the brainchild of a highly skilled mechanic named Bernie Rodgers, who later designed the now defunct Peerless car—a GT model.

The price tag on our Cooper-Bristol sports car was £2,000 (then about $7,000), a reasonable sum for a hand-built machine of this type, using the highest quality materials and the best technology available to us at the time. Our product, performance-wise, was the equal of the famous and very fast Le Mans replica Frazer Nashes. We could hold our own with such stalwarts as the Aston Martin DB3, which was pretty good. The body of our car was of eighteen-gauge aluminum with hand-beaten panels and we included such amenities as a nineteen-gallon gas tank, a tuned exhaust system and Armstrong shock absorbers. The upholstery and instruments were of very high quality. The general finish fully justified what we asked for the car. And this was not only our opinion but that of many satisfied buyers. If the Bristol engine was way low on power, it could be called extremely reliable and tough. That famous old British firm (AC Cars) whose origin is lost in the mists of time, also used the Bristol power unit in their sports car, which was known as the Ace-Bristol. Many of these machines were sold in the United States and run in competition with more than a measure of success.

But that's by the way. I think the credit for pioneering the Bristol-powered Formula 2 and sports cars rightly belongs to the Cooper name. We certainly left our mark in the book of automotive history. I sometimes wonder what Mike Hawthorn would have gained his experience on, had we not been there. The car suited him perfectly as he learned his way round. When Hawthorn first began making a name for himself with our Cooper-Bristol, he was twenty-three years old. Yorkshire born and bred, Mike with his tousled head of ash-blond hair and healthy complexion would have been regarded by the late, unlamented Hitler as a prime example of the Nordic "Aryan" race, but unfortunately he disliked Germans very much. His father, Leslie, had always been an enthusiastic motorcycle racer and tuner and when the family moved south to Farnham, Leslie Hawthorn found himself located within a stone's throw of Brooklands track, which was an ideal testing ground. Mike had an engaging personality, enormous determination and inborn skill for driving race cars which only needed development.

From the time he first competed in the Brighton Speed Trials with a Riley 1100, Mike lived only for racing, and when in 1953 he got a seat on the Ferrari team, he never looked back. Without question he was a great driver who proved his mettle by winning the Formula 1 World Championship in 1958. By then, he had returned to Ferrari via Jaguar and the terrible Le Mans disaster—suddenly and unconsciously triggered off by one of his lightning decisions—was already three years old. The decision was to make a sudden and long overdue pit stop, which caused him to swerve right on the narrow pit straight, in front of a much slower car driven by Lance Macklin. Lance, to avoid a collision, had no alternative but to swerve left, and in so doing slammed the gate on the veteran Frenchman Levegh, who was about to overtake him in an extremely fast Mercedes 300SLR. Levegh's reflex was also to avoid a collision and the only place where he could go was further left. The critical and tragic difference was that Levegh had no place to go except an abutment built up from piles of soil. The Mercedes stopped dead from perhaps 130 mph, killing its driver instantly, but the engine cannonballed out of the car like a projectile and mowed down a dense crowd of spectators, eighty-two of whom died, then or later. I was there in the pits and watched every foot of that ghastly accident unreel itself.

The 1955 Le Mans disaster is an old issue but was at the time the subject of violent emotional controversy which had far-reaching effects on motor racing, including its total ban by Switzerland. Hawthorn was shocked nearly out of his mind and refused to drive his factory D-Type Jaguar another yard. But by the end of that nightmare race his philosophical attitude to life was already reasserting itself. I knew Mike well and liked and respected him for his courage and splendid driving skill. Although he only won the World's Championship from Moss by the narrowest of margins, he deserved his success. I have often been asked my personal opinion of Mike Hawthorn, who later lost his life in a rather stupid and inexplicable road accident, but I have found it very hard to put that impression into words.

Everyone liked Hawthorn, and indeed how could one help doing so? He was full of fun and loved practical jokes and gave his all to driving fast cars. He suffered two serious crashes in his meteoric career, but neither left any mark on him. The first, which I have already mentioned, occurred at Modena track in 1952 while testing one of our Cooper-Bristols. He was recuperating in a London clinic when he got the offer to join the Ferrari team. The second accident was during the Syracuse Grand Prix the following year, when he suffered severe burns to his legs. Mike's popularity was at a low ebb because of a hate campaign launched against him for "evading" military service. Such was not the truth; it was a kidney ailment which made him ineligible, but the public would not buy that.

Not even the Le Mans disaster dimmed Mike's buoyant spirits for very long, and looking back, now, I would say he had a sort of built-in philosophy which enabled him to flow with events. He was perhaps blessed by the fact that nothing went really deep with him, nothing left a lasting scar, physical or mental. In fact, nothing bothered him with any degree of permanence. There was more than a touch of fatalism in this brilliant young driver who, in 1959, when only twenty-nine, lost his life in an accident that should never have occurred and had nothing to do with racing.

So far as I am concerned, his ready smile and ebullient spirits remain undimmed by time. And I am happy to think that his prodigious drives in our sadly underpowered Cooper-Bristol took him to the World Championship.

11

We Enter the Grand Prix Scene

Looking back over the years, we could say that our Grand Prix career was a distinct success, both for Cooper cars and their drivers. As I recall, our rear-engined entry into the Grand Prix racing scene really started in 1958, running 1759 cc and two-liter cars. We began by selling a car to my old friend Rob Walker of the Johnny Walker whiskey family. This car was prepared by a very famous mechanic, Alf Francis, while Rob retained Stirling Moss to drive for him when the latter was not tied up with the Vanwall team, then his primary commitment. Early in 1958, Rob Walker entered his two-liter Climax-engined Cooper for the Argentine Grand Prix, and the reason why he got Stirling Moss was either because the Vanwalls were not yet ready, or were not prepared to make that particular event.

I remember we were having some minor gearbox trouble at this time, and for a fairly obvious reason. The power put out by the Coventry Climax engine was straining our ERSA (Citroën) gearbox to its limit. We had tried various cures for this problem by fitting a special oil pump at the back which would provide the gearbox with extra lubrication, and we also had strengthened the ERSA gears and tried just about everything. But at this point the actual transmission cases began to split. I therefore had no choice but to stop off at ERSA's in Paris and ask them whether they might be able to make a casing of stronger alloy which at the same time would be thickened up a bit by scraping the mold at the factory.

Since ERSA were genuinely interested in "young" racing enthusiasts, they agreed to help me. This was about a month before the car was due to leave for the 1958 Argentine Grand Prix. I had gone to ERSA on the strong recommendation of Alf Francis, who told me, "I'm sure we're never going to finish a Grand Prix unless some way is found to stiffen up that gearbox."

And he was undoubtedly right.

A couple of phone calls to Paris in my pidgin French got me the assurance that if I showed up on Friday I would be able to pick up three beefed-up gearbox cases and could take them back with me. So I caught the early morning plane and duly arrived at ERSA to find the promised casings waiting for me. They had done a very good job, using high-grade aluminum and stiffening up these casings just where this was needed. Late the following evening I was back at London Airport, where a Customs officer asked me politely, "Have you read this notice, sir?"

"Yes," I said. "I have."

"Have you anything to declare?"

"Yes." Knowing what was going to happen, I was ready. "I bought a bottle of perfume, a bottle of whiskey, a cigarette lighter, two hundred cigarettes, a gearbox case—no, three of them—and some other small things of little value."

The Customs man was about to put his stamp on my suitcase when he paused and did a double take.

"What was that you said, sir? *Three* gearbox cases?"

"That's right," I nodded.

"Where are they?"

"In my suitcase."

"Would you mind opening it, sir?"

"Not at all." I did so as calmly as possible—far more calmly than I felt inside—and there, neatly tucked in my suitcase were three complete casings. "Well," I said, "I told you I had them."

"That's true," the Customs man nodded, "but that stuff is not supposed to come through here. You should have taken it to the Cargo Department."

From that moment on, I spent three hours in the Cargo Department before they would let me pay the duty on those casings and take them out. It was to say the least a harrowing experience, but that same night I rushed the precious load over to Alf Francis, who was waiting. With his customary genius he did a perfect transplant job, fitting our existing gears into the strengthened casings. He completed one unit in time to install it in the Cooper which otherwise was ready for the Argentine. All we had to do was fly the car over.

Quite frankly, I was dubious of our chances, especially in the company of such drivers as Fangio and Musso in 2.5-liter Maseratis. It seemed obvious that Stirling, despite his great skills, would be hard pushed in a two-liter Cooper. But what we had going for us was a rather twisty circuit and I thought, "Well, with Stirling you never can tell!"

On the evening of the race I was having a drink with Keith Challen, motoring correspondent for the *News of the World,* when he suddenly looked up and said, "Gosh, the Argentine Grand Prix is on, now. I really ought to phone the office and find out how things are going."

"That's a good idea," I said.

After a while, Challen came back beaming like a Cheshire cat. "Guess what!" he said. "I just got the news. The Argentine Grand Prix has been won by Stirling Moss, driving a British Cooper-Climax! My congratulations, old boy!"

Nothing could have pleased me more, since this was the very first World Championship Formula 1 Grand Prix that a Cooper had won. Naturally, to score such a victory on the other side of the world against opposition of the highest caliber was a real achievement. We actually got the news at midnight and immediately invited Ron Searles (who unfortunately was later killed in one of my center-seat sports cars while attacking the World's Record) to join me in the celebration of our victory. I also tried to get hold of Roy Salvadori and a few of us did open a bottle of champagne by way of a tribute to the occasion.

I suppose by this time we realized that it was possible for a Cooper car with a smaller engine and less power than the all-conquering Ferraris and Maseratis, to win a Grand Prix.

First thing Monday morning, I was on the phone to Mr. Lee of Coventry Climax and gave him the news. He was of course delighted, but already I had done some thinking.

"Look," I said, "I know we're playing around with a 2.2-liter version of your engine, but we've got to get a proper 2.5-liter job, built from scratch. Given that, I feel nothing can stop us from winning the World Championship. This may sound like big talk, but it's really no more than common sense."

Lee agreed and immediately set about designing a new, real, honest-to-goodness 2.5-liter Climax which we would be able to drop into the back of our cars. Of course the rest of the Climax team was roped in—men such as Wally Hassan and Harry Mundy, who all set forth with a will. They designed stronger connecting rods, larger bearings, bigger valves—in fact everything required to build a real twin-cam, four-cylinder Grand Prix engine with a piston displacement of just under 2500 cc. This was the engine with which we were destined to win the Formula 1 World Championship the following year and again in 1960, and to use at Indy in 1961.

In fact, the exact displacement was 2462 cc and the output (originally) 243 bhp at 6,800 rpm with a compression ratio of 12 to 1. It was a dry-sump engine, of course, and the twin carburetors were Weber double-choke, Type 38 DC03's. Under sustained and strenuous tests, this turned out to be one of the most reliable World Championship Grand Prix engines ever built. It got so that we could run two or three Grands Prix in a row with no teardown and only a minimal check and adjustment.

Our first Grand Prix in 1957 was at Monaco, where Rob Walker borrowed Jack Brabham from me to drive a Cooper with a two-liter Climax engine. We ourselves had entered a 1.5-liter car for Les Leston to drive and were obviously not competitive in Formula 1. Right away, during the first practice session around Monte Carlo Jack found that the power of his engine was quite adequate and this quickly showed in his lap times around the world's most difficult circuit. Unfortunately he got a bit carried away and as he rocketed up the Ste.-Dévote Hill toward the Casino, he ran into a patch of oil that one of the Ferraris had deposited there. Taking the right-hand corner by the Hotel de Paris, Jack lost the car in a big way and went through the scaffolding and straw bales hard enough to write off the machine.

That evening we had a quick meeting with Rob Walker and reached the obvious conclusion. Since Rob's car was now damaged beyond all hope of immediate repair, but luckily the engine was still intact, we decided to put Rob's engine in the 1.5-liter works Cooper that Leston had been driving but had blown up while trying to qualify it. Luckily, Jack had gone fast enough to qualify before his shunt, so we were okay there. But that left us with a big job to do and not much time to do it in. The upshot was that Alf Francis and I worked continuously, day and night, taking catnaps on the spot while we fitted Rob's two-liter engine into our chassis. Some of the modifications that Alf Francis had made to Rob Walker's engine gave us a hard time fitting it into the chassis. Anyway, this put Jack on the starting line, ready for this first Grand Prix with a competitive car.

I remember standing in the pits with my father, and although I felt pretty much exhausted, as did Alf Francis, we had enough energy left to get very excited about our chances. Rob Walker was in pretty much the same mood and we all kept praying that the car had been put together well enough to last through ninety grueling laps. The measure of the toll exacted by the Monaco circuit can be expressed in the ratio of finishers to starters, and if one third of the starting field of twenty cars is still there at the end, that's pretty good going.

Jack worked his way up during the race and what with his brilliant driving, cars dropping out and others having to pit, he found himself in third spot. Fangio was leading the race and I forget who was second, but we were more than satisfied. If we could do that well with a two-liter Climax and with Jack sitting very comfortably where he was, what could we have done with that extra half liter permitted by the then current Formula 1 regulations? Unfortunately, toward the end, the fuel pump quit and we waited on tenterhooks for Jack to appear. "Darn it!" we thought. "He must have smashed it up again, or something!"

But we were doing him an injustice. Suddenly we saw him along the side of the harbor, pushing the car as hard as he could round the Kiosk Hairpin, just before the pits. We weren't allowed to help him but I rushed out to get a verbal rundown.

"It's run out of fuel," Jack said between gritted teeth.

"It couldn't have," I said. "No way. We put enough gas in to last the whole race easily. It has to be something else."

Once in the pits we soon traced the fault to the pump and managed to get it working once more. Immediately Jack was on his way again and he did finish the race, but the incident served notice on all the other competitors that a rear-engine car with independent suspension all round was quite good enough to pose a serious threat in a World Championship Grand Prix. Far from being downhearted, the thought ran through our minds again and again, "Boy, just wait till we get our new engine next year. We'll show you fellows a thing or two!"

By this time, Climax had produced a second 2.2-liter engine and we had both these power units in addition to the regular two-liter line. If one of our bored-out engines was out of commission, or being overhauled, Jack and Roy would toss up as to who would use the remaining one. I must say that they always managed to sort things out amicably, so that the temporary shortage caused no problem between drivers. We went through the 1958 season "knocking on the door" at a few other Grands Prix and learning all the time. This enabled us to improve the Cooper chassis in many detailed particulars.

The usual 200-mile Grand Prix race may not seem very far, but in fact the constant braking, cornering, accelerating and gear shifting takes a lot out of a car. It puts loads and stresses on every part that no dynamometer can simulate, although a modern computer harnessed to the right equipment would probably come a lot closer. Still, to gain practical knowledge about a given design, I am a firm believer that there is no substitute for the racecourse.

Anyway, we learned a hell of a lot that year, not only in Grands Prix but also in just ordinary Formula 1 and Formula Libre races such as the *Daily Express* event at Silverstone, and so on. I was determined at all events that the following year we were going to make a real attempt to capture the World Championship on the International Grand Prix scene. Toward the end of 1958, during the British Motor Show, everybody in the game would buy the Esso and BP men gins and tonics and anything else, because they all hoped to pull off a big sponsoring deal for the coming season.

Aston Martin had meanwhile built a Grand Prix car which was not destined for great things. It was far too heavy to be competitive. But at the time a lot of people in the racing game got a bit scared. "If Aston Martin are going racing with David Brown's money," they said, "that means trouble for us. No one spends £50,000 [at that time well over $142,000] for nothing." It was further known that David Brown had offered Roy Salvadori a lot of money to join the new factory team. They had made an even bigger offer to our Jack Brabham.

At the time I was signed up with Esso, whose sponsorship

meant a lot to us and whose racing manager was Reg Tanner. I wasted no time in going to see him.

"Look, Reg," I said, "our Cooper team has a chance, next year, of putting up a really good show in Grand Prix racing. All we're waiting for is the new 2.5 Climax engine, which has been designed specially for us. Or at least at our request. Now, at what looks like the turning point, I stand to lose both my drivers to Aston Martin. What can you do about it? The Esso company has plenty of scratch and I need some help. I really do."

"Well," Tanner said, "how much money is involved?"

"A good-sized chunk," I said.

"Talk figures."

"Okay. I, myself, need at least £10,000 [$35,000] just to put a competitive Grand Prix car together. And that's only the beginning. I also know that Jack and Roy have been offered a lot of money to drive those new Aston Martins."

Tanner came to a quick decision. "I can't afford the car and *both* your drivers. So pick the one you want and that'll be it."

"Fair enough," I nodded. "One driver it is, then. Which one, I'll let you know."

But in my mind I had already made the choice. I would sign on Jack Brabham. He was younger than Roy and had a lot more mechanical experience. I felt we could work well together on the coming project. Of course I had to put it straight to Salvadori.

"I'm sorry, Roy, but the truth is I can only afford one of you. My picking Jack is in no sense a personal thing against you. So I don't want you to have any bad feelings about it. That's just the way it goes. You sign on with Aston Martin and, financially, you won't have much to complain about."

Roy, being a good sport and a personal friend, took it philosophically and it made no difference to our relationship. Meantime I also decided to sign on Bruce McLaren out of our own funds. This proved to be one of my wisest decisions because Bruce not only was a very good driver—he, too, had the kind of technical know-how that can be of enormous help to mechanics before and during a race. It's an ability to communicate clearly with the pit crew and draw their attention to whatever may be wrong with the car. Not many drivers have this gift, but those who do usually turn out to be brilliant people in the race game. That I was right about Jack and Bruce was proven not only on the world's Grand Prix courses, but because later both men quit racing to concentrate entirely on designing and building their own race cars. And both were very successful in their endeavors.

Bruce unfortunately was killed at Goodwood in 1970 while testing one of his world-famous sports racing cars.

Another driver we signed up was Masten Gregory, a young American who had made the big league with no other help than an enormous determination, great courage and a gradual honing of his skills through some crashes no other man would have survived. Masten was a charger, but outside a race car, a quiet, soft-spoken and very pleasant individual. One of his problems was that, thanks to a considerable inheritance in the United States, he had started at the top, not bothering to work his way up through MG's and so forth. He had gone straight out and bought himself a C-Type Jaguar and started from there. It proved to be a series of costly and sometimes painful lessons, but his tremendous grit carried him through.

So there we were, ready for the 1959 Grand Prix season, with a team of three Cooper-Climaxes to be driven by Jack Brabham, Bruce McLaren and Masten Gregory. It was a pretty good setup even though when you're a small manufacturer, such as we were, it does strain things a bit, running three cars. But the decision was made and my feeling was simply "If we don't do it now, we may never have another chance."

We therefore looked at the calendar for 1959 and made commitments to enter every possible Grand Prix that would count toward the World Championship. So, starting with 1959, which gave us our first Championship, here's a race-to-race rundown on what happened.

Our initial Formula 1 race for the 1959 season was not actually a *Grande Épreuve,* but what we thought would be a useful warming-up event with our new cars—the *Daily Express* Silverstone race for Formula 1 cars. This gave us only a week before the Monaco Grand Prix, which was running things a bit close. As a matter of routine, even if nothing went wrong at Silverstone, the three cars would have to be checked out for any minor malfunctions.

But we thought we would give it a try. As it happened, Jack put up fastest qualifying time and the new engines ran not only very well but without a falter. During the race it was the same and Jack won that event without having to beat off any serious challenge.

Naturally we felt pretty good and took this result as the best possible augur for what was to come.

Now came the wild rush to ship our cars over to Monaco in time for qualification and the Grand Prix itself, scheduled for May 10. This was, in fact, to be the first *Grande Épreuve* of the new season, counting toward the Formula 1 World Championship. We got there in time but our mechanics, Bill James and Mike Grohman, really had to work during the practice periods and in between. Although Jack had won at Silverstone the previous week with the new 2.5 Climax engine, which was a gem, we still were not sure of its many intricate details. For example, we did not know the exact clearance for the cylinder head sealing rings and our practice periods were followed by engine changes and detail modifications to get everything running smoothly as well as reliably.

Bruce McLaren, the "baby" of our team that season, had an amazing ability to learn quickly and could be relied upon to obey instructions. Still, one can imagine his disappointment when he arrived in Monaco and saw all three Coopers completely dismantled and the seat from his car already fitted into the frame of Jack's machine! When Masten Gregory tried out his car and found the engine ran like a charm, he at once insisted that Jack should take over the car. This was typical of Masten and of our team spirit.

12

World Championship—1959

There was no doubt that we had to survive a tremendous flap before the start of Monaco. But there were some compensations, nonetheless. We put up at a hotel in Roquebrune, about five miles up the beautiful Riviera coast from Monte Carlo, near where Lady Macklin (mother of Lance Macklin) lived. She had a luxurious villa with a very large double garage, which was made to order for us, and she did not hesitate to offer it.

"Keep your cars in my garage and work on them there," Lady Macklin said. "The chauffeur will clear the place out for you."

As a matter of interest, Winston Churchill used to stay at a villa next door to Lady Macklin's and did many of his interesting paintings there. It was an ideal setup for him. He was able for short periods to set aside and almost forget the heavy political burdens that he had to bear through most of his life.

Our modest hotel, too, suited us very well. It was clean, bright and inexpensive and we went back there several times on later occasions.

For the first day of practice we got up at 5 A.M. and towed our cars to Monaco in good time for the first session, which started at 7 A.M. We had done a fantastic amount of shuffling around of parts among the three cars, but it all turned out for the best. Jack used Bruce's frame and Masten's engine and brake system. Masten had our number two car, made up of Jack's original engine and the frame Bruce had used in England for the Aintree 200-Mile race; while Bruce drove the Silverstone car after the mechanics had worked all night to install a 2.2-liter engine.

Anyway, Brabham qualified in the front row—a habit which continued throughout that season, while Masten and Bruce occupied the fifth row, each with an identical time of 1:43.2, or 3.1 seconds slower than Jack. This shows how tight and competitive the grid was.

Behra in a Ferrari led from the start, but his engine went sour and this put his immediate pursuer, Stirling Moss, in the lead. Jack Brabham moved up to second, poised to make his move at the right moment. Unfortunately Jack ran into gearbox problems which began costing him two seconds a lap, mainly at the Station and Gasometer hairpins. (We later found out that there was almost no oil in his gearbox and this problem remained to plague us for quite a while, yet, until I finally hit on the solution. Still, ignorance is bliss, I suppose, and when Stirling Moss also quit, Jack took over the lead. Our worry, now, was Tony Brooks in second spot, who was gaining on Jack even though he was ill at the time and perhaps should not have been driving. But despite his gearbox problems, Jack responded splendidly and on lap 83 set up a new record of 1:40.4 for the race. Poor Masten had long since retired (on the seventh lap) with gearbox problems more serious than those Jack was trying to live with. Bruce McLaren drove extremely well, obviously the master of his car and taking care not to bend anything as the course was awash with spilled oil. He finished fifth and thereby earned himself two World Championship points.

So Jack Brabham won Monaco; Maurice Trintignant in Rob Walker's privately entered Cooper took third and Bruce McLaren was fifth. A pretty good start for us. We were in fact delighted and a successful day was capped by an invitation to a reception that evening, given by Prince Rainier and Princess Grace. It turned out to be a celebration of our first real Grand Prix win.

For our next event, the Dutch Grand Prix at Zandvoort, May 31, we decided to keep our entry down to two cars until that elusive gearbox problem could be properly sorted out. So it was Bruce McLaren who unfortunately was deprived of the reward for his excellent drive at Monaco. Seeing that Jack had finished the Monte Carlo classic with an almost bone-dry transmission which could have seized up at any moment, we improvised a temporary cure. This was a small gravity oil tank cradled directly over the gearbox. At a predetermined time the driver could switch it on. Practice at Zandvoort suggested that we might have found the answer (we actually hadn't!), but while Jack again got in the front row of the grid (with a 1:36 lap) driving our newly assembled "Number Four" car, Masten was unhappy with his lap time and felt certain he would have to start low down on the grid.

Still, the Weber carburetor man who had helped us out at Monaco, again showed up at Zandvoort and his know-how put a fine edge of tuning to our engines. Masten turned out to have been quite wrong. His qualifying time, only 1.6 seconds slower than that of Jack, put him in the third row. Also in the front row, of course, was Stirling Moss, only two tenths slower than Jack. What we had not exactly counted on was that Masten Gregory was loaded for bear. Using a "creeping" start as the flag fell, he jumped not only Jack but everyone else except Moss, and at the first corner he was second. On lap 2 he took the lead, pursued by Jo Bonnier in a BRM, and opened up such a gap that he began to wonder what had happened to everyone else. That was until lap 10, when third gear quit, so that on the following laps he was passed by Bonnier, Brabham and Moss. For fifteen laps Jack and Jo dueled for the lead, then gearbox trouble similar to Masten's overcame Brabham. But this time it was second gear. Taking hairpins in third was a pretty hairy business which put Jack sideways every time so as to keep up the revs. However, he managed to stick it out despite this handicap and finished second to Bonnier, with Masten Gregory in third place.

Stirling Moss also had retired with gearbox trouble, although he was using a specially made Colotti gearbox. So we didn't seem to have a monopoly of gremlins in that department. Anyway, the race was finally won by Jo Bonnier in his BRM, but with Coopers in second and third places (Jack and Masten) we had every reason to rejoice. What was more, once celebrations were over I vowed to locate the transmission problem that was robbing us of victory. And I did. A small modification to the gearbox lid performed the trick immediately.

The World Championship race of the season was at Reims on July 3, 1959, and was of course known as the French Grand Prix. It was and still is the fastest road circuit in the world. Because of the cancellation of the Belgian Grand Prix that year, we had a breathing space of nearly five weeks, which proved most welcome. After discussions with Jack, I gave immediate orders to start work on streamlining our cars so as to get more speed on the long straights of this fast circuit. However, we were not about to give away our secrets prematurely, so we arranged for the new body fittings to be quickly interchangeable with the old ones. Our panel beaters worked night and day, but when the job was done two men could make the complete switch in five minutes! We managed a quick test in the rain at Silverstone and got the answers we were looking for. Streaks of grime showed that the air was going in where it was supposed to. Where it was not, the body shape kept it out. But the whole thing proved to be an illusion. At over 180 mph on the straights, the nose of our streamliner began to float and cornering at any sort of speed became pretty dicey. In fact, Jack Brabham felt so unsafe that we discarded the "streamliner" and went back to his regular Formula 1 body. On the second day of practice, a Thursday, Jack responded by turning in fastest lap. That made us very happy, but Masten Gregory's estimates of his braking points apparently amazed Bruce McLaren.

"I think maybe where I have an edge on you, Bruce," Masten drawled, "is that I go a lot deeper into the corners before I start braking."

"You have to be kidding," Bruce said. "Nobody could leave their breaking that late and still get around those corners."

"Okay," Masten shrugged. "Have it your way."

The point was settled on Friday evening toward the end of practice. Bruce and Masten approached the famous (and highly dangerous) Thillois Hairpin at about the same time, but to Bruce's surprise and amusement, Masten's car dipped first under hard braking. Bruce decided to go deeper and as he expected ended up down the escape road. By the time he rejoined the circuit, Masten had disappeared up the pit straight! That ended the argument.

As expected, Friday night was livened by a Champagne Ball, but on Saturday our mechanics had their hands full, removing, dismantling and rebuilding all three gearboxes. We had used a new material for the bushings which looked like seizing up, so the original bushes were put back. On top of that, a new head gasket was fitted to Jack's engine.

The heat on race day soared to an unprecedented 98°F in the rare places where there was any shade. The road surface tempera-

36. John Rhodes leading Steve Neal in the Cooper Car Co. Mini at South Tower Corner, Crystal Palace, during a thunderstorm in 1968.

37. "See what I mean?" Famous trio taken in the Cooper factory at Byfleet, Surrey, in 1967. John Cooper, *left,* is making a point with the famous Juan Manuel Fangio and sponsor Jonathan Sieff.

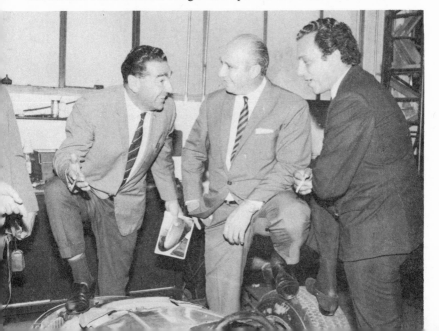

38. The late Pedro Rodriguez headed for victory in the 1967 South African Grand Prix with the difficult-handling Cooper-Maserati. Wins with this Formula 1 machine came too few and too far between and this led to a parting of the ways between Cooper and Maserati.

39. The Racing Car Show of 1968, held at Olympia, brought together as usual some interesting and famous personalities. *Left to right:* Wilkie Wilkinson, the BRM race manager, Ian Smith (dark hair and sideburns) of the BRSCC, John Cooper, the Duke of Edinburgh and an aide-de-camp. The Cooper-BRM on show was the firm's last exhibit before it phased out of racing.

40. Original Cooper Garage at Surbiton, Surrey, as it was in 1955. Business was founded by Charles Cooper in 1935.

41. Rebuilt and extended premises of the Cooper Car Company at Surbiton in 1961. Facilities were available for turning out complete racing and sports cars, except for the engines.

42, 43. A glance at these cutaways of the 1959, *left,* and 1960 Formula 1 Cooper-Climax Grand Prix cars—both of which won the Drivers' World Championship for Brabham and the Manufacturers' World Championship for Charles and John Cooper—reveals few striking differences mechanically. In fact, though they used similar components, suspension units and running gear, the tubular chassis of the 1960 car was extensively redesigned to produce a lower, longer line with reduced frontal area and wind drag. While the 1959 FPF four-cylinder, twin-cam Climax engine displaced 2495 cc (152.2 cu in) and put out 239 bhp at 6,750 rpm, the 1960 version had a fractionally shorter stroke of 3.5 in compared with 3.54 in, which resulted in a piston displacement of 151 cu in or 2462 cc. Yet the output of the latter was up 4 bhp to 243 at 6,800 rpm. Cam profiles, ignition timing and carburetor settings helped this minor power increase, but since the 1960 GP Cooper scaled 11.9 cwt (1,331 lbs) with oil, water and 33 gallons of fuel, a few pounds heavier than its predecessor, one must look elsewhere for the improved performance. Roadability was one factor; the front wheel rims were one inch wider and the rear wheel rims half an inch wider than the year before and lower profile tires were used. A new five-speed gearbox with magnesium castings was introduced which made better use of the engine torque curve. Weight distribution was improved front to rear to 44/56 per cent. The driver sat in a much more reclined position and the fuel tanks were reshaped to conform with the sleeker overall profile.

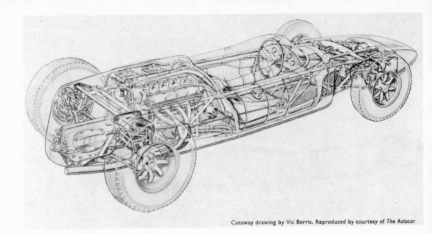

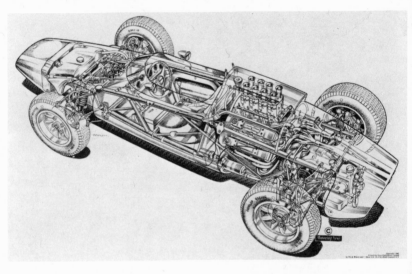

44. Constrained by a new FIA ruling which limited Formula 1 engines to a ceiling of 1.5 liters, the Coopers made the best of a difficult job by installing the only ready-to-go British engine of that displacement—the 1,498 cc twin-cam FPF Coventry Climax. Output was 150 bhp at 7,500 rpm, but since the 1960 chassis remained unchanged, performance necessarily suffered. The 1961 Ferrari 156 was too quick for the competition.

45. During the winter of 1961–62, the Coopers performed something of a miracle by completely redesigning their Formula 1 car and substantially reducing its weight. A Coventry Climax V-8 1.5-liter engine was installed which put out 190 bhp at 8,200 rpm through a new and much lighter six-speed gearbox. With Lotus coming on strong as well as Ferrari, it was a rough year; but the Cooper still registered two wins, a second and a third that season.

46. This cutaway of the 1966 Type 81 Cooper-Maserati shows an interesting composite of well-tried ideas brought together to conform with the then new Formula 1 displacement limit. Derek White of D-Type Jaguar fame, who had joined Cooper as chief designer, was responsible for the monocoque construction, running gear and brakes all beefed up to accept the Maserati 60° V-12 aluminum engine increased from 2.5 to 3 liters by enlarging the stroke from 56 to 69 mm. Fuel injection and a five-speed ZF gearbox were used. The car, though handsome and imposing, did not fulfill the Cooper hopes.

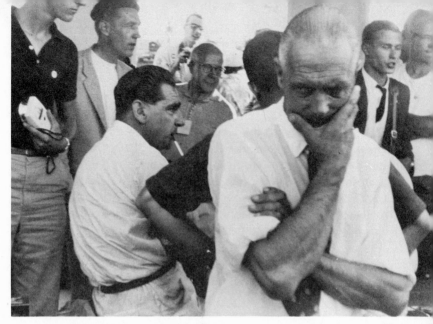

47. This photo, caught during practice for the 1961 U.S. Grand Prix at Watkins Glen, New York, was one of the last close-ups ever taken of the elusive billionaire Howard Hughes, but there's a story behind it. What's the Great Man (chin cupped in hand) thinking about as he stares pensively? "Shall I buy just this one Cooper that pulled into the pits—or write a check for the whole outfit?" John Cooper, enjoying a cigarette, isn't greatly concerned. He tells why in his story of a fantastic encounter with Hughes.

48. John Cooper and David Niven, old friends, at the 1976 Monaco Grand Prix.

ture was 130° to 140°F, while in the cockpits of our cars it was 170°F! Quite fantastic. What was more, our water temperature soared to over 100°C—the boiling point. In later cars, to insulate the drivers from this kind of engine heat, we fitted fiberglass bulkheads behind the radiators. (This improvement was so successful that later on during a race in England Masten complained of frostbite!)

Even before the start of the French Grand Prix, the incredible heat had melted the road surface and left the wet tar strewn with stones, especially in the braking areas. The whole event could aptly be described as a driver's nightmare, but when the flag dropped, Tony Brooks in his BRM catapulted into the lead and was never caught or even challenged by anyone. On lap 7, a flying rock hit Masten on the forehead and the effect of this jolt, combined with the heat, put him out of the race. Bruce's engine registered only thirty-five pounds of oil pressure, so he wisely kept from tailgating anyone so as to allow maximum air to enter the front of the car, from where it was ducted to the radiator.

Later in the race, while dueling with Gendebien's Ferrari, poor Bruce collected a small avalanche of flying stones but still managed to finish fifth, only a length behind his tormentor! Jack, clinging grimly to third spot, allowed no one to dislodge him, but he was driven to break the car's plexiglass windshield with his hands so as to let in more cool air! Or so he thought. In fact, more hot air and even greater numbers of stones found their way into the cockpit. On top of that, Jack had to fight clutch slip during the last twenty laps of the race, and afterward had no recollection of the final ten laps. But he made it, convinced that if there were ever a Grand Prix in the Australian desert, he would do pretty well!

So we ended up with Jack third and Bruce in fifth place, which was pretty good going.

Only thirteen days later, on July 18, we entered for the British Grand Prix at Aintree. The cars arrived in good shape but with the battle scars of Reims still showing. Our regular mechanics had been reinforced by a new man named Mike Barney, and for more than ten days a lot of hard work had gone into the Cooper gearboxes. Each was fitted with a special oil pump to stop the bushes from seizing up and overcome a general lack of lubrication which had been our main problem under heavy stress. We also replaced the ball bearings in each gearbox with tougher, more reliable roller bearings.

For the first time in more years than I could remember, I was not in the pits, watching over our cars. Illness kept me cooped up and I had to rely on TV broadcasts and phone calls. Would you believe? Somehow I had managed to catch the mumps!

On Thursday, the first practice day, it rained so hard no one was able to do more than motor around the course. By Friday, with the surface dried out, Jack Brabham in our Number One Cooper and Roy Salvadori (who had joined Aston Martin) shared the fastest lap in 1:58. Harry Schell (BRM) was 1.2 seconds slower, but fast enough to fill the front row.

Work continued into the early hours of Saturday on all three cars. Bruce had lost oil pressure and the mechanics dropped the oil pan to take a good look at the bottom of the engine. They also changed the gear ratios. Jack, too, got some new ratios while Masten Gregory's carburetors needed fine tuning. Then the front end of his car had to be readjusted to get rid of unwanted oversteer. Jack drove the newest Cooper as at Zandvoort; Masten had his usual car while Bruce was happily reunited with the machine he had had driven in an earlier Aintree 200. Bruce went well, storming through Becher's Bend with the rear end hanging out, but was startled when he saw Trintignant filling his rearview mirror. The Frenchman was tailgating him in Rob Walker's privately entered Cooper-Climax. Bruce quickly learned a faster line through the turns.

On the grid, Masten was in the second row with 1:59.4 while Bruce and Stirling Moss (Vanwall), both of whom were only two tenths of a second slower, occupied third row. Jack made a very good start, leading the BRM's of Schell and Bonnier. Masten also got off quickly, but was blocked by Schell, who fishtailed right in his path. When he did get clear he found himself dueling with Moss in a battle that lasted ten laps, until clutch slip set in. This, oddly enough, seemed to happen every other lap and produced some weird times. Then poor Masten's engine began overheating, but still he dueled, now with Roy Salvadori's heavier, slower Aston Martin.

Our crew knew that Jack, while in the lead, was worrying about tires, so they held up a ready-shod rear wheel to him as a reminder that they knew but he had better decide for himself. It was amusing to discover later that Jack had been worrying about tire treads from the fortieth lap on, whereas our sign didn't go up for another twenty laps! Anyway, Jack decided against stopping and won the race after a trouble-free run. Bruce, meantime, quietly slipped into second place when Stirling's Vanwall again pitted, this time for gas. A tremendous "dice" followed in which Moss regained second place and McLaren finished a smooth third. Masten Gregory (after a quick stop for a bucket of water) nursed his sick car into seventh spot. First, third and seventh was not a bad score. Our World Championship points kept piling up for Jack.

The next event, which was the German Grand Prix at the Avus Track, scheduled for August 2, came sooner than we would have liked. In fact all of us, except Masten Gregory, felt gloomy as our transporter headed for the coast and the Channel crossing. We had taken every possible precaution in the available free time, including the overhaul of all three engines by Coventry Climax, fitting higher gear ratios that would raise our top speed and installing modified shocks to withstand the tremendous "g" loads on the bankings. Masten was happy because he enjoyed charging along as hard as he could go and he thought of the Avus in the same terms as Reims with its long straights. In fact, only half the circuit was available, since the other half was in Eastern Germany. But in all other aspects there was no real point of comparison between the two circuits.

Surprisingly, there were two Coopers in the front row of the grid—Jack Brabham (2:07.4) and Stirling Moss with the privately entered Rob Walker car. The other two were Ferraris driven by the American Dan Gurney and Tony Brooks. Masten was in the second row, only one tenth of a second slower, while Bruce McLaren in the third row had clocked 2:10.4. So our three cars made the grid, but until our arrival the organizers had refused to confirm that we could run all three Coopers, which was another anxiety factor. During practice, Masten—the "charger" of our team—estimated that the Ferraris were about 14 mph faster at the top end than our Coopers. But Masten, who seemed to love situations with the odds stacked against him, figured that by slipstreaming Brooks (who was clearly out to win this one because of Championship points) he would be able to pass him just before the start of the main banking and keep ahead until just after.

During the first two heats which preceded the main event, Masten was able to coax better than 170 mph out of his car, and by taking huge risks he kept to his plan until the twenty-fourth lap, when a connecting rod bolt let go. Instantly, his engine blew sky-high and that was the end of a gallant effort. Masten got a big hand from the crowd for courageously splitting up the Ferraris, but his tactics came to nothing, unfortunately. We had time to install a spare engine in Masten's car and when the flag dropped for the actual Grand Prix he was right behind Brooks as the latter took the lead. On lap 3, Masten passed even Brooks but then tangled with Gurney's Ferrari on the banking when the latter misjudged things. The tail of the Cooper was crushed and so were Masten's hopes. Jack, whose car was undergeared, and who constantly had to over-rev his engine to stay in the running, slowed down on the seventh lap to give himself a chance to finish. But even that was not to be. On lap 15, his pinion gear, which had been incorrectly machined, came apart and that was the end.

Bruce McLaren, who had survived the first heat by finishing fourth, tried Masten's tactics in the second heat, doing his best to split up the Ferraris. But to no avail. His transfer gear assembly broke up and that wiped out the entire factory team. Still, the Cooper reputation was upheld by Maurice Trintignant, who was fourth in the Rob Walker Cooper. And by Ian Burgess, also in a Cooper, entered by the Scuderia Centro Sud.

Needless to say it was a sad day for us and we made ready to head for home less than happy. However, that evening we decided to go out on the town in West Berlin to drown our sorrow, and here at least we didn't do so badly. In fact we hit a couple of interesting night spots—one of them the Ricci Bar, where they had a water show on with colored fountains and a pretty good German string orchestra. Each table also had a phone with its own number. So, if you fancied the bird at table No. 75, you just dialed that number! Nobody knew where you were calling from—imagine about a hundred phones all going at the same time. So it was with reluctance that we headed for the next place, a club that had a sawdust ring something like a circus ring in the middle. You could have a meal there, and of course drinks. Then they put on a horse show and invited guests to ride bareback around the ring. Many of the race drivers ended up on their backs but it was very good fun, anyhow.

The Portuguese Grand Prix, three weeks after the Avus fiasco,

was next on our list for 1959. And since the Italian Grand Prix at
Monza would be due September 13, our transporter left Surbiton
equipped for a round tour which would cover both events. Bill
James had prepared Brabham's car before migrating to Canada, so
that left the two Mikes to carry the mechanics' load—Mike Grohman and Mike Barney.

Things didn't begin too well even before we started practice at
the Monsanto circuit, just outside Lisbon. Jack nearly lost a toe
while dragging a boat up on the beach; then his billfold was stolen
by a character who didn't even respond to an impassioned plea
over the local radio.

Of our three drivers, the only one immediately at home was
Masten Gregory, who had been there before. Naturally, we all
looked to him for information, but in practice he was still the
fastest of our team, although three seconds slower than Stirling
Moss with the Rob Walker Cooper. Masten's time was 2:05.6
with Jack just one second down. Bruce ran into immediate problems with the wrong gear ratio and an air-lock in the coolant system. It was again very hot and we carried out cockpit modifications to let more air into the cars so that we wouldn't suffer from
the same heat fatigue problems as at Reims.

On Saturday, Moss earned pole position with an extremely fast
2:02.8 lap; Jack was alongside him in 2:04.9, while Masten's
2:06.3 made him third man in the front row. Bruce was in the
third row with 2:08.1. Bruce and Masten drove their usual cars,
but Jack and Stirling both had their engines fitted with a new Climax cylinder head which gave an extra 12 to 15 hp.

Jack was first away at the flag, but Stirling passed him soon
after and held the lead to the finish. By the tenth lap our factory
Cooper team was running in line-ahead formation behind Moss—
the order being Jack, Masten and Bruce. Jack, however, decided
to concentrate on finishing second rather than risk trouble. He
didn't have to do any looking. Trouble came to him on lap 24
while he was trying to pass a slower car round a right-hand bend
at 130 mph. The other driver didn't see him and pulled across
right in front of the works Cooper. Jack was forced to swerve to
avoid a very bad shunt and he finished up skimming the tops of
the straw bales, then going end over end and knocking down a tel-
egraph pole, which threw him back into the middle of the road.
The car was completely wrecked but by a miracle Jack escaped se-

rious injury. Masten, who was following a few seconds behind, slid sideways to avoid Jack and also electrocution from the tangle of live wires that Jack's car had brought down! Luckily, they had already shorted out and Masten came past the pit with a thumbs up signal, meaning that Jack was okay.

On lap 39, Bruce, while still in third place, again lost a pinion gear and had to retire. Masten continued trailing Moss in second spot, though he kept a wary eye in his mirror for Gurney (Ferrari) who was doing his utmost to close the gap.

At the hairpin just before the main straight, Jo Bonnier, whose BRM had quit earlier, now set up a "refreshment bar" for the tired drivers. As they came past, crash helmets filled with water were thrown over them to cool them down. Masten made good use of this service during the closing laps and so the race ended with Stirling the winner and Masten a worthy second. But Rob Walker did better than our "works" team. Another privately entered Cooper of his, driven by Frenchman Trintignant, finished fourth.

Jack had been taken to hospital with some bad bruises, but after a checkup was released that same day. His car, as I've said, was a complete write-off, and this created problems loading it back onto the transporter. In addition, our overworked mechanics removed two engines and three gearboxes that Sunday night after the race. These were flown back to England, where one of our vans awaited to take them to London and Coventry, respectively. After overhaul they were returned to Surbiton.

Masten Gregory, happy with his second place at Lisbon, thought he would squeeze in a run in the Tourist Trophy at Goodwood before going on to Monza. That extracurricular event was to cost him dear, although I didn't learn about it at the time. I had to return to Surbiton before Monza to pick up a spare car which our works mechanics had hurriedly put together for Jack, following his accident. This was loaded on a trailer behind my Ford Zodiac, which was already filled to capacity with spare engines and gearboxes. Anyway, I set off on the trip to Italy on the Thursday prior to the Goodwood meeting where Masten planned to run, and that was why I didn't know of his accident until I reached Monza.

I was greeted with a telegram from Surbiton which said that Masten's shunt at Goodwood had been too serious for him to come to Italy. He was in hospital with a broken collarbone, a fractured leg and several cracked ribs, and if the truth be told he was lucky to be alive. But according to reports, what bothered him most was his inability to come to Monza!

Relieved by the knowledge that Masten would make a complete recovery, we set to work on our cars. One of the engines and all the gearboxes I had brought with me had to be installed—the other spare engine had already been fitted to the additional car built for Jack at Surbiton. New transfer gears, which had meantime been specially machined for Monza, again proved unreliable. When Bruce broke one during practice we changed all three of them. It then turned out that the cars were slightly overgeared, even for Monza, but there was nothing more we could do about it.

While all this was going on, I enlisted the services of Giorgio Scarlatti as the driver of our third car. The Italian had considerable experience behind him but not much luck. Perhaps things would now change?

Drivers and cars on our team were again shuffled around quite a bit, through force of circumstances. Jack drove Bruce's Aintree car while Bruce found himself in the Cooper that Masten would have occupied. Scarlatti was allocated the car that had been driven by Masten at Monaco. Jack, who had managed to squeeze in a drive at Brands Hatch between Lisbon and Monza, found his confidence quite restored and his bruises mending well. Bruce, in the absence of Masten, was saddled with more responsibility. In turn he tried out both his car and the one we had offered to Scarlatti. The Italian soon got the hang of things and was lapping at a very creditable 1:44, against Moss's 1:39.7 and Brabham's 1:40.2. So as to shorten pit stops in case a wheel had to be changed, Stirling had fitted hubs with knock-off spinners to the Rob Walker Cooper. Tire changes loomed as a vital factor at Monza and Jack planned his race strategy with great care. Tony Brooks in his Ferrari shared the front row with Moss and Brabham. Bruce's 1:42 was good enough to put him in the fourth row. Scarlatti, with a best lap of 1:43.3, was behind him.

Tony Brooks lasted exactly one lap before retiring, while the unfortunate Scarlatti also had to pit with a broken gear linkage which made shifting impossible. He lost two laps before we were able to get him going again. Jack, who was bent on saving his tires, let the leading group of cars go ahead and stayed in fifth place, awaiting the right opportunity and the likelihood that some of the leaders would break. Bruce (who was already in trouble with his second gear) tailed him for several laps, but it was not his day. A few laps later a piston collapsed and a rod came through the side of the engine. Moss drove a beautiful race, saving his tires wherever he could, just as Jack was doing, especially on corners. Phil Hill's Ferrari ran second and Jack moved up to third place. That was how they finished, with Brabham still top man on World Championship points. Once again, Moss gave Rob Walker's privately entered Cooper a victory. Scarlatti, considering his rotten luck and the loss of two laps, did well to finish twelfth.

With one more Grand Prix to go to complete the 1959 season, our transporter headed home for Surbiton. We had nearly three months to prepare for Sebring and the American Grand Prix. This took place at Sebring, Florida, on December 12, 1959, and it was an event to remember for many reasons. One was the on-again, off-again attitude of the promoters. At least three usually responsible organizations informed us during ten telephone calls that the race was off. But they were wrong and by the time we got the green light we were ready to ship our cars in some excellent crates which had been constructed specially for the job. However, we had only two drivers for three cars—the reverse of the usual problem team managers have to face. Poor Masten, whose Tourist Trophy injuries still had not healed properly, was forbidden to run. Stirling Moss in a Rob Walker car easily put up fastest time, lapping the 5.2-mile circuit in three minutes flat. Jack, with a gearbox ratio that was too high and some incorrect carburetor settings, as usual was the quickest of our team with 3:05.2. Bruce reported that his car handled badly and Jack, after trying it for a few laps, agreed. The front spring rates were way off and the chassis was out of line. This meant that the car had to be stripped down completely, giving our mechanics a lot of extra work.

The second day of practice saw temperatures climbing to a point where everyone was stifled, as often happens in Florida. This did nothing to cool our growing excitement. At last, after a year of World Championship ballyhoo, everyone was waiting for an answer to the sixty-four-dollar question. Would Jack Brabham scoop the title? He tried Bruce's car again on Friday, after the overhaul, but a cylinder head gasket blew. Bruce had to switch cars but his luck was just plain lousy. This time the ring gear failed. Another frantic strip down also revealed that a top shaft had broken in the gearbox. Luckily, this happened after Jack had improved his time to 3:03; but Bruce, whose car was laid up, was rated on his best time before the breakdown—3:08.6, which put him in the fourth row. On Friday night Bruce rolled up his sleeves and helped the mechanics put the gearbox together.

At the start, Saturday, Stirling grabbed the lead immediately. Tony Brooks (the third contender for the world's title) was shunted off into the boondocks by another member of the Ferrari team, but still managed to finish second to Jack in World Championship points, and that with a car that was less suited to most Grand Prix circuits than the Cooper. Stirling's Colotti gearbox again sidelined him and Jack took the lead after letting Bruce catch up with him in a "follow my leader" game. It was just as well that he did, yet the risk was great. The wily Trintignant (in a Rob Walker Cooper) closed the gap on the leaders in response to urgent pit signals. His calculations were only seconds out. Yards from the uphill finish, Jack's car sputtered as it ran out of gas. Bruce was so surprised that he actually slowed down, only to be waved on frantically by Brabham. Luckily he responded at once, beating Trintignant to the checkered flag by only six-tenths of a second! In a last-ditch effort to win, the determined Frenchman clocked fastest race time on his very last lap.

Jack, who had set his mind on finishing one way or another, pushed his car uphill to the finish line, gaining fourth place behind Tony Brooks. This plucky effort gained him two points which he was not allowed to add to his score for reasons I'll explain in a moment. But after collapsing from sheer exhaustion beside his car, Jack Brabham found himself World Champion anyway, with a total of thirty-one points. Paradoxically, Bruce who had finished last in his first Grand Prix was first in the last *Grande Épreuve* of the season.

By scoring in five out of seven events, up to and including Monza, Jack could only have added to that total at Sebring by finishing second or higher, or by putting up the fastest lap. Prior to Sebring he already had two wins, a second place and two thirds, and since a driver was only allowed to count his five best scores of the year, that was it. And it was a fairly close thing since runner-up Tony Brooks (including his Sebring third place for Ferrari) collected twenty-seven points.

Before the race, Jack had pondered about going for the fastest lap to assure himself an extra point at least. The logical man for this attempt would have been Masten Gregory, the "charger," but he was not yet well enough to drive, so Bruce became Jack's back-up man in a rather tricky situation. With Tony Brooks breathing down his neck for the title, Brabham rightfully felt uncomfortable about taking the risk of blowing up his engine. He decided against this and in the end, despite running out of fuel, he decided wisely. McLaren, by winning the race, effectively blocked any opposing team from collecting those nine valuable points, and that was enough.

Jack was destined to repeat his Formula 1 World Championship victory the following year, but as his skill and confidence grew even further, we tried to produce a car worthy of him.

Before closing the story of the first U.S. Grand Prix at Sebring, there is a story I must tell even though it means backtracking a little. It concerns the qualifications and starting grid positions and how the late Harry Schell threw a monkey wrench in the works that really caused something of a panic. That it was meant as a practical joke did nothing to mitigate against the wrath it provoked.

Schell's 2.2-liter Climax-powered Cooper was one of several private entries bearing our factory name but not connected with the Surbiton works. In the final grid, the front row was occupied by Moss (Cooper-Climax), Jack Brabham and Tony Brooks in a Ferrari. But suddenly, overnight, Schell was moved up into the front row along with Moss and Brabham, while poor Brooks was relegated to the second row. No one appeared to have noticed Schell's "fastest time" and the whole thing came as a bombshell which really angered Tavoni, the Ferrari team manager. Until that drastic last-minute change, the best time anyone had on Schell had been 3:11.2. There was no possible way he could have returned a time between 3:3 (Jack's fastest practice lap) and 3:5.8 (Tony's best). Leaving aside the driving, Schell's car just did not have enough steam and not even Fangio could have clocked the time he claimed, yet apparently there it was on the lap score charts, plain for everyone to see. If Tavoni was mad, so was Rob Walker, two of whose independent Cooper entries, driven by Moss and Trintignant, also were in the race. But Schell screamed loud and clear and his claim stood and there he was, in the front row, when the starting flag dropped.

Now as to what actually happened. Schell, who was given to

practical jokes in a big way, thought it would be hysterically funny if he could fool the official timers. And he did, by a very simple trick which no one observed, but which he freely admitted later.

At Sebring, just beyond the MG Bridge and before entering the Esses, there was a sharp right turn off the course that seemingly led nowhere. Certainly it was not part of the circuit, but Schell found out that it connected with the right–left elbow at the end of the Warehouse Straight, bypassing the entire straight and the Warehouse Hairpin with its tricky sandpile. So he quietly cut across, motored back onto the course during a momentary lull in the traffic—and cut about seven seconds off his lap time!

If a flagman noticed him, nothing was said about an incident which at the time had no particular significance to those on the course and was therefore simply forgotten. Drivers do tend at times to appear in odd places during practice sessions!

When Schell's escapade came to light, of course, the Sebring Grand Prix was over and his faked-up lap time made no difference to the outcome anyhow. But to him it was an abiding source of merriment, especially as the timekeepers were left with egg on their faces. There was certainly a funny side to this prank, but in all my racing experience I have never heard of anything to equal it in sheer brazenness.

13

World Championship—1960

The 1960 International Grand Prix season, which was to bring Jack Brabham his second consecutive World Championship in Formula 1 racing, marked the peak of both our careers, as driver and constructor. To get into detailed accounts of each of these exciting events would be repetitious, so I will merely mention the Grands Prix in their correct sequence (which was not the same as 1959), then relate some of the more interesting anecdotes connected with each event. There certainly was no shortage of them!

The season started with the Argentine Grand Prix (February 7, 1960), which was won by Bruce McLaren in a Cooper. This was followed by the Monaco Grand Prix (May 29), where Bruce placed second behind Stirling Moss's Lotus-Climax 18. In neither of these events did Jack finish. In Argentina he was sidelined early with gearbox failure. At Monaco, a gear jumping out caused Jack to hit the wall at Ste.-Dévote corner, where the uphill run begins. The car was not a write-off but it was too badly damaged to continue. After that, however, Brabham really came into his own. He won the next five Grands Prix in a row; these were the Dutch, Belgian, French, British and Portuguese events, in each of which he scored nine points, building up an unassailable lead of forty-five points to become World Champion for the second year. His record, by the way, has at this time yet to be equaled.

Bruce McLaren, having won the first *Grande Épreuve,* took second place not only at Monaco but in the Belgian and Portuguese Grands Prix as well, and finished third in the French event and fourth in the British GP for a total of thirty-four points, which made him runner-up to Jack.

During the Dutch Grand Prix at Zandvoort in 1960—the third *Grande Épreuve* of the season—there were some interesting she-nanigans. I remember that we were staying with the Lotus team at the Meyershoff Hotel, not far from the course. And this time the driver of a rival team held center stage. He was a great one for the birds, or, as they say in the States, chicks. Nothing got in his way—not even the overcrowded condition of the hotel, which forced him to share a room with an American journalist whose name escapes me but who was very straight-laced and rather religious. The situa-tion that developed was therefore most embarrassing to him, though it didn't bother his roommate much, and the rest of us found it hilarious in the extreme.

This chap, it seemed, had met some American bird and made a date with her for six o'clock on the evening of race day. During the Grand Prix, however, he had also made friends with a Dutch girl who was the organizers' secretary, and forgot all about the American chick. In fact he was so taken with his new discovery that as soon as the race was over he took this Dutch girl up to his room, where they had a pretty good time. Our friend was in the process of thoroughly enjoying himself when there was a knock at the bedroom door. It was of course the American girl, ready for what she probably expected to be a good reception. Our Lothario, however, was nothing if not resourceful. He told the Dutch bird to hide in the wardrobe while he made an attempt to get rid of the American girl. He didn't have much success, because the next thing that happened was that she slipped past him and closed the door.

"Crikey!" he probably thought. "What a hell of a situation. But still, this is too good to waste!" So he hopped into bed with the new arrival and was happily sampling his latest thrill when another knock sounded on the door. This time it was the American jour-nalist who wanted to be let in.

"I have to shave," he explained in all innocence, "so I can go to the prize giving. Come on, let me in, will you?"

His request was complied with and whatever happened next pro-foundly shocked the unfortunate roommate. He came down again soon after and sought me out.

"My God," he said, "that character! You'd never believe it.

He's got one chick hiding in the wardrobe and another one in bed with him! I've never in my life seen anything like this!"

Which was undoubtedly true.

Motor racing is a dozen heartaches and disappointments, a hundred frustrations for every joyous moment when you end up in the winner's circle. But in between races it can be a lot of laughs interwoven with some incredible experiences. Most of these I would not have missed for anything.

A couple of incidents come back to me which occurred during the German Grand Prix in 1960, both of which are worth the telling. After practice we had a lot of work to do on the cars to get them, as we hoped, ready. We toiled on our Coopers in some very elaborate lockup garages situated in the Paddock. We returned to the hotel in Adenau, a wonderful old fourteenth-century hostelry (called the Historic), there to have a meal, then went back to work on the cars. We didn't finish until about 3 A.M. and, of course, the hotel was closed up. Everybody had long since gone to bed. There happened, fortunately, to be a bakery in the courtyard which was still open. The people were baking next day's bread, I suppose, and one of them understood enough English to gather that I wanted to get into my room, overlooking the courtyard. I saw that my window was open, happily, and borrowed a ladder which the man held while I climbed up. It was all too easy and I put my leg over the sill, climbed in and turned to thank the German below. Then it hit me like a sudden icy blast. I was in the wrong room, and not only that but one occupied by a beautiful bird lying in the bed! She was quite alone but before things developed I hurriedly climbed out again and scrambled down the ladder. The man below must have thought I'd lost my mind, until I made frantic signs indicating the adjoining window. This time he got the message and I climbed into the right room—or at least toward it. The window was locked and I had to smash the glass to get in, but I finally released the latch and my troubles were over.

There was more to come before I got home from that race, and perhaps I should have been a little more wary, although it's smart to be wise after the event. Colin Chapman, like myself, happened to be returning from the Nürburgring, where, incidentally, none of our cars had finished. Just the fortunes of war, I suppose, but Colin wanted to get back to England in time to see the racing at Brands Hatch. He asked me if I would like a ride home in his plane as he had a spare seat and I said yes. It would save me a lot of bother. Jack Brabham had already flown back for this event, although it was not a Championship race. There were also some privately entered Coopers. Anyway, I remember being woken up early in the morning and at once realizing that the weather was terrible. It was drizzling steadily and on top of that there was a thick ground mist. Colin and I, together with Jim Clark and Trevor Taylor motored off to the airport about twenty miles up the road, and even this was quite a dicey business. When we reached the airfield, Colin's Piper Commanche could just be seen as a blurred outline in the swirling mist and the prospect of taking off in that stuff was not a happy one.

"We can never go in this weather," I told Colin, but it would have taken more than that to put him off. He was a qualified instrument flyer.

"Don't worry, John," he grinned. "It's going to be all right. No problem!"

He went off to see the commandant of the small German military airfield where he had been given permission to land in the first place, but this officer apparently shared my view. He wouldn't let Colin take off.

"No way!" was the equivalent of what he said in German. "It's just not on in this weather."

That, I suppose, made up my mind. "I'm going to Cologne," I told Colin, "and fly back in a proper airliner. And to hell with Brands Hatch!"

But Chapman was still undefeated.

"Just leave it to me," he insisted. "We're going, no matter what this fellow says. I'll talk him around."

So I waited another half hour against my better judgment and sure enough the commandant gave in.

"Take off at your own risk," he shrugged. "It's like this up to ten thousand feet. So your only chance is to keep climbing until you're clear of this stuff and fly above it."

"That's just what I plan to do," Colin said. "Thanks."

The commandant muttered something that sounded suspiciously like "Are you really tired of living?" and walked away.

We climbed in—I must say with serious misgivings on my part— and Colin fiddled with the switches, started the engine and let it warm up a bit before we taxied out. Whatever Clark and Taylor may have thought, they kept it to themselves, because they were obviously anxious to get home. Well, we took off all right but immediately found ourselves in the kind of soup where you could barely see the wing roots, let alone the wing tips! It really was blind flying but it didn't seem to bother Chapman much. He was keenly alert but very sure of himself.

"You take over," he told me after a while, "and I'll carry on with the map work, if need be, and keep radio contact. Just point the nose up and watch the altimeter."

"Okay."

Since at this time I had a private pilot's license, what he asked me to do was no great chore—provided we didn't collide with anything. Clark and Taylor, I must say, were pretty stoical about it, although I could tell that both were getting unhappier by the minute.

As predicted by the German commandant, the bad weather was just about 10,000 feet thick and eventually we climbed up above it into a beautifully clear blue sky and began to relax as we headed for the English coast. However, you have to get permission from "Airways" to cross the Channel. Colin made his request and got an affirmative, but the condition tied to it was far from reassuring.

"You must descend to three thousand feet," the controller's voice came over. "At the moment you're flying in airways—the path of commercial aircraft. We can't have you there. Sorry."

Colin tried to argue against this directive but got nowhere. Either we must descend to 3,000 feet or turn around and go back. That was it. So, muttering his displeasure, Colin shoved the stick forward and we began our descent. Uncomfortably soon we were back in the pea-soup mist which allowed us virtually nil visibility, save for a small occasional break. And there was worse to come. About halfway across the Channel (I computed this from our flying time) the engine began to sound rough.

"Do you hear what I hear?" I asked Colin. "The damn thing's shaking in its mounts. If it quits we're for the drink!"

Luckily for Trevor Taylor and Jim Clark, both had fallen asleep in the back, but Colin and I looked at each other and some unpleasant thoughts crossed our minds. We tried altering the pitch on the propeller, but that didn't make any difference. We then varied our height a little, several times, with no better result. Finally the real cause of the trouble struck us at the same moment. The carburetors were icing up!

Colin quickly switched on the carburetor heat and within a few moments the engine once more resumed its smooth rhythm. Both of us heaved a sigh of relief. When we arrived at Biggin Hill airfield in Kent, the weather was a lot clearer. The landing was uneventful and we found Andrew Ferguson (former secretary of the Cooper Racing Drivers' School but at that time working for Chapman) waiting for us with a car. So we got to Brands Hatch in time, after all. It definitely was one of those days when I promised myself I wasn't going to fly again, but I was back in a plane a week later.

At Reims in 1960, which was Jack Brabham's third consecutive win on his way to another World Championship, we certainly did not lack for amusing or interesting times. And I must say that in finishing first, second, third and fourth in the French Grand Prix, we were the only make in the world ever to achieve such a brilliant result, other than Mercedes-Benz. The latter had done the same thing with a team of W-196 open-wheel Formula 1 cars in the British Grand Prix at Aintree, five years earlier, the order being Fangio, Moss, Kling and Taruffi. Our four-Cooper finish involved Brabham, Gendebien (in a privately entered Yeoman Credit Cooper), McLaren and Taylor (with another Yeoman Credit private entry.)

But to get on with the story. Following the race there was a very large reception in the Town Hall at Reims, with all the drivers and race entrants invited and everyone drinking champagne as though it were going out of style. I had certainly had my full share, due to a very hot day and the fact that the local French people did not advocate drinking water when champagne was so plentifully available. You actually had to buy a Coke, whereas the champagne was free!

At all events, the reception took place in a huge and magnificent building with the Reims Philharmonic Orchestra supplying music at one end. There must have been at least thirty musicians in this orchestra, yet a hidden urge within me which surfaced due to the champagne, was so great that even this imposing sight did not deter me. I had always wanted, since my early youth, to conduct an orchestra and had nurtured this dream for decades. "Conducting" recorded music, which is what many people do for fun, is not the same thing at all. With me it had to be a real live orchestra on a platform, complete with conductor's podium. Anyway, Tim Parnell (son of Reg Parnell), who was with the BRM team, and Louis Stanley (a director of BRM) bet me I would not dare to step up on the rostrum and conduct the orchestra.

It was just what I needed by way of encouragement. The champagne had given me enough Dutch courage to try anything and the real orchestra leader took it all in good part, stepped down and handed me his baton. Perhaps he was impressed by the performance of our Coopers in the Grand Prix. I don't really know. All I know is that I got my wish—and was soon bewildered. With one accord the Reims Philharmonic Orchestra took off on their own, playing much faster than they were supposed to do and increasing their tempo so as to stay ahead of me! Finally, this huge group of musicians got completely out of hand and in trying to keep up with them I fell over backward off the podium! But at least my long-hidden wish was satisfied. I had conducted a full-blown Philharmonic orchestra.

There is more about Reims that eventful year. Lance Reventlow, son of the famous Barbara Hutton, was there with a Formula 1 team after having very successfully raced Scarab sports cars of his own design in the United States. This was his initial European Grand Prix attempt as I recall, and his lead driver was Chuck Daigh. Perhaps more interestingly, Lance's wife, the beautiful movie actress Jill St. John, was with him. She really was a stunning gal and when Lance, pleading tiredness, asked me if I would take Jill on a tour of the town, I was only too happy to oblige.

"That suits me fine!" I assured him.

I took Mrs. Reventlow to all the night spots I had visited in previous years, and a few more besides, and it wasn't in the least hard to take. Jill was so gay, spontaneous and appreciative, as well as being lovely, that it was not long before we picked up a few of my teammates and boys from other teams, too. They wanted to be introduced and "identify" and they had their wish. Among them was the handsome young Pedro Rodriguez, brother of the ill-fated Ricardo, who was killed in Mexico two years later. The boys were so stunned by Jill's beauty and charm that all they could do was sit around our table and gawk at her with open admiration. But I suppose she was used to it and by the end of the evening she came up with a very promising idea.

"John," she said, "you've treated me to a wonderful time. So when you come over to the States at the end of this season for the Riverside Grand Prix, I'll put on a party for the boys at our home. It's only about sixty miles from the course and I'll show you what parties are all about!"

This was sensational news and of course I agreed heartily. What happened at *that* party, I shall tell later.

The Portuguese Grand Prix at Oporto that year, which followed the British Grand Prix and took place on August 14, resulting in Brabham's fifth consecutive victory, brings to mind another interesting anecdote. Following Friday's practice, we had Saturday off to get rested up and fully prepared for the race on Sunday. Jack, Bruce and I were invited to visit the Sandeman factory in Oporto, where port wine is produced. It was to be a wine-tasting afternoon and I must say it was very interesting to compare the ancient chateau—home of Sandeman's port—with the British Vine Products factory in Kingston, Surrey, who turned out a popular product. Seeing the barrel makers actually hammering together or cleaning huge barrels was a sight in itself, and these people were quite amused because my name, Cooper, had long been given to the originator of that craft.

On such a visit they warned you beforehand not to swallow the wine you tasted. Swilling it around your mouth to get the bouquet would be enough. But it was not enough for me! Surreptitiously, I tasted and swallowed a little bit here and a little bit there, and some of that port was very old and tasted almost like liqueur brandy. Jack was very careful and only sampled a couple of the offerings, merely tasting them—and he proved wise. The next day I felt terrible! I sat on the pit counter before the Grand Prix, nursing the grandfather of all hangovers. It took me some time to shake off the effects of that wine-tasting tour, but I really think I was rewarded after all by the result of the actual race.

Both Jack's wife, Betty, and Bruce's fiancée, Pat, were in our pit when a potentially explosive incident took place. Though Jack led on points for the World Championship, Bruce happened to be leading the Grand Prix. Jack, Bruce and I knew what the score was and had everything pretty much sorted out before the start. But then Dean Delamont of the Royal Automobile Club happened by and looked at me in consternation.

"If you let those two drivers continue as they are, you're going to throw away the World Championship!" he warned. "Neither Brabham nor McLaren will get it. You're surely not going to let Bruce win, are you?"

This well-meant warning would have been all right if Delamont had whispered it in my ear, but he spoke loud enough so that everyone could hear, including Pat McLaren to-be.

"You're not going to slow Bruce down, are you?" she asked me with a very disturbed look. "If he wants to win this race he has a perfect right to do so!"

I tried to soothe her, but she evidently was not aware of the fact that if Bruce did win, neither of our drivers would become Champion. At that point, just to make things worse, Jack's wife got into the argument, which resulted in a terrific verbal "punch-up" between the two gals. It was so bad that I fled from our pit and left them to it. I took refuge in the BRM pit with Tim Parnell and stayed there until the race ended. In fact everything was quite in order. I gave Jack the required pit signal one lap before the end and he went ahead and passed Bruce so that they finished first and second.

The event that wound up our highly successful 1960 season was the Riverside Grand Prix in California, and it didn't take us long to find out that Jill St. John and husband Lance Reventlow had kept their promise to the hilt. The party took place at their beautiful home in Bel Air, overlooking Los Angeles, and we needed something to cheer us up after the financial fiasco faced by the promoter, Alec Ulmann, who simply could not meet his monetary commitments to the drivers and entrants.

For the convenience of all the drivers, mechanics and team boys who were anxious to attend the party, the Reventlows had laid on a special coach from Riverside to Bel Air. Lance, Jack and I flew back in Lance's twin-engine Cessna after practice and met Jill at Santa Monica airport. We soon found ourselves in one of the most elegant and luxurious houses I have ever seen. Everything was indeed ready for a party but it was breathtaking to absorb the character of the place. For example, the swimming pool came halfway into the bar and everything was of course electrically operated. If you wanted to dive from the bar straight into the swimming pool, all you had to do was push a button which caused huge glass doors to open. You could then dive over the barstools and swim out into the garden!

It was not long before the special coach arrived, carrying among others my father, Mr. Lee of Coventry Climax engines, Colin Chapman and several of the boys.

"Well," I told Jill after getting my breath back, "so far so good! I must say I'm impressed."

"Just you wait," she laughed. "You haven't seen anything, yet!"

Soon afterward I got her meaning when another bus arrived at the Bel Air house. Jill had organized an entire coach-load of beautiful young film extras from the studios, to entertain us for the whole evening. And, boy, that was some party! We spent a lot of the time in the pool, coming out to refill our glasses before taking another plunge. The revel went on all night and in fact in some cases personal interludes developed which lasted until after the Grand Prix was over.

But even that was not all. We capped the Riverside visit with one of the craziest and funniest stunts I have ever seen. Walt Hansgen, who was driving D-Type Jags for Briggs Cunningham and was quite a character besides being an excellent driver, had rented a car from Avis, and someone had spotted an advertisement of theirs that said in effect, "Pick up your rented car and leave it wherever you like!" The idea, anyway, was that the rental people would collect it from anywhere.

Some of the boys staying at a local motel, including Roger Penske and Hap Sharp, approached Hansgen with a brilliant idea. "If it really says you can leave the car wherever you like, why don't you leave it at the bottom of the swimming pool?"

"Okay," Walt came back. "Will you bet me a hundred bucks I don't do just that?"

"Sure thing." Sharp didn't even stop to argue the toss, and nor did Hansgen. He jumped into the car, drove it across the lawn and hurtled into the swimming pool. The car didn't sink immediately. It floated around in a great welter of air bubbles before going down with the lights still on. Walt had plenty of time to get out, but unfortunately forgot that he had left his camera and photographic equipment in the trunk. He managed to get them out after a few dives and the damage was luckily minimal. How Avis took that stunt was another matter. They were furious at the time but received so much free publicity that it smoothed their ruffled feathers. They just dismissed the whole thing as a crazy stunt and a big joke—and at the same time kept their fingers crossed that other people wouldn't return their rental cars in the same way.

After the Riverside Grand Prix fiasco, which netted us nothing as compared with the wonderful party thrown by the Reventlows, we headed back for England to get ready for the Mexican Grand Prix. We left again for this event a week before it was scheduled and flew to Jamaica, where Roy Salvadori and I decided to make an overnight stop. Tim Parnell met us at the airport and the overnight visit stretched into two or three days which made a very pleasant and colorful holiday. Then, on our arrival in Mexico, we flew down to Acapulco and spent three more days there. All the windows of our hotel overlooked the biggest and most lavish swimming pool I have ever seen. One of our games was to throw coins in this pool, when Tim Parnell would dive and retrieve them and everyone thought it was a huge joke. Every time Tim surfaced with a fresh coin, the crowd around the pool burst into enthusiastic applause. The only problem was that Tim happened to have a split in the back of his swimming trunks, and each time he dived for a coin the world was treated to a large, bare Parnell backside! To everyone's delight, of course.

At the end of the 1960 season, in January 1961 actually, I went over with Bruce and Jack for the New Zealand Grand Prix, following which they stayed on to run in the Australian Grand Prix as well. For my part I had a wonderful fourteen days in New Zealand, where I stayed with Bruce's mother and father and went to a lot of barbecue parties, met many of Bruce's friends and spent much time water-skiing. On one of the days that we went on an excursion, we flew out in an old seaplane with Jack, myself, Innes Ireland and Colin Chapman's father and went shark fishing off the Bay of Islands. I remember we lay about this boat all day and didn't catch a thing. I filled in the time with several good swims and had just come aboard when all of a sudden the bell rang. Jack, who was sitting in the back of the boat holding the rod, found himself hauling against something mighty heavy. It turned out to be a 300-pound mako shark! Crikey! I had only been swimming in there five minutes before. It took Jack more than half an hour to land this shark, after which we gaffed it with a hook and towed it back to the moorings, where the rest of our boys had taken other boats out. The shark was duly hung up with our name on it and we all had our pictures taken with this deadly great fish. I remember that I was leaning against the shark to have my photo taken, when its tail suddenly twitched and it scared me to death!

As a wind-up to those recollections of the 1960 season, I remember the occasion when Jack was testing one of our Coopers at Goodwood and Roy was there also, with another Formula 2 car. It was not an official practice date but just one of those days when people took their cars on the track to test them. Salvadori, who was in a privately owned Formula 2 Cooper, came in after a few laps and remarked, "I think it's a slow day, don't you, boys?"

It seemed that Roy was hoping at least some of us would agree with him. The track wasn't in first-class condition and so forth and there were general murmurs of assent from the other drivers, none of whom had done anything outstanding by way of lap times. In fact they were a second or two slower than usual. But then Masten Gregory, who happened to be walking by and overheard Roy's remark, spoiled it all.

"The reason why it's a slow day, Salvadori," he drawled, "is because Moss and Brooks ain't here!"

It was not, perhaps, the most tactful rejoinder to make.

I don't think this chapter would be complete without running into the following year, which brought us in close contact with an extraordinary character. He was none other than the great and mysterious—not to say eccentric—billionaire Howard Hughes. I first met him at Indianapolis in May 1961, by which time the name of Cooper stood fairly high in the racing world. The hard-bitten, rather skeptical Gasoline Alley boys knew all about our two World's Grand Prix Championships and our "funny" car with its rear-mounted engine, especially after its startling test performance around the Brickyard the previous year.

Anyway, we were back at Indy, this time to compete in earnest in the "500" and we were also entered for the U.S. Grand Prix Formula 1, scheduled in October at Watkins Glen, New York. My introduction to Howard Hughes came about through the late Eddie Sachs, who probably thought that Hughes was the right person for me to get to know.

Beyond doubt, Hughes was one of the most extraordinary characters I have ever met in a fairly eventful life. He was very tall—about six feet three inches—and for his size, rapier thin. He spoke with a Texas drawl, never smoked and didn't pay much attention to the bevy of alert young men who acted as his bodyguard or entourage. Their uniform, if one might call it that, was a neat gray flannel suit, white shirt, black knitted tie and something approaching a crew cut. But unless directly spoken to by the boss, they said little or nothing. Their job was to protect Hughes from unwanted people trying to intrude on his privacy. The only exception to this silent bevy of hard-faced men was a fellow named Ron, about whom more later—though not much!

It quickly became apparent to me that Howard Hughes was a mass of contradictions, although none of these seemed very important and in the thinking department he was not only far smarter than most people but also deceptively intuitive. You soon got used to his casual and rather odd way of dressing—his rumpled white shirt, gabardine slacks, loose-fitting sports jacket that hung in folds and worn-out shoes without any laces. It was the man who counted and his personality soon won you over.

From the beginning I got the impression that Hughes was interested in our little Cooper outfit, even though he didn't let on very much. But he wasn't interested in meeting people, except if they formed part of some idea he was pursuing at the time. So at first there was just some small talk about the weather and the huge crowd that came to see the 500 each year and stuff like that. Yet under it all I could sense in Hughes what was almost a small-boy enthusiasm for speed and Grand Prix cars and the thrill of racing.

Then, suddenly, on about the third day at Indy Hughes became much more talkative and began to open up. I got the definite feeling that he might well be in the market for one of our cars. Perhaps he was thinking of buying one or more of our new Formula 1 (1.5-liter) cars for Eddie Sachs to drive, more so because he knew that Andy Granatelli was also in the market and telling people openly about his interest in our Coopers.

I don't remember the exact dialogue I had with Hughes and it doesn't matter anyway; but I do recall that it wound up with an invitation from us that he come and see the Grand Prix at Watkins Glen in October.

"You know, that sounds like a good idea," Hughes drawled while his special aide, Ron, made some notes on a pad. The exact date and so forth. And that was the way it eventually came out. To my surprise and pleasure, Hughes arrived at the Glen in his private jet and landed exactly on time. Almost right away I discovered two more things about him: he loathed flies and had a consuming passion for big-breasted women. The sight of a well-stacked female was enough to send him into raptures and he would stop right in the middle of a sentence just to stare at her, utterly fascinated.

Anyway, the upshot was that Jack Brabham and I were invited to go aboard the Hughes jet and hold a conference while up in the skies. Unfortunately we both had so much on our plates, getting ready for the Grand Prix, that we had to refuse this tempting promenade on wings.

"Waal," Hughes drawled, "where else would you suggest? Do you-all have a car, here?"

We sure had. It was the rather classy Ford loaned to us for our personal use at the Glen.

"Would that suit you?" I asked.

"Why not? A private car is the best board room in the world," he grinned. "And it's less crowded than a phone booth!"

There were four of us in at the start. Hughes, myself, Brabham and the Hughes aide known simply as Ron. But the Boss didn't really open up until Ron left us on cue and made himself scarce. Even then we didn't get very far—at least not as far as I'd hoped. Hughes was interested, all right, but not so much in the Formula 1 end of our business as I had expected.

"How many roadsters are you going to build next year?" he inquired.

"I presume you mean the Cooper Monaco two-seater sports," I said. "We intend to build about fifty."

"How about building five thousand over here?" Hughes asked.

"Hang on a minute," I said. "It'll cost a lot of money to tool up for that number of cars."

"What kind of money would be involved?"

"Oh, about a million dollars," I said, pulling a number out of a hat. "Then of course there's the problem of engines."

Hughes replied, "I've in mind an American V-8 engine, the all-aluminum Buick F85. How does that grab you?"

I suggested there might be problems with General Motors over the supply of these engines, although as it happened they later became the British Leyland Rover power unit.

"Maybe," Hughes shrugged, "but it's nothing that couldn't be negotiated." The figure I had just mentioned didn't seem to phase him at all.

"Very likely," I said, doing my best to imitate his composure. "But meantime perhaps we can sell you one of our new Formula 1 Coopers or a team of them. Or the whole works, if you like!"

"Climax are going to have to squeeze more horses out of that ninety-cubic-inch engine," Hughes remarked. "Fitting a six-speed transmission isn't going to make you competitive with Ferrari. Nor paring down a little weight."

"Agreed," I said. "At the moment Enzo's got the jump on everyone in the new Formula 1. But our people are working on those extra horses. Rome wasn't built in a day."

"Let's hope it can be built in three years," Hughes kidded me. He was alluding to the length of time the new International Grand Prix Formula would be in effect. He was silent for a moment, lost in thought, then took a deep breath and appeared to reach a conclusion. "Let me think about the whole thing," he said. "I'll come back to you on it. Seems to me your car has a lot of potential."

Had we been lounging in Hughes's jet with unlimited time at our disposal to hammer out some agreement, I had the feeling I could have sold him the whole Cooper Company—at least the racing side of it. He was in a receptive mood and obviously interested. But as things turned out, I heard no more from him. This extraordinary man already had God only knew how many irons in the fire.

Still, that session in the back of my car was an unforgettable occasion. I certainly think it belongs in this story.

14

The Jonathan Sieff Era

Toward the end of the 1964 season, I was attending the American Grand Prix at Watkins Glen, New York, when the day before the race—or more precisely during the night—I was awakened by some shocking news. My father had died. I had, to be truthful, been expecting this to happen for some time, yet hoping of course that I would prove wrong. When faced with the grim reality of my father's passing, I felt bewildered and hurt beyond words. It couldn't be happening to me. There had to be some mistake. Besides being fond of my father I had always respected him as a dedicated, honest and hard-working man with some extremely bright ideas tempered by rare common sense. Until we had joined forces to become a world-beating combination—and that's not meant as a bragging statement—my father had done very well on his own, building up a thriving car repair business from practically nothing. It took a lot of guts besides hard work. It also took excellent judgment.

Fortunately, I had the moral support and practical help of Dr. Frank Faulkner, who attended most of the American races and many European ones as well, where we frequently met. It was Frank who had "organized" my sponsor at Indy and now he again jumped into the breach and took over the Cooper team for me.

I made New York airport early next morning and flew home at once. But Faulkner did a lot more than he had offered. He took our team on to the Mexican Grand Prix, a responsibility he had undertaken once before. Meantime, at Surbiton, there were many things for me to sort out—many decisions to make.

Early in 1965 I had a conversation with my old mate Salvadori, who had sold his motor business to Jonathan Sieff, son of Michael Sieff, the managing director of Marks and Spencer. (In fact, the Sieff family practically controlled Marks and Spencer. Jonathan's grandfather, Lord Sieff, was president of the company; his uncle was assistant managing director and so forth.) Anyway, following my talk with Salvadori he introduced me formally to Jonathan Sieff, though we were not unknown to each other. We had met at race meetings during Jonathan's earlier days, and I recalled a fantastic shunt of his at Le Mans in a Lotus that had nearly cost him his life.

During the meeting, Salvadori suggested it might not be a bad idea if I joined forces with the younger Sieff, who by this time had already bought out some twenty garages in the South of England. It seemed he was rather interested in getting involved with a racing team and perhaps having Marks and Spencer finance the venture under their St. Michael banner. From our standpoint at Cooper the idea was certainly appealing. Under the new International Grand Prix Formula due to go into effect in 1965, piston displacement of racing engines was to be increased to three liters. Most constructors foresaw a great deal of expense in perhaps redesigning their cars to four-wheel drive and their engines to twelve or possibly sixteen cylinders. In these circumstances a good sponsor would prove invaluable and at that time they were pretty scarce. The people who kept motor racing going were mainly the oil, fuel and tire companies. Firms outside the motor industry made comparatively small contributions to the sport, with two notable exceptions. These were the large finance companies Yeoman Credit UDT (United Dominions Trust) and Bowmaker.

In any case, our discussion seemed to progress very well and was livened up by the presence of Jonathan's managing director, Count Mario Tozzi-Condivi (that's a mouthful, isn't it?) who loved motor racing and was all for the idea of sponsoring the Cooper team. In those days, young Sieff was the United Kingdom distributor for BMW cars, Maserati, the Russian Moskvitch and Alfa Romeo. The operative words here were "Maserati," who had some very advanced engine designs that could be adapted to the new Formula, and the count, who spoke fluent Italian. But we'll come back to that later. The suggestion was soon put to me that Jonathan would like to buy the racing side of my company, and since I had already spent twenty active years in motor racing and was still not fully recovered from my terrible shunt in the twin-engine Mini, the idea held a strong appeal. Salvadori would take over as team manager; I would be the "engineering brains" and look after the design of the cars; and our Cooper team sponsored by Marks and Spencer would run under the name of St. Michael.

The subject of sponsorship money, about which we had talked only briefly, spelled something like £100,000 a year (well over $300,000 in those days), which was a fortune to me. So, after several meetings, one of which involved going up to London with my wife, Paula, and attending a dinner party with Jonathan's father, Michael, together with Count Mario, his fiancée and some other people, I more or less made up my mind. What clinched matters was a firm offer from the Sieffs for the whole racing side of my company. This was very substantial—something like £250,000 (I forget how many dollars in those days, but a very large sum).

"Well," I thought, "that's not a bad idea at all. I'll have a lot of money to invest and I'll still be involved in racing while someone else worries about the finances."

So the agreement was signed and I sold my entire Cooper racing organization with all the facilities and equipment for building cars. Roy, as foreseen, was appointed racing manager while I became technical director.

A year earlier, Jonathan had also bought a famous racing firm with premises at Byfleet near the old Brooklands race track and a garage in Cobham, Surrey. This was Thompson and Taylor, who specialized in sophisticated race tuning and preparation and could fabricate just about anything. Taylor was a well-known engineer who had designed several world record cars for famous drivers such as John Cobb and Sir Malcolm Campbell.

Jonathan Sieff's string of motoring companies was called the Chipstead Group, but since the name of Cooper was known throughout the world, its title was changed to the Cooper Group. So we not only kept our original Surbiton premises where my father had started his garage in 1935, but thus acquired a large factory at Byfleet. In any case, when I made the deal with the Sieff family I retained all my properties and sold only the racing business. For practical purposes it was decided to move the racing equipment and facilities out of Surbiton and into the Byfleet premises. I am not sure that I approved of this wholeheartedly, because it seemed to me that the Thompson and Taylor factory was rather too large for the type of operation we envisaged.

Still, the outcome was that I got back my old garage and rented it out to the police. It is, to this day, a Squad Car Station. The Langley Road premises, also in Surbiton, where we prepared the race cars in the old days, I rented to a printing works.

While we made ready to move to Byfleet, discussions cropped up about the engines which we proposed using under the new Formula. There was talk of Coventry Climax building a sixteen-cylinder engine, but this project was too nebulous and in fact never really got underway. At that time, only Ferrari and Maserati had suitable power units—and those built by Ferrari were, of course, tied up. It was therefore suggested that Salvadori and I, together with Jonathan Sieff, should travel to Italy and visit the Maserati factory. This company did have something close to the engine we were looking for, but it was in fact the old 2.5-liter, V-12 engine that Fangio had used several years earlier. This, in its day, had been a prodigiously powerful engine, but with the advent of the 1.5-liter Grand Prix Formula it had been "thrown under the bench" and forgotten.

At our request the Maserati people dragged this engine out and let us have a good look around. We did not take long to make up our minds.

"How about enlarging it to three liters?" we inquired. "We could use half a dozen of them to start with."

"What do you have in mind?" the Italians asked. "A Cooper-Maserati combination?"

"Exactly," we agreed.

Mario Tozzi-Condivi, who was also present, headed up a lot of talking in Italian and with the aid of some money passing "under the table" the Orsi family, who then owned Maserati, agreed to supply us with the six engines we needed for our Grand Prix team the following year.

We came home well pleased with ourselves but now faced another problem. The existing Cooper chassis would not be strong enough for the new power unit. It needed redesigning along monocoque lines, and in this we had only limited experience. The most we had tried until then had been a semi-monocoque chassis. A full monocoque construction is something else. It involves literally a stressed skin, riveted shell forming one compact unit and shaped like a giant tube with holes for the cockpit and engine compartment. A make known as the Cornelian first introduced the idea at Indianapolis back in 1915, but without success. Colin Chapman had picked it up in 1962 for his Formula 1 Lotus 25 with excellent results, the Belgian, British and American Grands Prix going to that world-beater, Jim Clark. So we had some catching up to do.

However, I got hold of Tony Robinson, a former Stirling Moss mechanic, together with Derek White, late of Jaguars, and the three of us set to and designed a new monocoque Cooper specially for the Maserati engine. Meantime as an experiment we converted and strengthened one of our earlier tubular chassis to accept the Maserati engine. We used this as a mobile test bench and even at that stage the result was very promising. We felt we might well have another world-beater.

By the time the Racing Car Show came around in January 1966, we had a full monocoque Cooper chassis on display, complete with the twelve-cylinder Maserati engine. I must say that our gleaming, immaculately finished chassis, superb in every detail, enthroned on the Cooper stand, drew many surprised admirers. This was really moving into the big league. Engineers from rival makes raised inquiring eyebrows and we probably stirred no small amount of disquiet among those who would be running against us that season.

But of course, no matter what you have achieved in the past, the demands of Grand Prix racing become ever greater and a new car is a new car until it has proved itself on the actual race track.

Looking back on the year 1966, we perhaps did not fulfill our expectations, confident as we were. Our drivers during that season numbered some of the greatest—Jochen Rindt, Jo Bonnier, John Surtees (who moved over to us on a one-shot basis) and Guy Ligier, the ex-Rugby player. However, the competition from Ferrari and others was extremely tough. That year Surtees won for Ferrari at Monaco and they were certainly the best prepared with an already tried 60° V-12, three-liter engine which put out 375 bhp and a smaller but equally reliable 2.4-liter V-6. Lorenzo Bandini won with the smaller car at Monaco while Surtees scored with the V-12 Ferrari in the Belgian Grand Prix at Spa, where Rindt was second. Surtees then left the Italian team and the season—albeit a bit late—began to swing our way until the Italian GP, when a revised 36-valve Ferrari engine made its appearance. These cars finished first and second with the checker going to Scarfiotti, who became the first Italian to win on home ground since 1952. If all this seems a little bit by-the-way, it still has a place here because Ferrari was really the thorn in our side. Our new Cooper, which was known as the Type 81, was perhaps not the easiest car to handle, but without making any excuses (since we did not lack driving talent), the "old reliables" were long gone. Jack Brabham had left us in 1962 to build and drive his own car; and Bruce McLaren followed suit two years later.

To get back to the actual 1966 calendar, Bonnier crashed one of our cars at Spa and finished sixth in the Mexican Grand Prix. So it was Jochen Rindt who bore the brunt of our efforts. The Cooper-Maserati was a reliable machine but rather heavy and massive, yet even so Rindt did well enough. He brought us that second place at Spa after a difficult drive in the rain; another second in the American Grand Prix at Watkins Glen, a third at the Nürburgring, fourth place in the French and Italian Grands Prix and a fifth in the British GP. It certainly was not his fault, for we still had much to learn (such as putting the Cooper-Maserati on a drastic slimming diet!).

At the end of 1966 we did manage to win the Mexican and South African *Grandes Épreuves,* but the latter rightly belonged in the 1967 calendar.

Looking back on 1966, I would say that but for a quota of the usual teething troubles and annoying things such as fuel pumps packing up, and of course the problem of unnecessary weight, which proved to be our worst enemy, we looked like having a fair chance of again winning the World Championship. But it was just one of those things and putting our new car on the track taught us a great deal.

During 1967 we retained Jochen Rindt, who was joined by Surtees later in the year and we several times found ourselves in pole position for a major Grand Prix. Maserati got busy designing a new V-12 engine for us which was much lighter than its predecessor. The original hemispherical head, four overhead camshaft layout was replaced by a flat (heron) head combustion chamber and a single overhead camshaft operating four vales per cylinder—a completely different configuration. But despite its radical redesign, this wasn't a very successful engine in competition. Its power increase was only modest and despite an appreciable loss of weight the opposition had by then caught up.

Late in 1967, when we were actually using the new Maserati engine in our Coopers, we decided to go all out at Monza, where the Italian Grand Prix was traditionally held. I therefore took our transporter and a lot of equipment to the Maserati factory in Modena and also brought along all our mechanics. As soon as a new engine came off the test bed we installed it in one of our cars and carted it off to the local track at Monza for a tryout. Eventually we got a lot more speed out of the Cooper-Maserati and during practice Rindt qualified third or fourth fastest. But we were now having terrible problems with the front end of the car, due to the greatly increased speed. At about 180 mph down the main straight at Monza we were experiencing serious troubles with the forepart of the car lifting as it got "light." I remember sitting in the bar with Signor Alfieri, the chief engineer of Maserati, and watching him shake his head disconsolately.

"If we could only stop that front end from lifting," he said, "we could get around Monza a lot quicker."

"Well, what about a spoiler?" I suggested.

"That's just what I was thinking," Alfieri agreed. "It would be a very good idea."

"Okay, let's try it, then."

So we built a large spoiler right across the front of the car, which bolted underneath the nose. Unfortunately we had no time to test it before the race, so we went straight into the Grand Prix with our untried innovation, hoping it might do the trick. That time we seemed to hit the jackpot. There was a tremendous improvement in high-speed handling. But unluckily Rindt ran into the back of the leading car, going out of the Curva Grande, and practically wiped out the spoiler. The immediate effect was to slow the car down considerably in order to retain control. I'm sure our little idea was one of the earliest examples of a design feature that is now part of every Grand Prix machine. At the time, of course, everyone thought the improvised spoiler was a big joke—some kind of a secret weapon! In fact, Alfieri and I, together with a couple of Maserati mechanics, had fashioned that spoiler with the help of a few bottles of Chianti!

By the end of 1967, I think we decided we had had enough of Maserati and they probably felt the same about us. So we switched to a BRM engine. We would have loved to use the aluminum overhead camshaft Ford V-8 engine, which looked like a Formula 1 world-beater, but we could not because of our association with British Leyland. Hindsight usually implies a twenty-twenty vision, but I am convinced that had we been able to use the Ford engine we would still be in Grand Prix racing today. However, it was decided that since all our eggs were in one basket with British Leyland we would stay out of the Ford camp.

Unfortunately the BRM engine was underpowered to start with, not only in our Coopers but in the BRM car itself. What's more, when you're using an engine which already belongs to a rival team, they just are not going to let you know about those little tricks that can squeeze out a few more horsepower for themselves. It stands to reason. As it was, we were at least 20 bhp down on the works BRM's, and even these were not competitive, so you can imagine the problems we faced.

In 1968 a Cooper-BRM V-12, driven by Lucien Bianchi, took third place at Monaco and we also managed to bring home a second and a third in the Spanish Grand Prix that same year with Bryan Redman and Vic Elford driving.

Still, after four years of racing under the Sieff family banner, the Marks and Spencer board of directors had, by this time, decided that perhaps it wasn't the thing to do to spend the public company's money on Grand Prix circuits. More so because fielding a World Championship team involved huge and ever growing expense. Possibly today the company would not be greatly worried, but at the time that was the decision and it stood. Prime concern was to keep the Marks and Spencer image intact and the Sieff name out of any risky enterprises. It was therefore decided to abandon the St. Michael team and the Formula 1 organization was disbanded. I did take up the Mini-Cooper racing and Rallye team again and finished the season with it. By this time, British Leyland had been taken over by Sir Donald Stokes and his interest in racing obviously was dwindling. As a result, the Mini team's activities also were dropped and the development of the racing Cooper "S" was curtailed to the level of a purely commercial enterprise.

To sort out all the interesting things that occurred during the Jonathan Sieff four-year era would be a gigantic task—perhaps a book in itself. A lot of interesting people came and went, not the least of whom was Count Tozzi-Condivi, who left under a cloud of some kind. What happened, I don't know. I saw him on a Friday and the next day he was gone. Two other people were brought in to replace the vanished managing director. These were Tony Towner, a banker, and Cliff Holden, a garage owner from Liverpool. They lasted about nine months before disappearing in their turn. David Blackburn, who was then managing director of the BMW organization in Britain, became managing director of the whole Cooper Group, but only with the intent of winding things up. Gradually, parts of the Group were sold to other interests until all that remained to Jonathan Sieff was the BMW organization. He is still chairman of that prosperous enterprise today.

As for myself, I virtually retired from motor racing and sought other interests. I had always had a very strong liking for Angmering near Worthing in Sussex, where I kept a weekend bungalow. And since by this time I had become involved to some extent in the real estate business, I sold my house in Surbiton and bought a pleasant home overlooking the sea at Rustington. Following this I purchased a garage in Ferring, about five miles away, with the idea of making it a property investment. But all my mates kept telling me, "Why the hell don't you open that place as a garage and showroom of your own?" And fortunately I did. My son Michael is now in the business, looking after the workshop side, while my son-in-law, John Angelo, who married my daughter Christine, is sales manager. As a result we have a nice little business that allows me a reasonable amount of spare time.

But this is by no means the end of my story or of what might be called the saga of the Grand Prix Carpetbaggers! Flashbacks keep crowding my memory as one thought leads to another, not necessarily in chronological order, but I think it would be a pity to leave them out, just the same.

For example, although the works Cooper-Maseratis did not fulfill our expectations, they were good enough to attract buyers such as Rob Walker, who had been running our cars as private entries for years. Jo Siffert drove for him and did very well, all things considered. When we first produced the Cooper-Maserati in 1966, with its overweight engine, handling was far from what we later achieved, yet Siffert managed, that year, to take fourth place in the American Grand Prix. Guy Ligier, who now manufactures his own cars in France, drove one of our Coopers as a non-factory entry also; and so did the late Jo Bonnier. I have mentioned these names earlier on, but the interesting thing was that in most of those later Grands Prix our representation rose to about six cars, or double the regular factory team entry. It was very good advertising for the Cooper name and it also brought home the bacon.

Another interesting customer I should mention here was a Japanese engineer from the great Mitsubishi company, whom I met one evening in a bar at Reims. He immediately told me he wanted to buy a Cooper-Maserati, but we did not then have one available. Privately sold cars were built to order, but this envoy was so insistent that we arranged for him to take a team car toward the end of the season. We completely reconditioned one of our machines and sold it to Mitsubishi for £16,000. The price—high in those days—was paid without argument and all the Mitsubishi engineers came to Goodwood for the trial. My driver and demonstrator was Innes Ireland, whom I employed for the day, and he put on an impressive performance. This was followed by lunch in a local hotel called the Richmond Arms, after which the car was shipped to Japan. And that was the last we heard of it. Just what the giant Mitsubishi firm had in mind, or whether they were seriously contemplating involvement in Grand Prix racing, I don't know. Honda was the only Japanese firm to enter the Formula 1 arena in a big way, with the Americans Ron Bucknum and Ritchie Ginther signed on as drivers.

Parenthetically and as a matter of interest, this first Japanese effort, which took place in 1964 during the 1.5-liter Grand Prix Formula era, came at a difficult time. But Honda was a very ambitious firm. They designed a 1500 cc, four-cam, V-12 engine that (with fuel injection) produced 230 bhp at 12,000 rpm. Power was transmitted to the road wheels via a six-speed gearbox, but the car was plagued with overheating and injection problems. Even so, Ginther finished sixth in the Belgian and Dutch Grands Prix that year and also won the final event, which was the Mexico Grand Prix. Bucknum finished fifth in the same race.

Honda went on to build an even more complicated engine for 1966, to meet the three-liter GP Formula. This was also a 60° V-12, but it was air-cooled and featured four valves per cylinder and roller bearings. The completed engine was so heavy that the car ran 243 kg (534 pounds) over the 500 kg (1,100 pound) minimum weight limit. So, despite its 400 bhp at 10,000 rpm, it never finished higher than fourth. In fact Ginther crashed at high speed on the car's first outing, luckily escaping unhurt.

However, engineer Nakamura of Honda was a very skilled and determined man and when John Surtees got into the act in 1968, Honda produced a new V-8 powered monocoque car called the RA-301. In line with Honda production cars, this had an air-cooled engine. Eric Broadley of Lola cars and Derek White, an experienced engineer, also helped design the chassis, but bad luck dogged this renewed effort. During the French Grand Prix at Rouen, Jo Schlesser crashed at high speed in the pouring rain and was killed. Surtees, far from happy, finished second. He also managed a third place in the United States GP and a fifth spot in the British GP, as well as putting up the fastest lap at Spa in Belgium. But that was the Honda's swan son. The reason why I have gone into the Japanese effort at this length is because their determination to break into the Grand Prix scene stamped them not as copycats but as originators capable of very significant technical innovations. Had the Honda people followed through in spite of these discouraging and at times tragic setbacks, there is little doubt that they were pointed straight in the direction of success in the toughest and most demanding of all sports.

15

The Cooper Driving School

I think our idea of starting a race drivers' school really came to a head at the time of the Suez Canal crisis in 1956. We began to worry about petrol once again being rationed, and if so, whether motor racing would be able to carry on in the form in which it had, by then, crystallized. We were still pretty busy building race cars to special order and I had an old friend working for me by the name of Ron Searles. He had done some racing and was very interested in the idea of running a school for budding Grand Prix drivers.

"Well," I said, "let's give it a try and see what sort of response we get."

We began with a display advertisement in *Autosport* which occupied a whole page. In it we informed the public that the Cooper Car Company was starting a "racing drivers' training division." Climax-engined, single-seat, open-wheeled cars would be available to students. Those interested should write for further particulars. Brands Hatch would be our chosen training center.

The response we got was staggering. So much mail arrived that it had to be delivered in a van. If my memory serves me right, we had at least 2,000 replies from that one advertisement! So obviously the name of Cooper had something to do with it. Also the fact that we were the first to start such a school, at least in England. Later, many imitators followed in our wake, but the early bird does seem to catch the worm. Some of those who came after us are worth mentioning, however. They included the Jim Russell School (which is still going strong), the Brands Hatch Training Division, the Bill Knight School in France and the former Sharp Racing School at Goodwood.

Anyway, once swamped by that avalanche of mail, we thought we had better make a start and get things organized. We had forms printed which we sent out to all those who had written to us and we set the initial fee to join the school at a modest five pounds. There was also a questionnaire to be filled in by the applicant. When the fees and forms began rolling in we knew beyond doubt that we were in the business of training eager beavers to drive race cars.

Our prototype training machine, which we quickly assembled, was a single-seat, rear-engined Cooper-Climax fitted with one carburetor to moderate the steam. Its displacement was 1250 cc. We also made available a replica of the Le Mans two-seater sports car successfully driven in 1956 by Hugus and Bentley. This was a central tube design which I was credited with having dreamed up "over a pint of beer," and it provided a seat on either side of the car's centerline, making it a genuine sports car.

Soon we had three single-seaters in addition to the Le Mans machine and also purchased a large ex-Bristol Corporation bus which towed a trailer with a race car in it. The bus we used as an office at Brands Hatch. I went along to talk to the track's owner, who, at that time, was John Hall, and explained the situation.

"I would like to use the course two days a week, if possible, so we can get the school started."

"What days would you have in mind?" Hall asked.

"How about Tuesdays and Thursdays?"

"I think we can arrange that."

"I shall want the exclusive use of the track," I said.

"Fair enough." Hall grinned. "I don't think we'd really want any other arrangement."

He and I then agreed on the fee that the Cooper Driving School would pay Brands Hatch for each pupil who used the track and how much the individual insurance would be. The business arrangement worked out very well. All we had to do was put together a curriculum of classes to cover the theoretical side of race driving. When everything was finally set up—the cars, Brands Hatch, the course of instruction—we had a big opening date for the Cooper Driving School. With Jack Brabham and Bruce McLaren pitching in to instruct and the prestige lent by the Honorable Gerald Lascelles, president of the British Racing Drivers' Club, we could hardly miss. Added to this we got full coverage from the daily and motoring press and even the BBC came down. The resultant publicity we obtained was enormous. We demonstrated how the school was going to operate and by that time we had also built up the required staff. Helping Ron Searles was Ian Burgess, a racing driver of note who came in as a regular instructor and also helped organize the school. Then, too, we had Dickie Samuelson, the son of Sir Francis Samuelson, one of my first 500 cc car customers. Sir Francis himself had been active in auto racing as far back as 1914 and knew the score. Andrew Ferguson, who was then on our regular staff as secretary of the racing drivers' school, pitched in to help while Jack and Bruce offered their services on a part-time basis. That was also the extent of my own involvement as I still had the Cooper race car business to run. The mechanical side was looked after by "Ginger" Devlin (whose red hair had earned him his nickname). Devlin was our senior mechanic, who had started with me and helped build the first 500 Cooper.

In fact, the team we got together in a very short time was virtually unbeatable for the job on hand. Every student of the Cooper Driving School was assured of full value for his money.

Predictably (though it still came as a shock) on our first regular school day at Brands after the grand opening, we shunted one of our cars. This was the kind of problem we didn't need, so we set about restructuring the course (I mean the curriculum) to minimize the risk of a repetition. Our method of instruction was to give each pupil a comprehensive lecture in which we explained gear shifting, rev. limits and the best line through the corners, especially at Brands Hatch, which was not easy. For this we charged a preliminary fee. We would then take each pupil around as a passenger in the sports car and get him thoroughly acquainted with the braking areas, acceleration points and so on, before we put him in the single-seater. His next step was to follow the sports car round the course while it was being driven by an instructor for two or three laps. Only then, if we were satisfied that the pupil was in full control and knew what he was doing, did we turn him loose. Obviously we could not run the risk of some eager beaver going out and killing himself, or even hobbling back to the pit with a handful of teeth while he left the car wrapped around a tree.

Later still, the trainee would be paced by another instructor, also in a single-seater. Our pace cars were fitted with large dual mirrors which kept the trainee in sight all the time. If he started to get sideways on a turn we would immediately slow him down and make a note of his problem, which would then be carefully explained to him.

This system worked very well and trainees made excellent progress, but inevitably we still had a percentage of over-eager beginners who plowed into banks or even turned cars over. To prevent anyone from getting seriously hurt, we evolved an almost foolproof method of building the school cars—after we had written off the first batch! We built the chassis of very heavy twelve-gauge tube, which was almost crash-proof, whereas the suspension wishbones were made much lighter than usual. So, if a car did go out of control and leave the road, the suspension was knocked off without hurting anything else. This kind of damage was easy to repair and comparatively inexpensive. Our mechanics became so skilled in effecting repairs that if a crashed car was brought back in the morning it could be made serviceable again the same day. Often, the work was done at the side of the track to save time. (The sight of what he had done probably made the offender squirm a bit, too, which was all to the good.)

As to the end results of our training, though we didn't produce a world champion, many up-and-coming Formula 1 and 2 drivers were the product of the Cooper School. We also had a variety of sedan and GT car drivers evolve through our tuition to become highly competitive.

Our worst days were the wet ones, for we operated in all kinds of weather. But one look at that slick track and our hearts sank.

"Crikey!" we would tell each other. "Today there are going to be several shunts. Nothing to do but grin and bear it."

On the other hand it was quite remarkable how well a pace car could control a student following it. Attendance, however, was always something of a problem. For no good reasons that we could fathom, some of our regular trainees would fail to show up, but their places would be taken by a host of new recruits who made it difficult for us to process everyone on that particular day. It usually meant a lot of overtime.

One of the boys who came down to our school actually did a bit of lecturing and instruction. This was none other than Jim Russell.

He thought our school was such a good idea and liked it so much that he went off and started his own school at Snetterton airfield. Today, his is the best-known race drivers' school in the world. Another of our supporters was Rob Walker, a wealthy race car owner who was very interested in helping to train new talent. He had provided race cars for several internationally famous drivers, so why not encourage new talent?

As a result, Rob Walker started a sort of rival school with Ken Gregory (Moss's manager) and Stirling himself. Then there was also Signor Dei of Scuderia Centro Sud, who started a school at Modena, not far from Monza. British Petroleum footed the bill for many of the expenses, but this school really did things in style. The headquarters was a lovely old villa near the Hotel de Ville in Milan which was really a very luxurious motoring club. In contrast with our method which charged a modest £5 to join ($17.50) and £1 per lap (about $3.50), Dei's idea was to have trainees stay at his beautiful club for about a week and charge £400 ($1,750). This was a far cry from our fees but for that sum everything was provided—instruction, actual driving, lodging and food. It was a very different approach from ours but it worked well and brought many new recruits.

Nor should I forget that famous Texan Carroll Shelby, either. Though he didn't do any instructing for us he spent some time at our school. On the basis of this practical experience he started his own race drivers' school in California. But that's another success story which sprang from small and precarious beginnings.

We ran our school for several years—from the time of the Suez crisis until the end of the fifties, when we became involved in racing and race car building more heavily than ever and our resources were stretched to the limit. One of the reasons why I decided to close the school was that if I couldn't give it enough personal supervision it might get out of hand and become dangerous. As it was we had cut down the rate of attrition to an absolute minimum and were proud of this.

What was more, by then there were a lot of other people doing the same thing as ourselves and well able to produce the required facilities for training race drivers. I could now see that the World Championship might be within the grasp of the Cooper firm and we decided to concentrate every effort in accomplishing that one job. So we closed our doors in what was obviously the right decision since, as the reader already knows, we did win the World Championship two years running, in 1959 and 1960.

I think the Cooper Driving School served its purpose by teaching many trainees a great deal. If one of our pupils left the school with a bit of capital in hand—not much—but still believed in his destiny as a budding Fangio, and felt that his next step was to go out and buy a car, that would be what he did. Our rates by going standards were pretty low. In fact they were so reasonable that many pupils came back for a "refresher course." Where else could they cover, say thirty laps for only £30 ($105) with car and instructor provided. And what other facility offered them any amount of theoretical and blackboard teaching at a mere $3.50 a session?

These rates gave the budding race driver of modest means ample opportunity to discover whether he liked motor racing and whether he was temperamentally suited to the sport. In the event that he showed promise and had the required capabilities, we were quick to tell him so and give him further encouragement. Driving a race car really well is a bit like being a ballet dancer who can *sense* the rhythm of what he is doing; or like being a musician with a natural ear for music. When we did discover a promising pupil who was anxious to come back for a second course of instruction, we always had somebody on our staff eager to help him take another step forward.

Believe it or not, by the time we closed our doors some 8,000 trainees had passed through the Cooper school—which was an all-time record for this kind of activity. I suppose that if I gave those 8,000 enthusiasts an opportunity to drive a race car under proper supervision, our idea must have had some merit. One of the things I always used to tell our pupils was that a race driver needed three things: the necessary ability, even if undeveloped, plus the facilities to get trained; the patience to spend the next year or two really learning his trade and working his way up to faster machinery; and thirdly the guts to carry out what he wanted to do and what he had been taught how to do. I always stressed the fact that the second prerequisite was the danger period—a parallel situation to that of the rookie pilot who breezes through a goodly number of solo hours without any trouble and becomes overconfident. That is the time when a driver, too, is most likely to write himself off. The easiest snare to fall into is to go faster than you are really capable of handling the car. But once that period was over, our trainee would be in the clear.

Funnily enough we had quite a number of girls pass through the school. I remember the first time a "Miss" appeared on an application form, I was horrified. "A woman driving a race car?" I thought. "Now I've seen everything."

But I was wrong. Some of our women pupils turned out to be excellent drivers. Looking back on those 8,000 trainees, probably 100 were girls. This worked out better than 1 per cent, which was not bad at all for the time. And of that number, only one had what might be called a serious shunt, though she personally was not badly hurt.

One of my early pupils was the Australian Frank Gardner, who later became several times the sedan (saloon) car champion of Britain and was also a very fast sports car driver. He is now retired, of course, and has gone back to Australia. Gardner drove one of our Cooper-BRM's for us on a couple of occasions. Another notable who went through the school was a young, small, wiry chap by the name of Roy James. He performed very well in the school and it was obvious that if he continued in this fashion he would develop great potential. In later years he proved out my belief by becoming involved in Formula 2 racing and drove his own Brabham car with outstanding success. Probably, had he gone on he might have won the Formula 2 championship. Unfortunately Roy got involved in a very negative way with a bunch of characters who planned what became known as the Great Train Robbery. This was in 1963 and it netted the plotters £2.5 million (then $8,750,000). James, I understand, was the driver of the getaway car but he did not go far enough. He was caught and sentenced to thirty years in Parkhurst prison on the Isle of Wight. Later, because of good conduct, this long term was reduced to twelve years. He is now out again and thinking once more about driving race cars.

One of the interesting things that happened while James was still in jail related to his trade before he got into trouble. He had been a skilled silversmith and he used his talent to fashion a beautiful trophy which he presented to the British Racing and Sports Car Club. A friend of his, Roy Bunting, supplied the necessary silver and the trophy is now awarded annually to whoever contributes most to the publicity side of motor racing, such as a journalist or radio or TV announcer. BBC's "Wheelbase" program won it one year, while the *Daily Express* also was a recipient.

I hope Roy James (who became known in court as "the weasel" because of his small size and great speed) performs as well as he did before his long rest. He really was a natural behind the wheel of a race car.

It would hardly be fitting to mention Roy James without citing the fact that he bought a Formula 2 car from Jack Brabham but unfortunately did not have much time to enjoy it.

Anyway, so much for the Cooper Driving School, another episode in a life so interesting that I would not trade my memories for a king's ransom. Each day brought something new—it might be a challenge, a success or a bitter disappointment; but it was action with a purpose. And that was what counted.

16

The Mini-Cooper and
the Famous "S"

After Sir George Harriman of BMC had successfully tried out the Mini prototype, the decision was made to produce the Mini-Cooper under different names but otherwise in almost identical form with the exception of the grilles. That was how the Austin Mini-Cooper and the Morris Mini-Cooper came into being, but from now on, for the sake of simplicity, we'll refer to both types simply as the Mini-Cooper. We got the go-ahead early in 1961 and set to work with the BMC engineers, since they were going to turn out this new model on the production line at Longbridge near Birmingham.

The modifications which were to be incorporated had already been decided upon, of course. Piston displacement was increased from 848 to 997 cc, with a bore of 62.43 and a stroke of 81.28 millimeters. Twin SU carburetors were fitted, the cylinder head was modified, the compression ratio raised to 9.5 to 1. This gave us 55 bhp at 5,800 rpm and a torque of 57 lbs/ft at 3,000 rpm. Power output was considerably improved over the original Mini's 37 bhp at 5,500 rpm. In addition, a tubular exhaust manifold was fabricated in place of the malleable cast component. We also had felt from the beginning that the rather wobbly shift lever in the original Mini would have to be sorted out and given a stiffer, more positive action. The existing three-foot gear lever was much too long and with a driver attempting a fast downshift on a corner, might cause serious trouble. We therefore designed a casting about two feet long which bolted up with the rubber mounting on the chassis' midship cross-member. This made possible a short and much more positive eight-inch gear lever which fell conveniently beneath the driver's left hand (these were, of course, right-hand-drive cars). A further advantage of the new unit was that it stiffened up the cylinder block by putting an additional engine mount in back of the gear lever.

Braking of the new Mini also was much improved by fitting seven-inch-diameter disc brakes up front and seven-inch drums on the rear. I think I've already mentioned that the disc brakes were produced by Lockheed, which was then under the chairmanship of Jack Emmott. His enthusiasm helped us greatly in fitting these disc brakes on such a small, ten-inch wheel. Right away the Mini-Cooper was equipped with braking which could easily cope with its increased power and speed, and this was more than many contemporary manufacturers of sporting models could claim.

Having sorted out the mechanical side of the car, we then went along to the Longbridge Styling Department (located in the corner of a building known as the "Kremlin" where a lot of the futuristic work was carried out. Sir George Harriman's office also was situated in this building, by the way). Anyhow, we decided almost at once to have two-color styling, using a different shade for the roof. Also, the interior trim was given an appreciable face-lift. Chrome strips were inset around the window frames while the bumpers were provided with special guards (called over-riders in England and bananas in France and Italy!).

A prototype completed body was soon put together for us to have a look at, and I remember also the unveiling, which was quite an event. We were all very pleased with what we saw. Now the Mini was really starting to look like an expensive product, much more in keeping with its enhanced performance.

The first 997 cc Mini-Coopers began coming off the production line toward the end of 1961 and I was then pushing BMC to produce 1,000 cars before January of 1962, since this was the minimum number needed to qualify for the homologation of the new model. It could then be entered in competition as a genuine Production Saloon Car.

The new Mini-Coopers were exhibited at the 1961 Motor Show but were introduced to the Press prior to that time at Cobham, Surrey, where they were received with much enthusiasm. In fact, during the Motor Show held in October, orders came pouring in and Bruce McLaren (then our number one works driver) took a Mini-Cooper over to New Zealand with him. His schedule called for him to run first in the New Zealand, then in the Australian Grand Prix, and incidentally enabled him to spend a good part of the winter close to home. On his very first appearance in a saloon car race with the Mini-Cooper, Bruce blew practically everything off the course and was never even threatened. On the other side of the world, the new Mini-Cooper proved a fantastic success.

When he returned to England, McLaren's first comment was, "Crikey! Why don't they build a lot of these little cars? They'd sell like hot cakes back home." Unfortunately at that time the import of British cars was restricted in New Zealand, but even so every available Mini-Cooper was snapped up at once.

Late in 1961, Bill Jones, one of the experimental engineers from British Leyland, and three of his colleagues, took a Mini-Cooper over to Montlhéry track in France and set up a startling new record. The little car with four people in it at all times—just to prove it really was a four-seater—covered 1,010 miles in twelve hours. This represented an average of 84.16 miles an hour—not bad for a standard production model of limited power and very compact dimensions. BMC derived a lot of encouragement from this performance, which proved that the Mini-Cooper was not only quick but also completely reliable. What was all the more surprising about this performance was that the car's claimed performance off the showroom floor didn't exceed 85 mph by much, while the 0-to-60 mph acceleration time was a modest 18 seconds through the gears. But in reviewing these performance figures one has to take into account the fact that this was fifteen years ago or more and that the piston displacement was very modest.

The 997 cc Mini-Cooper engine, however, did have one weakness and that was a crankshaft that didn't take too kindly to sustained high rpm and under certain circumstances was apt to come apart. Since, however, it was (rightly) not assumed that the average owner would want to cover 1,000 continuous miles at maximum speed, well enough was let alone until a new Mini engine made its appearance in 1962. This was a tuned version of the so-called 1000 cc unit, which actually displaced 998 cc, but was much more robust in all departments and had a better bore/stroke ratio.

As the demand for this amazing little car showed no sign of

slackening, but on the contrary grew apace, it was decided with George Harriman that we would race a team of three Mini-Coopers while the MG factory (part of the BMC group) would field a Rallye team from their competition department at Abingdon. The first season's racing (in 1962) was an unqualified success, which far exceeded our hopes. The Mini-Cooper in fact ended up by winning the British Saloon Car Championship.

Toward the end of that year I went along to see Sir George Harriman with Bill Appleby, who was in charge of engine design, and suggested that now might be a good time to produce 1,000 special Minis to be known as the Cooper "S." Basically the idea was once again to build enough cars so that we could get many important engine changes homologated and accepted for production car competition.

By increasing the bore to 2.7 in (70.6 mm) and the stroke to 2.68 in (68.26 mm) we got a piston displacement of 1071 cc. The compression ratio was raised to 9 to 1, requiring 100 octane fuel, but the output climbed to 70 bhp at 6,200 rpm and the torque to 62 lbs/ft at 4,500 rpm. With a strengthened crankshaft and camshaft and improved valve gear, this new engine could run up to 7,200 rpm before valve crash set in. The gearbox featured needle-roller bearings and by using Dunlop low-profiled tires on "wide" rims (5 × 10 alloy wheels), the tread was increased 4.5 inches for an even better road stance. Top speed rose to an easy 90 mph while the 0–60 mph time dropped to 13.5 seconds, even on a relatively new engine, not yet broken in.

We held long discussions with Alec Issigonis and Charlie Griffin, who was chief engineer at the time, together with Bill Appleby, the chief engine designer, and Eddie Maher (in charge of Morris engines), who had an experimental department at Coventry, where our Cooper Formula Junior engines were being produced. Also present was Daniel Richmond, a consultant for the new "S" type engine. Regularly, once a week, we sat around a big table and thrashed out all the problems connected with the Mini-Cooper "S" as they came up. It wasn't, in fact, until late 1962 that the decision was made to go ahead with the new car, and even then we had to insist on getting at least 1,000 examples built of this model so that it might be homologated. The job had to be done in time to enter the 1963 Monte Carlo Rallye. I remember this bevy of engineering talent seated around the table, scratching their heads and saying, "We'll never get a thousand cars out *that* soon . . ."

"Look," I said, "you don't have to actually *produce* a thousand of these cars. All you need is to *say* you've done so! What really counts is an honest intent."

"Right," was the quick response I got. "If you feel so confident about it, *you* handle all the homologation paperwork!"

"Okay," I agreed. "If that's the only problem, let's go ahead. From now on I'll take charge of all the homologation papers with the RAC."

And that was exactly what I did. Of course the fact that I was on friendly terms with Dean Delamont of the Competition Committee helped a lot.

The 1071 cc "S" Type Mini-Cooper, apart from its larger engine capacity and greatly improved performance, featured a nitrided crankshaft of enormous strength and also Nimonic valves. The SU carburetors were increased in size, as were the intake valves and the disc brakes. As a matter of interest, the "S" type engines were not built on the production line at Longbridge, Birmingham, but at Morris Engines in Coventry. This was a far more compact plant, where the engines were hand-built alongside the experimental department, a very handy arrangement. Here, Eddie Maher, whom I have just mentioned and who was a first-class engineer, took charge. It was largely to him that our Formula Junior and Formula 3 cars owed their success.

Yet from an administrative standpoint all was not quite as smooth-going as it seemed. The hierarchy at BMC were seriously concerned with whether we were putting too big a load on these new engines and might soon be reaping a harvest of mechanical bugs. As things turned out, these fears were quite unfounded. Eddie Maher and his team made sure that when an engine was put together it stayed that way. They were dead keen to see the new Mini-Cooper "S" win races and every kind of competition. In fact they did so good a job that before long buyers wanted the "S" Type regardless of whether they planned to go racing or not.

The new car was demonstrated to the Press toward the end of 1962 and was received with tremendous enthusiasm. It did not blight any hopes. Late in January 1963, Paddy Hopkirk won the Monte Carlo Rallye outright, a grueling event if ever there was one, and set the pattern for a long, almost unbroken string of victories in the Saloon Car class. This first win alone brought the new "S" more publicity than if we had bought whole-page advertisements in all the motoring magazines and daily papers combined! Sir George Harriman was beside himself with delight and the BMC management naturally shared his feelings.

During 1963, everyone at BMC became infected with a tremendous enthusiasm for racing and rallying, and Steward Turner, who was in charge of the BMC Competition Department at Abingdon (in the MG factory), made sure that the wins kept piling up. Turner, by the way, is now a director in charge of competition at Ford; but it can truly be said that in those days the Mini-Cooper "S" went from strength to strength. This inevitably led us down a one-way street and by the middle of 1963 we were looking for still more power. I remember again going to see Sir George Harriman and attending a board meeting at which Sir Lester Suffield was present, together with Alec Issigonis and Charlie Griffin (whom I had first met the previous year, when he was in charge of the BMC operation which introduced the Mini-Cooper to the United States). Also present was Joe Edwards, the assistant managing director of BMC.

Already, I was planning for two new "S" Types to go into production and I wanted to be sure that these would be homologated in good time for the following year. One of the newcomers was to be a 970 cc "S" Type which would be able to compete in the European Touring Car Championship and give us the best possible chance of success. Taking a look at the available competition, the under 1000 cc class was then the obvious one to go for. I also had in mind a 1275 cc engine, the maximum possible size to which the existing block could be bored and stroked. With such an engine we had every chance of cleaning up both in British races and international rallyes.

To get this extra capacity meant offsetting the cylinder bores and, of course, using longer connecting rods to increase the stroke. The initial reaction of the production engineers to the 1275 idea was, I suppose, fairly typical.

"This is going to be impossible!" they muttered in their beards. "It's just not going to work." One of the main objections was that the basic engine components were to be fabricated in Longbridge, then sent to Coventry for individual assembly. Even Sir George Harriman, who was a former production engineer, seemed dubious.

"I don't think this is really on," he said. "It's just stretching our resources to the limit. And after all, we still have to build production cars without all this fancy stuff."

The argument was undeniable but I scarcely felt that this was the happiest moment of my life. It was disappointment with a capital *D* and as I headed for the boardroom door to catch my train home, I told myself, "That was a wasted journey. I should have stayed in Surbiton and done something useful."

But at that moment the unexpected happened. Harriman tapped me on the shoulder and grinned. "Never mind, John, we're just bloody well going ahead with your idea anyway!"

Needless to say, I took a deep breath of delight and relief.

"I know you won't regret it," I said.

But once again I had the problem of getting this new oversized power unit homologated with the Royal Automobile Club to enable us to run in the "production" class, which meant without any special modifications. Dean Delamont came through as usual and the cars were duly homologated before the start of the 1964 season, meaning that at least the *intent* was to produce a minimum of 1,000 of the latest Mini-Cooper "S" with the 1275 cc engine. In the event a far greater number rolled off the assembly line.

To go back to the 970 cc model for a moment, my judgment proved right on this one, too. It did in fact win the European Touring Car Championship outright.

For those purists who enjoy a bit of technical history without going too deep into the engineering maze, I've jotted down a few particulars about the 1275 cc engine which was initially considered "impossible" to build. The crankshaft was beefed up even more than on the 970 cc engine, being both nitrided and forged. The journals were increased to a two-inch diameter and the connecting rods strengthened and given even bigger wrist pins. Nimonic valves were again used and these ran in special copper-nickel guides and were operated by forged steel rocker arms. The camshaft was redesigned with the idea of widening the torque curve rather than getting greatly increased top end power. The compression ratio was upped to 9.72 to 1 and the extra punch so derived permitted the use of a higher final drive ratio. Instead of the 3.76 rear end used with the 1071 cc engine, a 3.44 ratio was substituted. The same 1¼-inch SU carburetors were fitted as for the smaller engine, a fact which restricted breathing a little, but helped with mid-range power, which was the 1275 engine's greatest asset. Peak power soared to 76 bhp at 5,900 rpm with 79 lbs/ft of torque at only 3,000 rpm—a much lower rpm peak torque than with the 1071 engine.

In August of 1964 the first 1275 cc Mini-Cooper "S" to be given a thorough road test came through with flying colors. On a two-way run, a mean top speed of 96 mph was reached and the car took only 11.2 seconds to reach 60 mph from a standstill. To us as well as to the Press and public, the 1275 model was the ultimate. Compatible with reliability of a high order, we squeezed just about all we could out of the engine, certainly in terms of enlarging the cylinder block. The 970 "S" engine, by the way, which was in every detail a smaller replica of the 1275 version, produced 65 bhp at 6,500 rpm.

Once again, in 1964, we won the Monte Carlo Rallye outright, and this was to prove the second of four wins, although not in a row. The following year our car was disqualified because of so-called "illegal" headlights, which were the subject of protest by another competitor—the Citroën firm. In my opinion, both the protest and the verdict were frivolous, if not ridiculous, and the obvious conclusion was that Citroën really needed to win the Monte Carlo Rallye that year, come hell or high water. Still, BMC got by far the most publicity and by this time our cars were winning events such as the Tulip, Alpine, RAC and Polish Rallyes and the Tour de France. They also cleaned up at rallyes in Finland and even in the United States. So, by then, the public was thoroughly spoiled. Every buyer wanted the "full house" 1275 Mini-Cooper "S" because it had so much power to spare and was therefore a very flexible road car.

At Surbiton, we went ahead with our own factory competition plans, running a team of three Coopers in England and another team on the Continent of Europe. Not content with all the improvements already made, we also got a fuel injection system and a new cylinder head homologated. This was a cross-flow head with separate inlet and exhaust ports on opposite sides of the combustion chamber. The result was staggering. Toward the end of the 1275 Mini-Cooper "S" reign in 1968, we were getting 135 bhp out of this engine! Actually, Ken Tyrrell, who had very successfully run my Formula 3 works team, also took charge of Mini-Cooper competition activities in Europe. I remember when he took the team over to Spa in 1963 with Sir John Whitmore as number one driver, backed up by Bill Blydenstein (an excellent amateur driver who later became an automotive development engineer and today heads up a thriving business in Hertfordshire) and Jimmy Blumer.

Tyrrell got the drivers together and spelled out his plan before the start of the race. "Whatever happens," he told them, "you've got to make sure that Bill wins this race. Otherwise the European Championship is going to slip out of our hands. So don't pass Blydenstein, don't push him and force him to blow up his engine!" The trouble was that our cars were so much quicker than anything else in the class that such a thing might easily have happened. In addition, it turned out that Bill Blydenstein had easily the fastest of the three Minis. Unfortunately, even our carefully laid plans went awry. Bill was in fact leading the race when his gearbox started to act up, and going into the La Source Hairpin he found it very difficult to get into a lower gear. This slowed him considerably and on the following lap he was down to a crawl, which made matters very difficult for our other drivers. They almost had to use their brakes to avoid passing Bill, but they stuck to what Tyrrell had told them to do.

That last lap was an agonizing experience, especially as the only opposition to the three Minis was Holvoet's DKW, which simply did not have the speed on the straights and hung on gamely in the hope that something might happen to at least one of our three cars. Most of the time he wasn't even within striking distance and posed no threat at all.

To quote from a letter I recently received from Bill Blydenstein, recalling that Spa race in some detail:

"About an hour before the start we were summoned into the presence of Ken Tyrrell and Daniel and Bunty Richmond (the owner of Downton Engineering, who did the Mini engine development work, and his wife). We were told that we were going to try to make a spectacular finish, three abreast across the line.

"Having blown up two gearboxes in practise (the second and third gear layshaft bushes were constantly seizing at high speed, before needle rollers were introduced) I agreed that this would be fine provided all of us stayed out of trouble. I did suggest that should anyone get into trouble, the others should continue and finish the race in as good a position as possible overall."

Tyrrell conceded that if there was no alternative that arrangement would be the best, but he was hell-bent on a three-car, line-abreast finish.

In the event, Blydenstein's gearbox packed up one lap before the end of the race, and all he could find (with a great deal of trouble) was third gear. Looking along from the pits we could see the procession coming slowly up the straight with Whitmore and Blumer doing their utmost to allow Blydenstein to limp across the line with them in a triple dead-heat finish. The final few hundred yards became a farce as these two, unable to hold down their speed any further, came alongside Bill, grimly determined to let him win by "just a few inches," which would be enough yet would not detract from the line-abreast finish.

Then, suddenly, before the team could take the flag, the DKW came through on the grass from somewhere back in the field, passed all three Minis and won the race! (The photo tells its own frustrating story and is probably unique.) So we finished second, third and fourth instead of one-two-three. I don't think Ken Tyrrell's ever forgotten that incident. I certainly haven't.

Perhaps at this point it might be interesting if I talked a little about the financial arrangements between Cooper and BMC. Just to give the reader an example, I'll skip forward for a minute to 1968. During that year alone there were nearly 20,000 Mini-Coopers and "S's" produced. And if we extend the manufacturing period to the present day, probably more than 130,000 Mini-Coopers have reached the public and innumerable rallye drivers in one form or another. That's saying nothing of race drivers.

Although production of this basic model ceased in 1971, when my agreement with British Leyland came to an end (perhaps because Lord Stokes and I didn't go to the same school, or something), the car passed into the capable hands of Innocenti, in Italy, where production was continued at the rate of about 8,000 units a year. And a very nice and potent little machine it was, with just that touch of Italian flair for styling. Then, a couple of years ago, the great Bertone got out the drawing board and completely restyled the Mini-Cooper, giving it a new, rather boxy body, a rear-opening door and a new model designation so that it still came in 1000 and 1300 cc versions but was renamed to 90 and 120L. Then strikes (in 1976) halted not so much production as delivery of a large inventory of completed cars, which were not allowed across the picket lines and couldn't leave the factory at all, although the public was eager to get them. That trouble is now over, I gather.

By 1968, incidentally, I had already renewed my contract two years earlier, and as of August 1, 1966, it had been agreed that this new contract would run another five years, thus terminating in 1971. During that period I was to act as consultant to BMC on British Mini-Coopers with a consultation fee based on £2 (at the present rate of exchange about $3.40) per car, regardless of the number produced. This in fact was not a bad arrangement at all and in the days of Sir George Harriman it worked very well. It's a pity, really, when things have to change, but they always do reach that point, sooner or later.

The only real modification to the chassis design of the Mini-Cooper during all those years was the introduction in 1964 of what was called Hydrolastic Suspension. This fluid-filled type of suspension proved very successful on the 1100 cc cars and was, in fact, quite suitable for rallying as well as for daily use. Even in circuit racing it was a help under certain conditions. Also, the 997 cc engine was replaced in January 1964 by a 998 cc unit with a new bore and stroke. The bore was 2.54 in (64.58 mm) and the stroke 3 in (76.2 mm) and the result was a much improved production engine for the "man in the street." Concurrently, the 1071 cc "S" engine was dropped, leaving the choice of the 970 "S" engine, the 1275 "S" and the standard 998 cc unit.

It's rather interesting to recall at this point the strong negative reaction I encountered from engineers when I suggested offsetting the centers of the cylinder bores within the block so as to permit larger pistons to be fitted; and also the stroking which resulted in the 1275 "S" unit. As things turned out, the idea proved so successful that it is now the standard production bore–stroke ratio for all British Leyland 1300 cc engines. Virtually millions of these cars have since been produced, giving the lie to the original arguments put forward against this design at the conference table. Oh well.

This may be hard to believe, but people who bought 1275 cc Mini-Cooper "S" Types for road use were often owners of Aston Martins and Ferraris, with a lot of money to spend. A firm named Radford's, who were coachbuilders, soon started a lucrative business modifying the bodywork of our "S" Type saloons and providing luxurious upholstery (leather, of course), beautifully lacquered finish, electric windows, sunroofs and the like. It was in fact quite common for wealthy Radford clientele to spend up to £4,000 (even today well over $6,800) in customizing our Mini-Cooper "S" saloons. One name that comes to mind is Peter Sellers, who at one time or another owned two or three of our cars. Curiously enough, another illustrious Mini-Cooper "S" fan who had the front of his car specially restyled by Pininfarina was none other than the great Enzo Ferrari himself. When he wanted to let off steam, the Commendatore would climb into his Cooper "S" and go belting around the mountains for a while, then return and think up something new for his own cars.

Lord Snowdon was another Mini-Cooper enthusiast and we also built a special station wagon version of the "S" for Steve McQueen, who planned to use it in one of his movies.

Interestingly enough, ladies found the Mini-Cooper a very easy car to drive and made full use of its performance. One of the fastest Mini-Cooper drivers was Christabel Carlyle, a piano teacher from London. She was a small-built and very attractive woman whose quick reflexes were ideally suited to the Mini-Cooper. Christabel Carlyle won a number of races and at times even gave some of our works drivers a run for their money.

Among the special extras that we homologated for the Cooper range and which was much in demand, was the ZF-type limited slip differential. Our gearbox man, Jack Knight, and I sat up one evening and designed this thing on the back of an envelope. Naturally, it had to be a very compact unit in order to fit into the gearbox and I remember talking to Issigonis about it. His reply at the time was fairly characteristic.

"Well, we'll just have to see what happens. Don't forget that no one has ever tried a self-locking diff on the *front wheels* of a car!"

Anyway, we eventually had the prototype model made to our specifications and put it in a Mini. We went down to Silverstone to try it out and as usual it was a wet day. This gave us a good opportunity to test out the idea in practice. The result was quite fantastic. We also brought along a standard Mini-Cooper "S" without the diff, and the modified car was much quicker in the wet. There was simply no comparison. So as to really nail this thing down, we went back to Silverstone the next day, in the dry, and again ran a comparison test. Even in these circumstances the limited slip diff cut our lap time down by two or three seconds. No doubt about it, the improvement went way beyond our hopes and we had this piece of equipment homologated at the earliest possible moment. Later, when Jack Knight simply could no longer cope with the orders, we turned over the whole thing to the Salisbury Axle Company.

Another "goodie" which we produced for the "S" was a ten-inch magnesium wheel with various rim widths. The width ranged from four and a half to six inches and in fact the Minilite wheel produced at a later date was almost an identical copy of our rose petal type alloy wheel, also used on our Formula Junior and Formula 1 cars. A further improvement which we made available as an optional extra on the "S" was adjustable front and rear sway bars, and this too was homologated so that the racing Minis could benefit from it. Larger fuel tanks were adopted and made available on all production Mini-Cooper "S" models, while fiberglass moldings could also be fitted where the use of wide wheels and low-profile tires caused the latter to stand out from the body sides, violating FIA rules. These moldings were called spats and everyone with a "go-quick" Mini who had adopted wide wheels asked for this modification, whether they raced or not. The spats gave the Mini a very sporty appearance and that was the "in" thing to do.

One improvement inevitably leads to another and we began experimenting with a new type of cylinder head which used hemispherical combustion chambers and cross-over pushrods. This head featured eight ports, of course—four intake and four exhaust—while the twin SU carburetors were moved from the rear of the cross-mounted engine to the front, and replaced with twin double-choke Webers because of the four inlet ports. To accommodate these new carburetors, a slight bulge had to be made at the front of the hood, but this was not unsightly. I think, looking back, that had we pursued the development of this engine it would have made a very good substitute for the time-honored basic "A"-type unit. Politics, however, were such that we only produced half a dozen of them.

The next thing to come out of the hopper in those days—I am speaking now of 1964—was a new twin-cam, four-cylinder Formula 2 engine. This was produced by BMC at their experimental engine shop in Longbridge, not at the Morris works located in Coventry. We tested one of these engines in a Cooper Formula 2 chassis, but despite its modern concept it wasn't a very successful power unit. At least not right away. So it, too, was shelved.

Before Lord Stokes took over BMC and amalgamated with Leyland in 1968, forming what is now known as British Leyland, I was working with Sir George Harriman and Charlie Griffin on two new Cooper models. One was to be known as the "1300 Cooper," which was basically the 1100 cc Morris sedan with the 1275 "S" type engine; while the other was a twin-carburetor version of the 1800 which would be known as the "Cooper 1800." When Lord Stokes assumed command, he shelved both these models but later produced them under the nomenclature of "1300 GT" and "1800 S." The Cooper name was dropped from both these cars, as I expected it would be. So I was not too surprised or disappointed.

Still looking back, things began to wind up in 1969, when the standard Mini-Cooper was phased out, while, as I have said, upon termination of my agreement in 1971 the Cooper "S" also was dropped.

An incident which sticks in my mind, less because it was of any grave importance than because there were undercurrents of humor, was in the 1967 Yugoslav Touring Car Championship. We took the team of three Cooper Minis to Yugoslavia, which is of course a Communist country, and found on arrival that one of the other entrants in our class had failed to appear. As the last practice period loomed up, we began to get worried, since to obtain maximum points in the European Saloon Car Championship, a minimum of eight starters was required in each class. If the number dropped below eight, then those who did show up earned fewer points. It looked at the time as though there were going to be only seven starters in our class for the Yugoslav event. Ginger Devlin, who was my chief mechanic at the time and had been with the Cooper firm right from the early days, came up with a brilliant idea.

We had a 1000 cc Fiat, which I believe we had rented at the airport, and this happened to be what might be termed in racing parlance a "Group Two Production Car."

"So," said Ginger with a big grin, "why don't we enter that one in the race, too? No need to flog it. Just take it around the course nice and easy and that way we'll have another entry."

"Think we can get away with it?" I wondered. It seemed like a pretty bold expedient, especially as the car wasn't even on the entry list at that point.

"Sure we can," Devlin insisted. "All we need is a bit of nerve."

I couldn't help seeing the funny side of the situation, but my main objection was pretty obvious.

"Suppose they find out?"

"Who's going to know?" Ginger parried. "One of our mechanics has just got his competition license. So we enter him as the driver. Legitimate, isn't it?"

Truth to tell, I didn't require much pressure to convince me that the idea was feasible, so we rushed along to the organizers and asked them if they would accept a 1000 cc Fiat entry with one of my mechanics driving. This would take the place of the missing foreign entry.

The committee raised no objection, so we quickly installed a rollbar in the car (easily detached, of course), stuck some numbers on its sides and made other minor modifications to comply with the requirements of the scrutineers. When the flag dropped for the start of the event, my mechanic ran a few leisurely laps, then retired, having convincingly achieved our objective, which was to comply with a minimum of eight starters in that race.

That's one way to go motor racing and to the best of my recollection we never got any backlash from the rental company—who almost certainly had no idea of the good use we had made of their car.

Looking back on the years during which the Mini-Cooper "S" swept all before it in every kind of competition, I don't think I would be exaggerating if I said that we created a new dimension in motoring. The basic idea—and a brilliant one it was—came from Alec Issigonis, but our little group at Cooper certainly deserved credit for taking it on from there.

Mini-Cooper successes have been dealt with so thoroughly and in so many publications that I am not going to start all that again, here. In fact, this is as good a place as any to end the present chapter.

17

Random Recollections

This chapter is, I think, appropriately titled since it really does consist of recollections through the Cooper racing years, set down at random and without regard for chronological order. Truth to tell, when it comes to remembering dates and places (and sometimes names too) I am not at my best. Don't ask me why. Or rather, don't ask me *when!*

At all events, while I was attending the 1958 Grand Prix at Monza, I had lunch during practice with the great Enzo Ferrari himself and also that internationally known motoring correspondent Bernard Cahier. It was a kind of trackside meal with no formality, and since Ferrari spoke very little English, Cahier acted as the translator. In passing it is interesting to note that to this day, despite heavy racing involvement, especially in Grand Prix events, Enzo keeps away from race meets with the exception of a yearly pilgrimage to Monza, which is, so to speak, almost on his doorstep. And even then he usually confines his visits to practice periods.

On this occasion, however, rather an amusing incident occurred while various drivers were trying to set up times which would put them in a good position on the grid. There was Ferrari, standing in front of the pit, wearing mainly his pants and suspenders, and of course without a pit pass because the great Commendatore hardly required anything so trivial. Unfortunately, however, the Army (who used to control the pits) descended on him in a routine check and asked for his credentials.

"I'm Enzo Ferrari," the great man said. "What else do you want to know?"

"Your papers, please!"

"Get lost," Ferrari told them in Italian, or the equivalent.

Whereupon, without further discussion a pair of heavy *carabinieri* lifted him up bodily and carried him out toward the exit. Ferrari was so incensed that minutes later he had withdrawn all three of his cars from the race—a disastrous move from the standpoint of the organizers. Naturally, they lost no time getting on their hands and knees to him and uttering the most profuse apologies. Meanwhile, the guilty soldiers, who had only been doing their duty, got a terrific tongue-lashing and were practically banished to Siberia. But the imperious Commendatore wanted the lesson to sink in. Nobody, but nobody was going to treat him like that and it was fully half an hour before he forgave the cringing officials and reinstated his team.

It was on that day that the lunch I referred to earlier took place with the great Enzo and that polished Frenchman Cahier. We were discussing Grand Prix car design, and in particular the Cooper rear-engine layout, when Ferrari threw up his hands and made an unforgettable statement which, translated, amounted to this: "I for one will never build a rear-engine Grand Prix car! You're entitled to your opinion, Signor Cooper, but I have the experience!"

As we were only on the way up, and still a year from our first World Championship, I held my peace. But times have certainly changed since that fateful statement.

After Carroll Shelby had retired from motoring racing, in 1960, he decided to get involved with building race cars. Given Ford's limitless backing he succeeded beyond his dreams; but at the time he came over to see me he was not there yet.

"I've a great idea," he said. "Why don't you beef up your Cooper Monaco sports car chassis to take a 427-cubic-inch Ford V-8 engine? Stock, of course."

"Our car would need too much redesigning," I said, "and we're fully committed as it is to a Grand Prix racing program."

"Think about it," Shelby drawled. "Ford are interested and you could turn out a large batch of Coopers powered by their engines. What's more, the market is wide open."

I knew that what Shelby proposed was beyond our capability at that time, but he was very insistent.

"Those cars could be supplied to all the Ford dealers in the States. Think what that would mean."

Suddenly an idea came to me. I was on friendly terms with the Hurlock brothers, who owned the very ancient firm of AC at Thames Ditton, just down the road from us. Their AC Ace model had been a carbon copy of our front-engined Cooper-MG chassis in the first place, and things just then were a bit slow for them. They might well be interested.

"There's a chance I may know the very people who would go for your idea of a British chassis and body with an American engine," I told Shelby. "Let me make a phone call."

As a result, I sent him along to Charles Hurlock, one of the AC directors. It so happened that there were a number of spare chassis lying around at the AC premises and the Hurlocks listened with enthusiasm to Carroll's proposal. Perhaps that Texan drawl of his fascinated them, but I don't think they quite realized there and then what they were letting themselves in for. Still, the deal eventually gave them the financial transfusion they needed and proved very profitable.

What none of us knew at that time was how clever Carroll Shelby could be at dreaming up ideas and manipulating people. I believe he had already approached Ford and told them in effect: "We need a top-selling American sports car to really dust off those foreign imports. And the market is there for it. If I can find you the right chassis and body in England, will you supply me with a few trial engines to see how things work out?"

Ford were ready to give it a go and promised him two lightweight V-8 engines of 3622 cc (221 cu in) displacement, so when Shelby came to see me he had the deal already half sewn up. And when AC Cars fell for the proposition, Shelby was able to deliver the Ford engines. And that was the birth of the world-famous Cobra, but for the Hurlock brothers it was something of a painful birth, nonetheless. By stages, the entire AC tubular chassis had to be redesigned to accept the weight, torque and power of the big Ford V-8 unit. And this was quite a job. It was not enough to use heavier-gauge tubing. The suspension needed beefing-up considerably, then the brakes, the rear end assembly and finally even the steering underwent drastic changes. That's not to mention the gearbox and clutch, of course.

During the seemingly endless series of tests which ultimately produced the prototype of the great Cobra sports car, designated CSX001, every time something was strengthened a corresponding weakness showed up in another component. The car was unmistakably of AC origin and derivation, but by the time it was ready for production and had also been approved by Ford (in 1962), it reminded one of the Slim Jim who takes a body-building course by mail and eventually ends up flexing huge muscles! It was a magnificent machine, nonetheless, with a quite shattering performance. Ford's Donald Frey, in charge of engineering planning, was sufficiently impressed to start supplying Shelby with the larger V-8, 4261 cc (260 cu in) engine, and after the first 75 cars, with the 4736 cc (289 cu in) unit. But even when Shelby had, himself, opened up a factory at Los Angeles airport, California, and taken most of the production load off the AC firm so that only a few complete AC Cobras were built in England, he still did not forget us.

He had only shelved the idea of building a mighty rear-engine Cooper (which he named King Cobra) and at the opportune moment he approached me again.

This time (in 1963) we went along with the idea but did not get involved with producing complete cars. We stuck to suitable chassis and bodies strong enough to take the Ford V-8, and we probably had a better idea of what was needed than did the Hurlocks originally. What Shelby had in mind, of course, was the racing publicity certain to accrue, which in turn would help the sales of the Cobra. And he was right. We built in all twenty-five complete (but engineless) chassis and bodies for him, which were then fitted with special Ford engines. The King Cobra was a winner from the outset and proved it by winning the Riverside Sports Car Grand Prix in California, driven by the late Dave McDonald, who was later killed at Indianapolis. So Carroll Shelby ended up with two winners—the AC Cobra (as it was first called) and the Cooper-designed and built King Cobra, both Ford-powered.

Another interesting recollection I have concerns Roy Lunn, a high executive in charge of engineering planning for the Ford Division at Dearborn. (In a corporation that size, turning out several makes and models, it is an American custom to give each make a separate Division, even though it is part of the corporate group.) Interestingly enough, Lunn had worked in England for the ancient firm of Jowett's, long since extinct, and for the AC Company. He was married to a second cousin of mine on my father's side. But Roy had long since decided that his possible fortune lay in the States—a fully correct judgment. In 1963 he came over to see me at Surbiton and suggested that the Ford Motor Company wanted to get into big-time racing. They had already approached Ferrari with an offer to buy him out, but he had more or less told them to get stuffed, perhaps because he already had financial backing from Fiat, but mainly because he found the Ford bureaucracy "suffocating." Thus, on the very point of signing the agreement, Ferrari dropped his pen and walked out of the office determined not to go through with the deal.

So Lunn remembered me and here he was, wondering if the Cooper firm would be interested in building a car for the large Ford V-8 engine. At that time there was no hope of our getting involved. We were fully committed to Grand Prix racing and race car building; but a sudden idea came to me.

"I think I might know someone who would be very interested in your proposition," I said. "Chap named Eric Broadley, who owns a small car manufacturing concern called Lola, at Slough. He's just built a really beautiful monocoque rear-engine GT car which is still in prototype form. In fact I think he plans to fit a Ford V-8 engine in it. Could be just what you're looking for."

"Sounds too good to be true," Lunn said.

"Why don't you go and see him? What can you lose, except time?"

"I will."

It was not long before a swarm of Ford engineers descended on the Lola plant and the next thing Broadley knew was that he had sold out, lock, stock and barrel to the giant FoMoCo. Roy Lunn and John Wyer took over production and went from there (via a lot of Dearborn engine development and track testing) to the world-beating Ford GT40, which made its initial appearance at the Nürburgring in 1964, driven by Phil Hill and Bruce McLaren, and ended up with a dramatic prearranged finish at Le Mans, two years later, getting the checker first, second and third. Broadley, meantime, was unable to stand the pressures put on him by Ford's gigantic organization and divorced himself from the whole thing. He later started again on his own while Ford moved their operation to John Wyer's place until eventually he, too, regained his freedom. Ford, it is worth recalling, sponsored the first two GT40 victories at Le Mans in 1966 and 1967. After that, the automotive giant retired from GT racing and it was John Wyer (under Gulf sponsorship) who won the next two Le Mans events in 1968 and 1969. Still, taking one thing with another, those four Le Mans wins cost Ford (directly or indirectly) about $15 million, even though they had little to do with the last two victories.

It's not everybody who meets Prince Philip, Duke of Edinburgh, but I have been privileged to do so on a number of occasions—three to be exact. The first time goes back to 1952. I had been a member of the British Racing Drivers' Club Committee for four years and on the twenty-fifth anniversary of the club we had a big white tie dinner at the Royal Festival Hall on the river Thames. This was attended by the Duke of Edinburgh, president-in-chief of the BRDC. We were all waiting for him to arrive for the special reception the committee was holding in his honor, when I suddenly realized that one of the studs on the front of my stiff white shirt had popped out. Most embarrassing, especially at that moment, but I had no choice except to get down on the floor and try to retrieve the darn thing. As so often happens when you drop something, it acquires a mysteriously elusive quality that is very aggravating. At any rate, I was still on the floor, groveling around after that wretched stud when the Duke arrived. And the worst of it was that I was not even aware of the august presence.

The Duke smiled and pointing to me asked, "What's he doing on the floor? It's a bit early, isn't it?"

"Oh," several voices chorused, "that's old Cooper looking for his shirt stud!"

That was my introduction to His Royal Highness.

My next encounter with the Duke took place under rather different circumstances. I am an honorary member of the Club des Anciens Pilotes, which in French has nothing to do with aircraft but refers to retired Grand Prix drivers. (Incidentally, Prince Rainier also is an honorary member and so was that famous ex-motoring journalist, the late Tommy Wisdom.) Theoretically, how-

ever, in order to belong to this select group you must have won a
Grand Prix at some time.

Every year a different country promotes a special party for the
Anciens Pilotes at the time of the European Grand Prix held in
that country, regardless of nationality. On the occasion I recall, in
1966, it was Britain's turn to stage the European Grand Prix and
the reunion meeting of the Anciens Pilotes. The president of the
British Racing Drivers' Club at the time was the Honorable Gerald
Lascelles, cousin of our present Queen and a good friend of mine
who lives at Fort Belvedere, the hideout of the Prince of Wales in
his prewar courting days. On this occasion it was decided to hold
the party for the Anciens Pilotes on the Sunday after the race at
Silverstone. Fort Belvedere is a lovely place, and in addition to the
stalwart ancients some of the modern drivers also were invited.
About thirty or forty of us were about to enjoy an excellent and
stimulating luncheon at Fort Belvedere when an incident occurred which set back our schedule a little. I happened to be gaz-
ing out of the window along the winding driveway when I saw an
elderly Alvis sports car which must have been at least fifteen years
old. The top was down and the driver could be seen wearing a
trilby hat. When the car braked to a stop, lo and behold, he turned
out to be none other than the Duke of Edinburgh. He soon joined
our party, which also included Juan Manuel Fangio and Sammy
Davis, who won Le Mans in 1927, when I was four years old. We
had a most interesting chat with the Duke, who showed a genuine
interest in our sport. After lunch, however, he excused himself.

"I'm afraid I've got to rush, now. I'm playing polo just down
the road at Windsor." Then he added, "Why don't you all come
and watch? It's an open house."

This was too good a thing to miss, so we piled into our cars and
followed the Duke to the Windsor polo grounds. There we were
introduced to Queen Elizabeth since we had been given the status
of special guests. The Duke acquitted himself very well in that
game, about which I know little or nothing, except that it's pretty
fast.

The third time I met His Royal Highness was at a get-together
of the British Racing and Sports Car Club, of which I am the life
president. This very active organization puts on a Racing Car
Show every two years at Olympia. On this particular occasion,
which was, I think, in 1968, the Duke graciously agreed to open

the show. It fell to me to take him around the many glamorous exhibits at the opening of the show and to introduce him to some of the people on the stands. Unfortunately it's very difficult for me to remember names—not to mention dates, as I have already said—especially when I panic. I recall that we walked on to the Champion Spark Plug stand, where an old friend mine stood waiting. He was the managing director of this famous firm and there he stood, attired in his best suit, but although I knew him extremely well and we had many times gone out together, at that moment I completely forgot his name. My memory simply dried up and the harder the effort the bigger the blank I drew. It was a most embarrassing situation as I walked over with the Duke to effect the introduction, so I made a desperate effort to cover up.

"Prince Philip," I said, "this is Mr. Champion."

My friend brushed it off very well. "I'd like to be that," he smiled, "but my name is only Herbert Starley."

That's one way to handle the situation when you can't even remember a friend's name!

Another time (in 1964) Lord Snowdon, Princess Margaret's husband, came to the Racing Car Show. He didn't actually open it but arrived the day after with none other than Sir Alec Issigonis. These two, incidentally, were great friends, and I spent the whole afternoon with them going around the show. While we were chatting, Lord Snowdon suddenly asked me if I would make some modifications to his Mini-Cooper.

"Of course," I said.

"Could you arrange to have the car picked up, Mr. Cooper?"

"Certainly," I agreed. "In fact I'll do it myself."

At that time the Snowdons were living at Kensington Palace and when I showed up at the garage, which was near the house, I thought I spotted a familiar face sitting on the running board of a Rolls-Royce.

The man's name escapes me but I recognized him at once and asked, "What are you doing here?"

"I work in this garage," he grinned. He was a former Lotus mechanic who had since got a job as one of the Royal Family chauffeurs.

Anyhow, I did the work on Lord Snowdon's Mini-Cooper as requested and I believe he was very pleased. He happened to be a great Mini enthusiast.

In my younger days we used to spend many of our evenings at the Steering Wheel Club in Brick Street, London. The racing fraternity met there regularly for a drink and a chat, but the only drawback was that the club closed its doors (as did many genteel enterprises of that kind!) at 10:30 P.M., a ridiculously early hour. So we later would meet at another club, which wasn't quite so particular about closing time. It was located in Kensington, directly on my way home. This club was run by an attractive young woman named Ruth Ellis, who came to a tragic end at the age of only twenty-eight. At the time she was—if not engaged to—at least the steady girl friend of a man named David Blakely, son of Sir Humphrey Cooke, who had financed the ERA (English Racing Automobile) firm in prewar days. Blakely also was a race driver in his own right.

As so often happens, the pair fell out and had a big argument over another woman with whom Blakely was said to be carrying on. But this was at a later date. In those days we would all repair to Ruth's club and drink till the early hours of the morning. She was a great gal, friendly and gay, and we were stunned by the news that she had shot her boyfriend. On April 10, 1955, in a fit of jealousy, apparently, she emptied a revolver into him with fatal results. There were extenuating circumstances and it was pretty well known that Blakely had treated her badly; but the law in those days called for capital punishment where a defendant was found guilty of murder. That was the jury's verdict in Ruth's case and she was condemned to death. Her appeal was turned down and in July that same year she was duly hanged at Holloway prison. Incidentally she was the last woman in Britain to undergo this barbarous form of capital punishment. We unanimously felt that they should not have carried out the sentence, but we were helpless to intervene. Ruth was a charming person and on one special occasion I was invited to her birthday party, cake and all. It was a tragic ending to the life of a young woman who had everything going for her, but momentarily lost control of her emotions over a man to whom she was devoted.

My father had a cottage in Cornwall on the river Fal near Falmouth, where he used to go down for a week's rest and sometimes a fortnight. I, too, would come down for the odd week when I could get away. It was a lovely and restful spot which my wife,

Paula, also enjoyed, as did our children, Christine, Michael and Sally. On one occasion in 1960 I invited Jack Brabham to come and visit us and by means of a map carefully explained to him where the place was.

"Yep, yep, yep!" he replied, totally confident of finding his way—by air, I should explain.

To make doubly sure, I told him that at eleven o'clock on a Saturday morning I would mark out a big white cross in a field that was somewhere behind the cottage. Brabham should have no trouble landing his Cessna there. Incidentally, he planned to bring along his wife, Betty, spend the weekend with us and then fly back. At a quarter to eleven on the Saturday, I marked out the field as agreed but the weather was not very good. Scudding clouds obscured the view from above. Sure enough, though, at about eleven-fifteen Jack flew over and took a good look at the field. There were a lot of cattle about at one end which I couldn't very well move, so after a couple of dummy runs Jack decided it wasn't the place for him to land. He dropped an airline carrier bag out of the plane window, which incidentally landed in the river mud nearby, but I was able to retrieve it. There was a note in the bag saying, "I'm flying off to St. Morgan. Pick me up."

This airfield was about forty-five minutes' drive from our cottage, so we got going. When I arrived at St. Morgan there was a hell of a row going on. The police were there together with a number of outraged BOAC (British Airways now) officials, and everyone was milling around. The cause of all this bother was that St. Morgan's was being used by BOAC to train pilots on 707 jets and they were doing "circuits and bumps"—the English for practice takeoffs and landings. Jack, completely unperturbed, had simply flown in and landed his Cessna 180 on the grass beside the control tower. The officials were horrified.

"Do you realize," they bellowed at him, "that we could have been forced to write off an aircraft worth several million pounds?"

But when they found out who Jack was, everything was forgiven. I picked him and Betty up and we had a wonderful weekend at my father's cottage. Most of our time was devoted to water-skiing and fishing.

During the 1961 American Grand Prix at Watkins Glen, New York, it was customary for Americans to lay on cars for everybody when they landed from Europe at Kennedy Airport in New York. That year everyone had a Ford car, including the mechanics, so that they could get to Watkins Glen with a minimum of bother. In fact the cars were made available to contestants for the duration of the Grand Prix as well. I remember that after touchdown, following the usual seven-hour flight, which time-wise was only two hours later than it had been in Europe, we picked up a large Ford car—I forget which model. Bruce McLaren was driving and the passengers consisted of Innes Ireland, myself and two of my mechanics. We were belting along the freeway (which in those days permitted cars a reasonable 70 mph speed limit, strictly enforced) but Bruce paid no attention. It was already dark and we were actually doing about 110 mph, anxious to get to our hotel as quickly as possible, when a police car caught up with us, siren blaring ominously. Bruce slowed, of course, and the cop car swung directly in front of us, forcing us to a quick stop. A very angry patrolman swaggered up to our Ford and barked, "Who's the owner of this car?"

"The Ford Motor Company," Bruce said innocently.

The patrolman wasn't buying anything. He stood back from the car, hand at the ready on his gun holster and said, "Get out of the car—all of you!"

Bruce and I sidled out but the patrolman took no chances.

"*All* of you get out of the car!"

We complied and were then told to face the car and put our hands on the roof. A second patrolman frisked us carefully to see if we were carrying any guns. This was a bit much and we asked, "What's the game? What's the big idea? We were going over the speed limit—so what? There's a fine, isn't there?"

Finally the first cop responded. "When you've got five people piled into a car, doing better than 110 mph at this time of night, boy, you must have robbed a bank someplace!"

We then carefully gave proof of our identity and explained that we were on our way to Watkins Glen for the Grand Prix. This time we were in luck. The two cops happened to be motoring enthusiasts and they began to ask questions about our cars—and forgave us. No ticket. Things could have ended a lot worse, like spending the night in jail till someone came to bail us out!

Switching back to the Italian Grand Prix at Monza in 1956, an amusing incident comes to mind which concerned the late Graham Hill, a really great guy and a gifted speaker as well as a champion driver. Hill was then driving for the Gold Leaf, tobacco-sponsored Team Lotus. It was their first year with John Players and the cars were painted up like cigarette ads.

Since the following day would be Graham's 100th Grand Prix, they were having a party at Monza and I was invited along with most of Graham's friends. It was a beautifully arranged party which must have cost Players a lot of money. I remember when Hill got up to reply to the eulogies and say thank-you for this lavish celebration. What he actually did was stand up, take a packet of Gold Leaf Players out of his pocket, extract from it a cigarette, light it—and lapse into an endless cough that was superbly stage-managed. It lasted just long enough to be really funny. Graham then stubbed the cigarette out in an ashtray without yet having said a word, after which he calmly announced, "Now the commercial's over!"

His audience howled with glee but I don't know how the Players management took it. As usual, however, Graham made a fluent and amusing speech that left everybody in a good mood. It certainly was an original introduction to Lotus racing with a cigarette company, but I can well imagine the reaction of numerous doctors and anti-smokers.

I seem to be working backward, because the year 1947 has just flashed across my mind. That was back in the early 500 cc Cooper days and we journeyed to a place in Wales called Aberystwyth, where a race meeting was being held. We arrived at the hotel fairly late at night—around ten o'clock, I think it was—and found the hotel manager, an ex-naval commander, sitting in the bar with his feet resting on the washing-up sink. This seemed to me a pretty good start.

"If you want a drink," he said, "help yourselves."

Anyway, it was not long before we made friends with him and also took a peek at the hotel register. To my surprise I saw that a "Mr. and Mrs. Barnes" were among the hotel guests. I knew a young fellow named Barnes who had come into our shop and bought a new 500 Cooper and he had cut quite a dash with his bowler hat and pinstripe suit. However, I also knew that Barnes wasn't married, so I thought, "What bloomin' sauce, this chap putting up at the hotel with some bird!"

So around midnight, after quite a few drinks, we wheedled the passkey to all the hotel rooms out of the owner and made our way up to Barnes's room. Our party consisted of John Coombs, a red-headed garage owner from Guildford who did a lot of racing; Eric Brandon and Alan Brown. We approached the Barnes "hideout" armed with a soda siphon, let ourselves in, switched on the light and stood around the bed, taking aim. Luckily, before we actually squirted any soda we discovered that this was not the Barnes we had expected but a total stranger. So we all rushed out of the room and scampered off, hoping that the occupant would forget the incident. But no such luck. Next morning at breakfast our victim appeared at the entrance to the restaurant and gave Coombs and his mop of ginger hair a pretty cold look.

"What the hell were you doing in my bedroom, last night?" he wanted to know. "It's an outrage!"

"I wasn't in your room," Coombs lied, not very convincingly. "You must be mistaken."

"I'd know your mug anywhere," the man retorted.

Luckily he didn't insist and that was the end of the incident.

Another great character I recall—probably one of the greatest in my two decades of racing—was Earl Howe, president of the British Racing Drivers' Club. In 1962, which is the year I have in mind, I had served on the club committee for many years and as a result knew this wonderful old character very well. When he was "under the doctor," he was not supposed to drink and he did in fact keep to one drink a day. We had our own supply of liquor and Earl Howe would save up his drink to enjoy during the committee meeting. I remember that he had quite a large whiskey glass and when someone poured for him and asked, "Say when?" he let them nearly fill the glass with whiskey before exclaiming, "Ah, that'll do!"

He would then be asked, "Water or soda, sir?"

To which his reply invariably was, "Water—but don't drown it."

With only an eighth of an inch left at the top of the glass, that would have been difficult.

Another amusing little quirk of his lordship's was that he carried around an ancient Craven "A" tobacco tin, the lid of which was secured by a rubber band. This tin contained his supply of cigarettes and he went through the ritual with great solemnity, taking the old tin out of his pocket, slipping off the rubber band and "selecting" his cigarette. He would then insert it into a long cigarette holder, light it deliberately and puff away. One would have thought that Earl Howe would carry an elegant gold cigarette case around with him—probably a family heirloom. But not a bit of it. The Marquess of Curzon, as he was also known, disliked pretension of any kind and unlike many aspiring race drivers he had started his racing career quite late in life—when about forty years old. Yet he was very successful and much respected for his driving skill.

Going back to one of my first races on the Continent, in France to be precise, at La Bouille in 1948, there was a motorcycle race just prior to the 500 cc event. The start was always interesting to watch. The bikes were lined up across the track and when the flag dropped riders pushed their machines and jumped on. To make sure of an immediate start, the trick was to pull back the bike on compression beforehand so that it would fire as soon as the rider cocked his leg over the saddle.

On this occasion the width of the road was minimal, with a high grandstand on either side, packed with French people. When the flag dropped there was a great roar and a lot of smoke as the machines fired up and scooted away. But one unlucky starter was left on the line with a dead engine. I remember that in the relative quiet following, while people held their breaths, this rider looked up and shouted at the top of his voice, *"Merde!"* And that was my introduction to the French language.

Whenever the boys were in Paris, whether we planned to spend the night there or were on our way through to a race meeting, we found time enough to whoop it up. If it was an overnight stay, we didn't even bother to put up at a hotel but spent the entire night at various joints on the Place Pigalle.

I recall being there one night with Mike Hawthorn and Ivor Bueb and some of the Dunlop boys, including Harold Hodgkinson, the man who invented the Dunlop disc brake. Our favorite watering hole was Fred Payne's Bar, a nightclub frequented by most British drivers and a really smashing place. You could always find some nice birds there, much to the delight of Mike Hawthorn. If my memory serves me right, on this particular occasion we were all at Fred Payne's Bar around 3 A.M. and after a few drinks Mike went out for a breath of air. Parked directly outside was a beautiful Triumph Speed Twin motorcycle which caught his eye at once.

"Whose is that?" Mike inquired.

"It belongs to Fred Payne, the boss," he was told.

Whereupon he started up the bike and shot off on a tour of Paris in ever widening circles around Pigalle. He had a good time, no doubt about it, but I don't think the gendarmes showed any particular joy.

When Steve McQueen and Sir John Whitmore (who was also one of my Mini team drivers) shared an Austin-Healey Sprite in the 1962 Sebring 12-Hour Sports Car Race, Whitmore was already at the hotel when Steve arrived in a big American Lincoln. It was late at night and Whitmore must have been watching for McQueen's arrival from the bedroom window, which was located at the front of the hotel. Anyway, dressed only in his pajamas, John vaulted onto the roof of McQueen's car, directly outside the window. It was a wrong move because McQueen knew what had happened and at once took off and shot down Sebring's main street while Whitmore clung to his precarious perch for dear life. Eventually the Law caught up with them and Steve had to stop. The local cops were convinced he had a madman on the roof of his car—until they recognized Steve from some of his movies and he got away with it.

Another interesting personality of the late forties was Alan Brown. When I first met him he was a major in the Army—or rather he had just returned to civilian life and was working as a salesman for Dennis trucks in Guildford. He soon became interested in motor racing and persuaded one of his customers in Leicester (the sales area where he operated) to buy him a Cooper 500 and sponsor him in 500 cc races. He did quite well and one weekend finished second in a race at Rouen which I happened to win. His boss happened to see this in the paper and was curious.

"How could you be racing on the Continent," he asked, "when you're supposed to be selling trucks in the North of England?"

"Well," Alan shrugged, "it's just one of those things. The racing end helps me to sell trucks."

I don't think his boss ever knew the truth; he certainly would have blown a fuse had he found out that one of his customers was footing Alan's racing bill.

Sometime later, Alan's boss again called him into the office and said, "I think I've got just the job for you."

"Oh, what's that, sir?"

"I believe you're a great con artist and certainly have the gift of the gab. So I want you to have a go at selling a lawn mower to a very famous person."

"Who's that?"

"His Majesty the King."

"You must be joking," Alan said, aghast.

"Not a bit of it," his boss said. "I was never more serious."

What he had in mind was pretty far-seeing. The traditional custom is that if the Royal Family orders something for themselves, of their own free will and unofficially (it mustn't be a gift), then the supplier has the right to use the royal coat of arms with underneath the words "By Appointment."

Alan didn't have much choice, so he proceeded to entertain the royal gardener at Windsor and really whooped it up with the expense money. The result surprised even him. He got an official order from the King for a lawn mower! Unfortunately, only a couple of days later the King died and poor Alan had to go through the same process all over again with the Queen.

Another recollection I have about Alan Brown was after the 500 race at the Nürburgring in 1951. But I had better put things in their right order. I happened to meet there an interesting character named Walter Sleuter, who knew the course pretty well and later became a great rallye driver in Germany. His wife, Christine, a beautiful German girl, also made a deep impression on us. In fact—perhaps because she knew everybody—my wife (who had originally met her in Luxemburg) named her "Mata Hari." Christine it was who met Alan and me at Cologne airport on our arrival from England.

"While you're in Germany," she informed us, "I am going to look after you."

"Well, that's lovely," we agreed.

Walter Sleuter had promised to show me the way round the Nürburgring, which in itself proved an interesting experience but had unhapppy repercussions for him during the actual race. The winner was Eric Brandon. I ran in fourth place, immediately behind Sleuter. I kept station all through the race, passing him only on the last lap. Needless to say, he wasn't very pleased about that, but he concealed his displeasure perfectly. After the race we stayed at Sleuter's elegant hunting lodge, up in the mountains, on our way back to Cologne. Alan and I shared a room with twin beds while Walter and his wife slept in another room. But in the middle of the night something happened which gave me a bit of a shock. Christine simply came into our room—visiting. I think she was quite struck with Alan but that didn't make things any easier for me. In fact I really got scared and hurriedly left the room.

Walter, however, was not in the least perturbed. He was sitting up in bed, reading the paper and smoking his pipe as I passed his room.

"Crikey!" I thought. "If he could see his old woman now, with all those hunting guns pinned to the wall that would be the end of us!"

But he apparently didn't realize what was happening and a good time was had by all.

Then there was the occasion when we were attending the Moroccan Grand Prix in 1958. We met some American officers, one of whom was a colonel and another a major, and they scrounged pit passes from us for the race. As it turned out we managed to get many of their friends in as well. So our pit was more like an American army camp. They thoroughly enjoyed the race and we all had an exciting day, even though we were not yet competitive in the true sense and Moss won the race with a Vanwall.

When it was over the colonel told us, "We'd like to express our appreciation before you go back to England. Maybe we can show you how we live, here."

"Here" was a NATO air station about fifty miles into the desert out of Casablanca. Some thirty of us piled into a coach and were driven out to the encampment. There we were shown all around the place and it was some setup. You could even buy a Cadillac there, if you wanted one. They sold them at the PX. Our hosts entertained us to a most marvelous lunch and after that to the most fantastic air display I have ever seen. Some of the latest U.S. jet fighters went through hair-raising evolutions while ground control talked to them.

We could hear the squadron leader's voice asking, "What d'you want us to do now?"

Control gave precise instructions and the aerobatics continued with breathtaking accuracy and daring. To top it all, there was a sprint meeting—a sort of drag race—held on the main runway among members of the base with a variety of cars, some of them Porsches.

Well, that's certainly one way to run an air force!

In 1961 we were flying into Honolulu in a 707 when the captain announced that he would like everyone to remove their glasses and put a cushion in their lap and their head in the cushion while landing. He called the problem a "minor malfunction" but I knew there was trouble of some sort brewing. The mechanic who was traveling with me, Noddy Grohman (who had acquired his first name, by the way, from a character in a popular TV program of that time), tried to find out what the problem was, but he couldn't make any sense out of the stewardesses. I did notice, however, that while the pilot made several low runs over the control tower, there were people looking up at us with binoculars. This to me indicated problems with the undercarriage, or the flaps or something. After several more passes over the airport we headed out to sea and dumped most of the fuel, then returned on a very low and slow approach. The pilot was obviously an expert at his job. He dropped the plane exactly where the runway began and made a very quick stop using maximum reverse thrust. At least he tried to but we continued on, despite this, to the end of the runway, where the pilot did a neat ground loop on the grass. So our problem had obviously been hydraulics, causing brake failure. Everyone, by then, imagined that the undercarriage was stuck, hence the approaching sense of panic.

I must say that the thought that such a thing could happen in a regular airline with every service facility, as well as in my own plane, put the wind up me.

On another of our many flights, coming back from the Argentine with Jack Brabham in a Comet during January of 1960, we also had some anxious moments. Argentine Airlines had bought four of these Comets, but now only three remained. One of them had overshot the runway at São Paulo in Brazil, and as we were landing there on our way home, a big cutting showed up in the woods below that certainly was not natural. In fact it looked like an ugly scar. We had asked one of the crew what this signified and had been told with a wry smile, "Oh, that was our fourth Comet . . ."

This put Jack and me off somewhat, but we were still on our way home and still in one piece. The pilot and crew were Argentine and I don't think they quite had the hang of these Comets. However, we continued across the Atlantic and landed in the early morning in Spain. That's to say, we made ready to land. In fact a ground mist several feet deep covered the runway and on our first attempt it seemed as though the pilot was trying to land on top of this mist as if it were a solid runway. He obviously didn't know how deep it was and was trying to "feel" his way down. As a result we overshot and came around a second time. But with no better result. The pilot went lower into the mist yet the wheels still did not make contact with the ground. So we tried yet again and this time were lucky. We found the ground without too much bumping and Jack and I got out of the aircraft very happy to be "on the deck."

What really was the inside story of former World Champion Phil Hill and his short "drive" with the Cooper Car Company? Hill was with us for about nine months, actually, and I am well aware that the American Press came down on me rather heavily for "insulting" Hill publicly in the pits after his dual shunt in the 1964 Austrian Grand Prix at Zeltweg in August. Also for "firing him on the spot." This was rather less than the truth, so I would like to tell the story from my side as well.

Beyond doubt, Phil and I were temperamental opposites that could never mesh properly. In addition, we were both quick to flare up and during the time he drove for me we were going through a lot of teething troubles because of having to readjust to the new 1.5-liter Grand Prix Formula. We had enjoyed considerable success and gained two World Championships with the 2.5-liter Coventry Climax engine and now things were a lot tougher.

We took only a couple of cars to Zeltweg, so when Phil had his first shunt it meant working all night to repair the damage. He had run into some straw bales on the last turn, knocking the car completely out of shape, but this had not seemed to worry him at all. His excuse was that he was "relaxing" while getting the car warmed up. That didn't seem very convincing to me but Phil had a way of rationalizing events and a split second of inattention or misjudgment is enough for anything from a mild shunt to a catastrophe. Luckily Phil was unhurt and since the car was repaired in time, although I was far from happy I tried hard to inhibit my anger.

But then what did Phil do but crash again at the very same spot on the very first lap of the Grand Prix! Again he escaped unhurt but this time the car was a total write-off. It burst into flames which could not be quelled. I immediately ran over to the scene of the accident to see if Phil was all right and found him just standing there, seemingly indifferent to what had happened. I forget exactly what he said but it was something like, "Oh well, it's only a Grand Prix car anyway. Who cares?" These may not have been his precise words but the message came across loud and clear. Then I'm afraid I just blew my top. Hill responded indignantly and the sorry thing was that the argument took place in front of a lot of spectators. By the end of the race I had already forgotten about it, because bearing a grudge is not one of my weaknesses, but it was evident that the business festered pretty badly with Hill. His dignity was affronted as never before. As I recall that shunt—and I would as soon forget it—Phil took the view that Grand Prix cars did get written off and if they did, so what? It happened all the time. It was a risk that the entrant had to accept in the same way that a driver lives with the risk of injuring or killing himself.

Well, fair enough, I suppose, but what really got my goat was having a driver make precisely the same mistake at the same spot twice running, then treating the whole thing as a mere incident.

Looking back objectively on Phil Hill's racing career, there's no doubt that at times, when the mood took him, he was a brilliant driver, especially in places like Le Mans at the wheel of sports cars. But I don't think he had anything like the same virtuosity in a Grand Prix car, although to win a World Championship, no matter what the circumstances, one *has* to be good. Ferrari, the previous year, had enjoyed the advantage of being ready with an extremely potent 1.5-liter engine, but to be totally honest I don't think Phil would have won the 1961 World Championship had not Von Trips been killed in the Monza accident. Yet the fact

remained that he did win it and that when Ferrari failed to renew
his option a year later (and Hill had spent a miserable 1963 season with the abortive ATS project*) I did hire him as one of my
drivers. So to that extent the responsibility was mine. On the other
hand that second shunt at Zeltweg was not the act of a responsible
driver, either. I know from experience that most drivers—even the
best of them—have off days. But how many off days can they allow
themselves? How many such days can a team afford? Race cars
cost a great deal of money and the economics of racing are a factor that is continually nagging at car constructors and team managers. At best you're walking a tightrope, even with ample backing
—a fairly rare occurrence.

It is true that I did not offer Hill a car for the Italian Grand
Prix, which followed a month later; but he was back in a works
Cooper T73 for the U.S. Grand Prix at Watkins Glen, on October
4. He was the slowest qualifier and retired with ignition problems.
Our other driver, Bruce McLaren, was six seconds faster in practice but also retired when his engine dropped a valve. Phil, however, continued his run of successes in Ferrari sports prototypes
and Group 7 cars such as the Chaparral until 1967, when he retired.

A year or so ago I ran into Phil Hill and I am glad to say that
we greeted each other with a spontaneous friendliness which indicated both of us had buried that sad episode at Zeltweg.

I don't think I should leave out an incident which occurred during the 1960 French Grand Prix at Reims, especially as it concerns the late Harry Schell, who was then driving for BRM. Schell
arrived in a small German mini-car called the Goggomobile. This
pint-sized machine apparently was too much of a temptation for
some of the boys and this time Harry was on the receiving end of a
practical joke. During one of the evenings after practice, Schell
went out with the most beautiful bird, leaving his car outside the
hotel. While he was enjoying dinner in one of the many good res-
taurants nearby, the boys seized their chance. They bodily carried
the tiny, lightweight Goggomobile into the hotel and up the stairs
and dumped it outside Harry's bedroom door. What was even

* The ATS was a car manufactured in Northern Italy, designed by Chiti,
one of the ex-Ferrari designers.

worse, they placed it so that he couldn't even open the door to get into his room when he returned. It was a long time before he was able to get the car down and back on the road again, and meantime he was denied the use of his bedroom and even a change of clothes!

A somewhat similar thing happened to me on that trip. I had driven a new Mini-van to Reims with a spare engine in it and also parked my vehicle outside the Hotel Lion d'Or. The trees planted along the main road were about six inches further apart than the length of the van. So the boys lifted it up and stuffed it between two of those trees so that there was probably less than three inches clearance, front and rear. When I came out next morning I saw at once that it was impossible to get the van out by any known maneuver. To make things worse, the mechanics declined to help me lift it clear—at least for a couple of days. So there it stayed until they finally relented.

If the reader is having half as much fun reading about all these Cooper shenanigans through our racing years as I am having recalling them, perhaps I'll be forgiven for harking back to the 1958 Moroccan Grand Prix at Casablanca. The fantastic air display put up for us by our American friends was not all that happened during our stay. We were also invited to a party at the British Consulate and there enjoyed a fine and plentiful selection of drinks. Attending to our needs was a most charming girl who made sure that our glasses were quickly refilled. Roy Salvadori, not unexpectedly, was chatting her up, but that's another story. Prior to this party we had met a chap by the name of Don Christie, who was the skipper of Lord Tredegar's yacht. He previously had captained David Brown's yacht and that was how we knew him. Anyway, Lord and Lady Tredegar and their daughter, together with a friend of hers, had sailed into Casablanca to see the Grand Prix. They were also anxious to meet some of the drivers and get involved in that way. So we were asked whether we could bring a few of the boys back to the yacht for a party that evening. It sounded like a pretty good idea and we readily accepted and made our excuses at the British Consulate.

Before we left, the delightful creature who was keeping us supplied with drinks inquired, "Where is this other party being held?"

"It's Sir Henry Morgan's party," we told her, getting things thoroughly mixed up. Actually that was the name of Lord Trede-gar's boat but we did not realize this at the time. Nor did we stop to think that Sir Henry Morgan, the pirate, had died two centuries earlier.

Anyway, our young lady went off and told the Consul about "Sir Henry Morgan's party," to which he replied with a smile, "I didn't know he was in port."

It turned out that the girl we had been talking to was the Consul's daughter, which left us in a rather embarrassing situation since we were obviously trying to edge out of the party.

We got away, though, and on arrival at the yacht were intro-duced to his lordship by Don Christie. We also were introduced to her ladyship and her daughter, a stunning gal named Bridget. Also present was Bridget's girl friend, who was a lovely blonde. Because of her hair we promptly nicknamed her "the straw bale," behind her back of course. Jack Brabham took a fancy to her and it all went very well. We had a wonderful evening on board the yacht and the Tredegars made it clear that they wished to attend the Grand Prix the following day. I volunteered to get them tickets and Lady Tredegar said to me, "If you don't mind, Mr. Cooper, I would like you to be responsible for my two young ladies and see that they come to no harm."

"Of course," I agreed. "I'll be delighted. No problem at all."

The Tredegar clan added a great deal of color to the Cooper pit, I must say, and since we felt that one good turn deserved another, we invited the Tredegar girls to dinner the night after the race. My father and mother, who had both come over for the event, were expecting us for dinner. So they had to readjust to the new ar-rangement as so often occurs after a Grand Prix. Salvadori was sharing a room with Jack Fairman and while these two were out the girls used their room to take off their slacks, brush up a little and get into something more formal. At this point my father—not knowing there was anyone in that room—just opened the door and barged in. He beat a hasty retreat and at once collared me.

"What's going on?" he wanted to know. "Those two buggers have a couple of girls in their room—one on the bed and the other in the bathroom. And neither has any clothes on!"

So I had to explain. "Don't worry about that. The girls are only changing for dinner anyhow."

As things turned out, everyone had a good time and I later ran into Bridget, Lord Tredegar's daughter, when she was working for Graham Hill. I also attended her wedding party at the Savoy. She really was a most attractive girl.

In the wintertime, the boys almost always organized stag parties around the time of the Motor Show, in October. On this occasion (it was 1968) there was an excellent party hosted by the racing mechanics and the trade at the Connaught Rooms in the West End of London. As usual, a couple of strippers were provided for the boys to goggle at, but the moment they started to undress, Graham Hill, who was feeling no pain, did likewise. At least down to his underwear and socks. It ended up with Graham chasing one of the girls along the tops of the tables with glasses flying off in every direction. Then the inevitable happened. Graham trod on some broken glass and cut a bad gash in his foot that needed stitching. So we wrapped an overcoat around him and took him to the local hospital—something of an anti-climax for a party ending!

But all was not over yet. As Graham lay on the "operating table" awaiting the ministrations of a doctor, a tough-looking matron came in and inquired, "And what has happened to you, my young man?"

To which Graham replied, "Well, it was like this. I was chasing this bird along the top of the tables when I got my foot caught in a glass!"

The matron stared at him disbelievingly, not at all sure that he was telling the truth.

Appendix

EVOLUTION OF THE COOPER

Type Nos.	Category	No. built	Year	Notes
T1	Austin 7 Brooklands Special	1	1936	Built by Charles Cooper
T2	Cooper-JAP 500 cc F3 prototype	1	1946	
T3	Mk 1 500 F3 production model	2	1947	
T4	Sports car (Triumph engine)		1947	
T5	Mk 2 500 F3	7	1948	
T6	Cooper-MG sports car		1948	
T7	Mk 3 500 F3		1949	
T8	Cooper trailer		1949	Cooper wheels
T9	Mk 3 F3 with 1100 cc engine		1949	
T10	Cooper sports-racing car		1949	
T11	Mk 4 500 F3		1950	
T12	Mk 4 F3 with 1000 cc engine		1950	
T13	1100 cc JAP-engined sports-racing car		1950	
T14	Cooper-MG sports-racing car	1	1950	Developed by Lionel Leonard
T15	Mk 5 500 F3		1951	
T16	Mk 5 F3 with 1100 engine		1951	
T17	Streamliner on Mk 5 F3 chassis	1	1951	Used for record breaking
T18	Mk 6 500 F3		1952	
T19	Mk 6 F3 with 1100 engine		1952	
T20	Mk 1 Cooper-Bristol F2		1952	Front-engined
T21	Cooper-MG sports-racing car		1952	
T22	Cooper-Bristol sports-racing car (converted T20)	1	1952	For Alan Brown
T23	Mk 2 Cooper-Bristol F2		1953	
T24	Cooper-Alta F2	2	1953	
T25	Cooper-Bristol sports-racing car		1953	Central-seater

Type Nos.	Category	No. built	Year	Notes
T26	Mk 7 500 F3		1953	
T27	Mk 7 F3 with 1100 engine		1953	
T28	Streamliner on Mk 7 F3 chassis	1	1953	Used for road racing and record breaking
T29	Sports car	1	1953	
T30	Vandervell chassis	1	1953	Built by Cooper for the first Vanwall F1 car
T31	Mk 8 500 F3		1954	
T32	Mk 8 F3 with 1100		1954	
T33	Mk 1 Cooper-Jaguar sports-racing car	6	1954	Total includes Mk 2 (T38) versions
T34	Cooper-Norton sports-racing car		1954	
T35	Cooper-Lea Francis sports car	1	1954	
T36	Mk 9 500 F3		1955	
T37	Mk 9 F3 with 1100 engine		1955	
T38	Mk 2 Cooper-Jaguar sports-racing car	†	1955	† see T33
T39	1100 Climax-engined sports-racing car		1955	Manx-tailed
T40	Cooper-Bristol F1/2	1	1955	Rear-engined; built for Jack Brabham
T41	Mk 1 F2	5	1956	
T42	Mk 10 500 F3		1956	
	Mk 11 500 F3	19	1957	
	Mk 12 500 F3	6	1958	
	Mk 13 500 F3	4	1959	
T43	Mk 2 F2	29	1957	28 production and one prototype—chassis F2-P-57
T44	Cooper-Bristol F1	1	1957	Built and raced by Bob Gerard; known as the Cooper-BG-Bristol—chassis F2-21-57, 2.5-liter Bristol
T45	Mk 3 F2	26	1958 –59	The two works T45's were built in 1957
T46	F1 streamliner (2.5 Climax FPF)	1	1959	Works car for Brabham
T47	Cooper-Anzani three-wheeler		1958	Experimental road car
T48	Sports-racing car (1.1/1.5 Climax)	2	1958	Sold to America
T49	Mk 1 Monaco sports-racing car	8*	1959	Rear-engined
T50	Cooper Dauphine	1	1959	Cooperized version of Renault Dauphine saloon with Climax FWE engine
T51	Mk 1 F1/2	28	1959 –60	Used by works in 1959 and put into production in 1960

T52	Mk 1 Formula Junior	17*	1960	
T53	Mk 2 F1/2		1960	Works cars
T53P	Mk 2 F1/2		1961	Production version of T53
T54	Indianapolis car (2.7 Climax FPF)	1	1961	
T55	Mk 3 F1	11	1961	
T56	Mk 2 F1	22*	1961	
T57	Mk 2 Monaco sports-racing car	2	1961	
T58	F1 Climax V-8 prototype	1	1961	
T59	Mk 3 F1	28*	1962	
T60	Mk 4 F1	3	1962	Two works cars and a third used by Honda as a test-bed for a Honda V-12 F1 engine
T61	Mk 3 Monaco sports-racing car	3*	1962	
T61P	Monaco s/r with Maserati engine	1	1964	For Tommy Atkins
T61M	Monaco		1962 –63	
T62	Tasman/Intercontinental	1	1962	Built for F1 1.5 BRM V-8, but only used with 2.5 Climax FPF
T63	Mk 4 FJ prototype	1	1963	Hydrolastic suspension
T64	F1 prototype		1963	Hydrolastic suspension
T65	FJ prototype		1963	Hydrolastic suspension
T66	F1	1	1963	Coil-sprung
T67	Mk 3A FJ		1963	
T68	Cooper Monaco GT	1	1963	
T69	F1 prototype	1	1963	Monocoque
T70	Tasman/Intercontinental	3	1963 –64	
T71	F2	3	1964	
T72	F3	20	1964	
T72L	F3 prototype	1	1963	
T73	F1	3	1964	Two works cars and one Gerard Racing
T74	F3	1	1964 –65	Interim car used by Stewart at the end of 1964
T75	F2	7	1965	
T76	F3	20	1965	
T77	F1		1965	
T78	Monaco s/r	1	1965	
T79	Tasman	1	1964 –65	
T80	F1 prototype	1	1965 –66	Maserati 3-liter engine
T81	F1—Maserati V-12	6	1966	
T81B	F1	1	1966 –67	
T82	F2	2	1966	

Type Nos.	Category	No. built	Year	Notes
T83	F3	7	1966	
T84	F2	1	1967	
T85	F3	2	1967	
T86	F1 Maserati	1	1967	
T86B	F1 BRM V-12	3	1968	
T86C	F1 Alfa Romeo V-8	1	1968	
T87	Hillclimb/libre chassis	1	1968	Daimler 2.5 V-8 for M. Brain
T88	Formula C (1.0 BRM 4)	1	1968	
T89	F3		1968	Prototype; not built
T90	Formula A/5000		1968 –69	
T91	F1 (3-liter Alfa Romeo)		1969	

* Denotes total exported only, as some British cars did not carry chassis numbers.

Index